DISCARDED

THE MOTOR INDUSTRY

In the same series

EFFECTS OF MERGERS

Six Studies
by P. Lesley Cook
in collaboration with Ruth Cohen

CAMBRIDGE STUDIES IN INDUSTRY

THE MOTOR INDUSTRY

GEORGE MAXCY
Lecturer in Economics
University of Hull

AUBREY SILBERSTON
University Lecturer in Economics and
Fellow of St. John's College, Cambridge

HD
9710
G72
M3

Ruskin House
GEORGE ALLEN & UNWIN LTD
MUSEUM STREET LONDON

↑ 946423

FIRST PUBLISHED IN 1959

This book is copyright under the Berne Convention. Apart from any fair dealing or the purpose of private study, research, criticism or review, as permitted under the Copyright Act, 1956, no portion may be reproduced by any process without written permission. Enquiry should be made to the publisher.

© *George Allen & Unwin Ltd 1959*

PRINTED IN GREAT BRITAIN
in 10 pt Times Roman by
SIMSON SHAND LTD
LONDON, HERTFORD AND HARLOW

FOREWORD

IT is impossible to study every aspect of an industry in the course of a single book, especially when the industry has as many ramifications as the motor industry. In this book we have confined ourselves to those aspects of the motor industry which are likely to be of the greatest interest to economists, but even within the limits we have set ourselves we have been selective. In deciding what to put in and what to leave out we have been influenced partly by our views on the relative importance of different subjects, and partly by what has already been written about the motor industry by others. We have not dealt in any detail with individual export markets, for example, and have not attempted to make detailed estimates of our own of the possible future level of demand for vehicles in home and export markets. In discussing such questions, we have leant heavily on the studies made by others, and have referred the reader to these studies if he should want to examine these matters in greater detail. Where we hope we have ourselves made a worthwhile contribution is in the study of costs of production in the motor industry. This is a subject which has not, in our view, been dealt with very satisfactorily in previous studies, and we have therefore given a good deal of space to a discussion of the structure of costs in the industry and its implications. We have also devoted a good deal of space to the form which competition takes in the motor industry, another subject which has not been dealt with very satisfactorily in previous studies, at least in the British context.

The book has been written with particular reference to the British motor industry, although frequent reference has been made to the motor industries of other countries. We have included a discussion of some of the problems of the retail motor trade, but the main emphasis is on vehicle manufacture. Since the greater part of the book was completed during 1957, most of the calculations contained in it relate to 1956 and earlier years, but we have, where possible, taken the story up to the end of 1957.

The preparation and publication of this book has been made possible by a grant under the Conditional Aid Scheme for the use of Counterpart Funds derived from United States Economic Aid. In making this study we have had help from a great many firms and organizations in the motor industry. Those who have helped us would not wish us to mention them by name, but we should like to express our gratitude to them for the ready way in which they have given us information, much of which took them a good deal of time to assemble. One firm in particular helped us in every possible way, and provided us with the detailed estimates which enabled us to construct the long-run cost curve for the firm contained in Chapter VI.

Cambridge and Hull   G.M.
February 1958   A.S.

CONTENTS

FOREWORD *page* 7

I. *Historical Introduction* 11
II. *Structure of the Industry* 21
III. *The Demand for Vehicles* 38
IV. *Technique of Production* 53
V. *The Structure of Costs* 62
VI. *Economies of Large-scale Production* 75
VII. *Competition in the Car Market, 1929–1956* 99
VIII. *The Nature of Competition in the Industry* 125
IX. *Profits and Sources of Funds* 151
X. *Future Prospects* 182
XI. *Conclusions* 190

APPENDIX A 206
The Capital-Output Ratio in the Motor Industry

APPENDIX B 210
Comparative Productivity and Prices in the British and American Motor Industries

APPENDIX C 216
The Relative Prices of British and Continental Cars

APPENDIX D 223
Statistical tables

LIST OF CHARTS, FIGURES AND TABLES 231

INDEX 234

CHAPTER I

Historical Introduction

THE British motor industry effectively came into existence in 1896, the year which saw the repeal of restrictive legislation which had hitherto throttled the development of the industry. Since that time, the industry has grown out of all recognition and is today one of the most important in the country. It consumes about 10 per cent of all deliveries of finished steel in the United Kingdom and is responsible for about 10 per cent of the total value of British exports. It employs directly some half a million persons, and many hundreds of thousands more are closely dependent on its fortunes.

The passing of the Locomotive on Highways Act in 1896 gave the 'all clear' signal to an industry in which there were already a number of British pioneers, such as F. W. Lanchester, but the first car to be produced on any scale in this country was a German car—the Daimler. This reflected the fact that the initial steps in the development of the internal combustion engine had taken place on the Contintent, where such men as Lenoir in France and Otto, Benz, and Daimler in Germany had pioneered important advances. The Daimler patent rights were acquired for Great Britain in 1893 by F. R. Simms, who sold them in 1895 to the British Motor Syndicate. The Syndicate became the parent company of the Daimler Motor Company which was formed in 1896 and began to produce Daimler cars at Coventry in the same year. Through its control of the Daimler rights, the Syndicate made a determined attempt in the late 1890s to gain a patent monopoly in the new industry, but a Court decision of 1901 put an end to this manoeuvre and ensured that entry into the industry should remain free.

In the early years, it was not difficult to enter the industry. A knowledge of general engineering techniques and a modest amount of capital were all that were required. Both general engineering firms and firms engaged in cycle manufacture, such as Rover and Humber, were well fitted for making motor cars, and in the years that followed 1896 a large number of firms entered the industry. These firms were less fortunate than their counterparts in the United States, where the engineering industry had developed a system of standardized interchangeable parts and of extensive sub-contracting that had no equivalent in this country. The first British manufacturers were forced to make a high proportion of their own parts and components. Their capital requirements were appreciably greater than they would have been if they could have relied more on component suppliers with capital equipment of their own. They produced cars in small numbers and at high prices. Many of them failed to keep up with the rapid technical advances that were being made in these years, or failed to survive the intense competition from other manufacturers. Before 1913, nearly 200 makes of car had been placed on the market, and of these over 100 had disappeared.

The output of the industry expanded slowly in the early years of the century. By 1911, the combined output of cars and commercial vehicles had risen to 19,000. In that year, an important event occurred when the Ford company began to assemble and partially manufacture their Model T car at Old Trafford, Manchester. The Model T, which had been introduced in the United States in 1908, had been designed as a cheap, workmanlike car, and had had enormous success in America. In the years following 1911, a number of British manufacturers brought out inexpensive vehicles. By the time the war came, Ford had become the largest producer, with an annual output of 6,000 cars, followed by Wolseley, with an output of 2,000 to 3,000 cars. Other sizeable producers were Morris, Austin, Singer and Rover, with outputs in the region of 1,000 cars each.

The production of commercial vehicles developed at first more slowly than that of cars. The first petrol-driven vehicle, a Thornycroft, was not produced until 1902. Most of the important present-day producers in this branch of the industry entered the industry in the period before 1914, several of them as producers of cars as well as of commercial vehicles. Their commercial vehicle production was greatly stimulated after 1912 when the Government, with the possibility of war in mind, introduced a scheme for subsidizing the buyers of certain types of commercial vehicle.

By 1913 the production of cars and commercial vehicles had risen to 34,000, of which possibly some 25,000 were cars. This was a good deal less than production in France, where about 45,000 cars were produced in 1913, and far less than in the United States, where the combined production of cars and commercial vehicles reached 485,000 (462,000 of which were cars) in the same year. Clearly, the situation in the United States, with its vast potential demand, was not comparable with that in this country. Almost certainly, however, the achievement of the British industry was less than it would otherwise have been because of the lack of an efficient components industry. William Morris, who pursued a deliberate policy of buying a high proportion of his components from outside suppliers, had to turn to the United States in 1914 when he could find no British firm which could produce large enough quantities of standardized parts to fulfil his growing requirements.

The growth of the British industry, unlike that of the American industry, was checked by the 1914–18 war, although its potential capacity to produce vehicles was increased as a result of wartime expansion to produce munitions. Perhaps the most striking wartime event, from the long-run point of view, was the imposition in 1915 of the McKenna duty of $33\frac{1}{3}$ per cent *ad valorem* in the landed cost of imported cars. This duty, which still exists[1] has had the effect of practically removing foreign competition from the British home market.

As soon as the war was over, the industry quickly resumed its upward progress. A large number of new manufacturers entered the industry in the period 1919–25, but growing competition from such firms as Morris, together with the effects of the 1921 slump, led to the elimination of a very large number of firms between 1922 and 1925. For the industry as a whole, however, recovery from the 1921 slump was rapid, and production increased greatly during the 1920s. In 1922, 73,000 cars and commercial vehicles had been produced; by 1929 production had reached 238,000 units, of which 182,000 were cars. The 1920s was a particularly important period in the development of the industry because during it the transition occurred from an industry composed of a large number of small firms with a rapid rate of mortality, to an industry composed of a few large firms with a comparatively low rate of mortality. The number of car-producing firms fell from 88 in 1922 to 31 in 1929, and in the latter year three firms alone—Morris, Austin and Singer—accounted for 75 per cent of the industry's total output of cars.[2] Morris and Austin were by far the largest producers of cars and Morris and Ford by far the largest producers of commercial vehicles, although they concentrated on the lighter types only.

During the 1920s, the components industry was also beginning to take on its modern shape, with the growth of specialist concerns such

[1] It was reduced to 30 per cent at the end of 1956.
[2] *The Economist*, October 19, 1929, p. 720.

as Joseph Lucas. By itself, this development was one which was favourable to small as well as large vehicle manufacturing firms, since the small firms were able to draw on the resources of the parts and component firms equally with the large. The factor which sealed the fate of the smaller concerns, however, was the growth of mass-production techniques on the part of companies such as Morris and Austin which had succeeded in producing models that were successful with the public. In these companies, very rapid developments were made in the adoption of American flow-production methods, and this enabled costs and prices to be considerably reduced. Car prices fell, on the average, by 25 per cent between 1924 and 1929.[1]

The most remarkable feature of the period that followed 1929 was that the great depression affected the British motor industry far less than it affected the motor industries of the other main producing countries. Comparing the best and worst years in this period, the production of cars fell by only 15 per cent and of commercial vehicles by 10 per cent. In the United States and Canada, on the other hand, vehicle production in 1932, the worst year of the depression, was 75 per cent below the 1929 level. In Germany, the fall was nearly as great as this, and even in France, which was less hard hit, the fall was of the order of one-third. This difference between the experience of the United Kingdom at the one extreme and the United States and Canada at the other can be accounted for, in part at least, by the relatively slower development of the British vehicle market before 1929 and by the relatively small fall in real income per head in this country during the slump. The buoyancy of the British market can be seen by the fact that after 1932 production rose well beyond the 1929 level, and by 1937 the output of both cars and commercial vehicles was twice as great as in 1929. In the United States, Canada and France, on the other hand, although some recovery from the slump did take place, the 1929 level of production was never again reached before the outbreak of the Second World War.

The period between 1929 and 1939 saw a further consolidation of the industry. By 1939 there were only 33 car-producing firms left, and since a number of these were under common ownership the number of independent car-producing firms was only about 20. Important changes also took place during this period in the relative importance of the different firms. Ford, which had begun production in a new factory at Dagenham in 1932, Vauxhall, which had been acquired by

[1] Society of Motor Manufacturers and Traders *Motor Industry of Great Britain*, 1939, p. 46.

General Motors in 1928, Standard and Rootes, all grew in relative importance as car producers. By 1938, six firms only were responsible for 90 per cent of the output of cars. They were, in order of size as car producers, Nuffield, Austin, Ford, Vauxhall, Rootes and Standard, although there was not much to choose between the last three. On the commercial vehicle side, there were a number of new entrants as a result of the introduction in the early 1930s of the diesel (heavy oil) engine for the larger vehicles, but the most important entrants into the commerical vehicle field were Vauxhall and Rootes, particularly the former, which had become the country's largest producer of commercial vehicles by the end of the period.

An important development in the car market during the 1930s was a decreased emphasis on price competition and an increased emphasis on quality competition and variety.[1] Commenting in 1933 on this last development, *The Economist* stated[2]

'The number of models in production of the ten largest manufacturing groups, controlling over 90 per cent of the market, increased from 46 in 1929–30 to 55 in 1931–2, 60 in 1932–3, and 64 in 1933–4. The old game continues—everybody endeavouring to catch the public's fancy with at least one of their range of models.'

The pattern was repeated after 1933. By the end of the 1930s, the variety of models produced had increased even more. It is significant that in the United States, where production was ten times as great as in the UK, a considerably higher degree of standardization was achieved during this period.[3]

The outbreak of war in 1939 brought about an abrupt change in the position of the industry. The output of cars was reduced to very low levels, while the output of goods-carrying vehicles rose as a result of military demand. Tractor output was also increased as part of the drive towards greater agricultural output. At the same time, vehicle manufacturers used their existing capacity, plus a considerable amount of new capacity, to produce a wide variety of military goods. Much of this additional capacity, in the form of machines as well as buildings, was retained in the industry after the end of the war, and provided the industry with the ability to expand its production to well above pre-war levels.

[1] *v.* Chapter VII below for an analysis of competition in the car market from 1929 onwards.
[2] October 21, 1933.
[3] *v.* Chapter VII.

The reconversion to peacetime activities was carried out very rapidly by the British industry. In 1945, the production of cars had been negligible, but in 1946 it rose to well over half the level of output in 1937, the best pre-war year. By 1949, the 1937 output had been surpassed and by 1950 car production was one-third above the 1937 level. Commercial vehicle production rose at an even greater rate than car production during the period 1946–50: it very nearly doubled, while running all the time at a level well above that of pre-war years. In these years also, tractor production increased fourfold, to over six times the highest pre-war level of output. There was a check to the industry's expansion in 1951 and 1952, when the shortage of steel, particularly sheet steel, became acute and a fall occurred in the output of both cars and commercial vehicles. However, production rose again after 1952, and in 1955 it reached a new peak of nearly 1,400,000 vehicles (898,000 cars, 341,000 commercial vehicles and 133,000 tractors).

The year 1955 was a record one for all the main vehicle producing countries. In that year, their total production of cars and commercial vehicles was more than double the 1937 level.

TABLE 1
Car and C.V. Production—UK and Main Producing Countries
(1937=100)

	UK			France, Italy Germany			Six Main Producing Countries*		
	Cars	C.V.s	Total	Cars	C.V.s	Total	Cars	C.V.s	Total
1947	74	134	88	21	105	34	83	137	93
1950	134	223	155	114	221	132	162	165	163
1955	230	289	244	299	413	317	215	177	208

* UK, USA, Canada, France, Italy, West Germany (1937 figure for all Germany). These countries produced between them in 1955 very nearly the entire output of cars and commercial vehicles in countries other than the USSR, China and Eastern Europe.

It should be borne in mind when comparing the rise in UK production since 1937, as revealed in this table, with that of the six main producing countries taken together, that 1937 was the pre-war peak year for the UK but not for the United States, Canada or France. If a comparison had in each case been made with the pre-war peak year, it would have been more favourable to Britain than is indicated in the table. Perhaps the most striking fact brought out by the table, however, is the very rapid rise in vehicle production on the Continent between 1950 and 1955—a rise very much greater than that which took place in the UK. In 1950, the total number of vehicles produced in France, Italy and Germany taken together was practically the same as in the UK. By 1955, it was over 50 per cent higher.

In the period immediately following 1955, the UK suffered a setback. In 1956 a combination of factors—the credit squeeze, import restrictions in overseas markets, and the Suez crisis—caused a severe fall in British production, although German, French and Italian production continued to expand. New registrations of cars on the British home market fell by 20 per cent and of commercial vehicles by 3 per cent, while exports of cars fell by 14 per cent and exports of commercial vehicles by 8 per cent. In 1957, however, the industry made a strong recovery, although production did not reach the 1955 level.

Before the war, a setback in overseas markets would have had far less impact on the British motor industry than it had in 1956. This is because overseas markets have taken a far larger proportion of the industry's output since the war than they ever did before. In 1937, the best pre-war year for exports, 86 per cent of the industry's production of cars and 78 per cent of the industry's production of commercial vehicles were sold on the home market. The number of cars exported was 78,000 and the number of commercial vehicles was 21,000. In 1950, on the other hand, the best post-war year for exports, only 25 per cent of the output of cars and 40 per cent of the output of commercial vehicles were sold on the home market. The number of cars exported was five times, and the number of commercial vehicles nearly eight times the 1937 level of exports. By 1950, the United Kingdom had displaced the United States as the world's chief exporter of vehicles. In that year, world exports of cars and commercial vehicles were over 50 per cent greater than in 1937, and the British share of the increased volume of trade had risen to 52 per cent as compared with under 15 per cent in 1937. Great credit must be given to the industry for the vigour with which it expanded its exports after the war, in dollar and European markets as well as in its traditional Commonwealth markets, but it must be recognized that the industry was aided by a number of exceptionally favourable circumstances. Of particular importance was the shortage of dollars, which limited American exports, and the relatively slow initial recovery of the German motor industry.

In the years since 1950 the dominance in export markets that the British industry achieved in the early post-war years has lessened considerably. German exports rose very rapidly after 1950, while British exports fell, partly as a result of import restrictions in the very important Australian market. Even a recovery in 1954 and 1955 failed to bring British car exports back to the 1950 level. Although world trade had risen by 1955 to a level 130 per cent above that of 1937, the British share in 1955 had fallen to 34 per cent of the total while the German share had increased to 25 per cent. In 1956, when British exports were once more hit by import restrictions in Australia, German exports went on rising, and in that year German exports of cars were, for the first time, greater in number than those of the United Kingdom. Germany retained her leadership in 1957, despite the rise to record levels of British car exports. An outstanding feature of the latter was the great increase in sales to the United States, which took nearly one-quarter of all British exports of cars.

The concentration of British motor manufacturers on export markets had important repercussions on the home market in the years following the war. Demand on the home market was naturally very strong, but the supply of vehicles was severely limited by Government pressure on manufacturers to export as many cars and commercial vehicles as they could. The supply of commercial vehicles was easier than that of cars, and civilian registrations on the home market exceeded the peak pre-war level by 1946. New registrations of cars, on the other hand, were at less than half the peak 1937 level in the years before 1952. The 1937 level was not approached until 1953 and not exceeded until 1954. Since there was a high level of consumer and business demand for cars, and a backlog of very old pre-war cars to be replaced, the consequences were long waiting lists for new cars, a very frustrated motoring public, and prices for second-hand cars which at the peak (the nadir as far as motorists were concerned) were for many models double those of the list price of a new car. This was in spite of the fact that the list prices of new cars included a purchase tax that, at its height, reached two-thirds of the wholesale value of the vehicle. The keen desire to own cars was also reflected in the fact that from 1948 onwards there were more cars on the road than there had ever been before the war, many of these, of course, being pre-war cars.

After 1953, the new car position on the home market became easier, but it was not until the end of 1955 that anything approaching normality returned to the car market.[1] In that year, new registrations

[1] There were well over a million pre-war cars on the road in 1955 out of a total of 3½ million (the 1939 total had been just under 2 million), so that even after the high level of registrations in 1955 the age composition of the car fleet was still abnormal.

Historical Introduction

surged up to a record figure of 511,000 cars and 163,000 commercial vehicles. Sales were so buoyant in 1955 that new registrations in 1956 might well have failed to reach the 1955 level even if unfavourable factors had not intervened. As it was, new registrations on the home market in 1956 were severely curtailed by stringent hire purchase restrictions and the fear of petrol rationing, which finally came in December. There was some recovery in 1957, but new registrations were well below the 1955 level.

In the situation in which the British motor industry found itself in the years between 1946 and 1957, competition on the pre-war scale, at least in the home market, did not exist. Competition was by no means absent, however, and some of the smaller firms, such as Jowett and Singer, were compelled to cease production as separate entities in the early 1950s. The 'Big Five' (as they became after the merger between Nuffield and Austin in 1952) strengthened their hold on the market, accounting between them by 1955 for over 95 per cent of the industry's output of cars as compared with less than 90 per cent in 1946 and 1947.

A feature of post-war years has been the number of mergers that have taken place.[1] In the first place, there has been a good deal of backward integration. The race to expand production in the face of a steel shortage impelled a number of firms to absorb their suppliers of car bodies. The amalgamation of Ford with Briggs Motor Bodies in 1953 and the BMC merger with Fisher and Ludlow within six months, were events of major importance, leaving Pressed Steel the only remaining supplier of mass-produced car bodies. Six other smaller mergers took place between car manufacturers and body builders in the decade after the war. It is quite plain that this absorption of body builders was not motivated by cost considerations, or for any wish to integrate for its own sake. Despite the fact that a finished body may represent as much as 40 per cent of the cost of a car, those companies which still lacked body building facilities of their own made no move to acquire them until they felt that their sources of supplies were threatened. As had been the case with Morris in the 1920s, vertical integration took place because of the need to assure supplies in an expanding market.

In the second place, there have been a certain number of horizontal mergers, easily the most notable being the merger of Austin and

[1] For a detailed historical discussion of mergers in the motor industry, see the chapter by George Maxcy included in P. L. Cook and R. L. Cohen, *Effects of Mergers* (Allen & Unwin, 1958).

Nuffield in 1952 to form the British Motor Corporation. The merger gave the new company control of some 40 per cent of the market. The evidence suggests that the motive for this merger was primarily a defensive one, in the face of increasingly strong competition from the American-controlled companies, Ford and Vauxhall. Competition between vehicle manufacturers is a subject which is discussed more fully in later chapters.

Another feature of the pattern of production in the post-war period that deserves particular mention is the far greater emphasis on standardization than was the case before the war. Nearly all manufacturers have cut down their range of models and have used common parts in models which appear different on the surface. Considerable progress has also been made in the standardization of parts and components, and a standardization committee of the large mass-producers of cars has been in existence since 1948. It is true that, from about 1950, there has been a tendency for vehicle manufacturers to extend their range of models, but for nearly all manufacturers the number of basic models they produce is still a good deal less than before the war.

CHAPTER II

Structure of the Industry

ANY economic analysis of an industry immediately raises the familiar problem of defining what that industry is, and what it produces. Unfortunately, in this respect, it is never possible to find convenient groups of completely integrated firms, whose activities are entirely devoted to the manufacture of a homogeneous product. All concerns rely, to a greater or lesser extent, on suppliers, and most of them produce a range of products which, in some cases, may not even be roughly similar in nature. Motor vehicle manufacturers, in particular, are peculiarly dependent upon the services of a number of suppliers of parts and components who, in turn, may also be important contributors in other fields of manufacture. The output of motor vehicles is, of course, widely heterogeneous, and the concerns engaged in their manufacture do not necessarily confine themselves to this type of product, however broadly it may be defined.

Nevertheless, it is easy to exaggerate these difficulties. It is often the case that useful definitions emerge from a working knowledge of the situation and the relative importance of producers in the particular field under investigation. This task becomes easier the more highly concentrated that field has become, for an industry tends to be the big firms, together with their principal suppliers; and the products of that industry tend to be what these big firms produce. The following examination of vehicle production in this country suggests that such an approach is particularly applicable to the motor industry.

1. CARS

At the 1956 Motor Show in London, at which all the UK producers of cars were represented, there were 31 different British makes exhibited on the stands, and a considerably greater number of distinct models. Despite this somewhat surprising display of variety for a mass-production industry, the output of cars is highly concentrated in the hands of a few manufacturers. Although there were 31 makes, some producers were responsible for more than one make, so that there were only 21 independent companies represented. Out of this number, five—popularly known as the 'Big Five'—account for about 95 per cent of the total UK production of cars. The unit sales and market shares of these companies for 1954, together with those of the sixteen other car producers grouped together as 'Specialists' are shown in Table 1.

TABLE 1
Estimated Unit Car Sales and Market Shares, 1954

Company	Unit Sales	Per cent
British Motor Corporation	290,030	38
Ford	204,150	27
Rootes	84,860	11
Standard	81,380	11
Vauxhall	72,600	9
Specialists	36,145	4
UK Total	769,165	100

Even within the 'Big Five' there are significant differences in output, with BMC and Ford each producing two to three times as much as any single one of their main competitors, and nearly 65 per cent of the total. Nevertheless, the similarities in products, prices, production methods, and degree of dependence on the sales of motor vehicles are so great as to warrant grouping these five companies together. By British standards, they are the mass producers. Each one has a combined car and commercial vehicle output of at least 100,000 units per annum, or more than twenty times the volume of any of the specialists, except Jaguar and Rover.[1] The five big companies compete among themselves for the mass market and the great majority of their output is not directly competitive with that of the specialists.[2] The latter aim primarily at two narrow markets and concentrate on the production of (i) sports and racing cars, and (ii) big, luxurious, high-quality saloons and limousines. Both these categories are protected to some extent from the mass producers by the appeal of special performance characteristics and exclusiveness. This appeal is partly ensured by the price which, in most cases, is over £1,000 basic, well outside the price range of all but a few of the products of the 'Big

[1] Jaguar output was said to be 10,000–15,000 in 1954; Rover 10,000 cars and 25,000 Land Rovers.

[2] There are important exceptions, however. BMC produces 'semi-specialist' cars such as Austin-Healey, Wolseley, Riley and MG, as well as Austin and Morris cars; Rootes produces Sunbeam and Humber cars as well as Hillman; Standard produces Triumph as well as Standard cars.

Five', and more than twice the price of the average popular make.

It is significant that almost all the expensive saloon makes are produced by companies whose main interests lie outside the industry. The Rolls Royce Company, for example, is primarily concerned with the manufacture of aero engines and devotes only about a tenth of its resources to the production of the Rolls Royce and Bentley cars. Similarly, the Bristol Aeroplane Company (Bristol cars) and the Hawker Siddeley Group (Armstrong Siddeley) are more closely allied with the aeroplane industry than with cars. Alvis Limited (Alvis) also produces aero engines, and in addition armoured fighting vehicles, so that passenger cars are a minor interest. BSA (Daimler) belongs more properly in the fields of machine tools, weapons, and cycles. David Brown (Aston Martin, Lagonda) would probably be best classified as a general engineering firm, although its tractor production, and its manufacture of gears, gear boxes, and other mechanical components, gives it a more important interest in the motor industry than perhaps any of the others.

This is not meant to imply that these specialist producers are not part of the motor industry. Much is owed to these manufacturers and their predecessors in the way of innovations, and much of the world-wide prestige of British cars stems from their efforts. Nevertheless, it is important to note that their production is now an offshoot, or a by-product of other industries, and their survival depends partly on financial success elsewhere. Indeed, doubts have been expressed of the ability of a number of these car divisions or subsidiaries to survive without financial help from the parent company.[1]

The sports and racing car specialists appear to be independent financially but, because of their very small scale of operations, tend to rely on the major car producers for engines, gear boxes, and other mechanical components. The Morgan is supplied with either the Ford Anglia engine and gearbox or the Triumph TR3 engine. The Allard is equipped with either a Ford or a Jaguar engine; the Lotus, with a Coventry Climax or Ford engine, and so forth. Such firms do not so much manufacture cars as design and assemble them, using modified standard mechanical parts obtained from other car producers and their suppliers.

From a volume standpoint, Rover and Jaguar have been the most successful of the specialists in the post-war period. Both have contrived to find a lucrative market in a price range in between that of the mass-produced cars and that of the typical specialist product. It is

[1] *The Economist*, Motor Supplement, October 22, 1955.

a market, however, in which demand is relatively limited, so that further growth for these companies, at least in the home market, can only be moderate unless they enter the popular-priced field. Such a move is highly unlikely—no specialist producer in a mature car industry has yet succeeded in bridging the gap between small-scale and big volume production. What is much more likely is that the mass producers will continue to invade the specialist markets with specially adapted versions of their own standardized products, a process which may lead to the elimination of a number of the small producers.

2. COMMERCIAL VEHICLES

Commercial vehicles can be usefully divided into two quite distinct categories. The first consists of fairly standardized, mass-produced vehicles ranging from light vans to trucks with up to 6 tons carrying capacity. Some 90 per cent of the total commercial vehicle output consists of vehicles of this nature, and the 'Big Five' account for the bulk of them, although Standard, a recent entrant into this field, is responsible only for a relatively small number. Rover, with a utility vehicle—the Land Rover—is the only specialist car producer of any importance in this section. The dominance of the large car-producing companies in the manufacture of light commercial vehicles is not surprising in that their vans are, for the most part, merely commercial adaptations of passenger models, and some of their trucks have mechanical parts in common with the heavier cars. Clearly, economies of scale have played the major role here in reserving this area for the mass producer.

The second category encompasses a tremendous variety of vehicles including medium and heavy duty trucks, single and double-decker buses, coaches, trolley buses, road tankers, articulated tractor and trailer units capable of carrying anything up to 100 tons, fire engines and other municipal vehicles of all types. A group of about twenty companies cater for this market with two firms, Leyland (Leyland, Albion) and ACV (AEC, Maudslay, Crossley) supplying over 50 per cent of all the vehicles. Many of the smaller producers do not make their own engines but buy them from outside suppliers such as Perkins, Meadows, Gardner and Rolls Royce. The 'Big Five' have been gradually penetrating the lower reaches of the heavy commercial vehicle section, and now all but Standard are producing trucks up to 7 tons carrying capacity.

Table 2
Estimated Unit Commercial Vehicle Sales and Market Shares, 1954

Company	Unit Sales	Per cent
BMC	94,000	35
Vauxhall	58,000	21
Ford	42,000	15
Rover	25,000	9
Rootes	24,000	9
Leyland	10,000	4
AEC	5,000	2
All others	12,000	5
UK Total	270,000	100

Although the heavy vehicle section of the industry is responsible for only about one-tenth of commercial vehicle output, it is considerably more important than the volume figures suggest, since unit value is high—it was some five times that of the lighter products in 1948.[1] This is due primarily, of course, to the greater size of these units, but a contributing factor is their largely non-standard nature. Often they are 'tailor-made' to the specifications of customers who usually buy directly from the manufacturers. This wide variation in product makes batch production the general rule in most cases. AEC, for example, despite its success in instituting line production methods for its three basic types of engines, found itself making 211 different types of vehicle derived from 60 basic models in 1954. Furthermore, because of consumer insistence, the trend appeared to be towards even greater variety. The difference between such a company and any one of the 'Big Five' in type and price of product, and in production and distribution methods, is so great as to warrant, for many purposes, an entirely separate analysis.

In some respects, the position of the heavy vehicle manufacturer in the structure of the industry is akin to that of the specialist car producers. Like them, he is subject to increasingly severe competition from the mass producers. Before the war, for example, none of the 'Big Five' made a truck with a carrying capacity of more than five tons. Now four of them produce seven-ton trucks and there is a tendency to 'chase the heavy vehicle producers up the ladder'. So far,

---

[1] PEP *Motor Vehicles* (London, 1950) p. 32. PEP figures for 1947 (*ibid.*, p. 34) suggest that the heavy vehicle builders produced 90 per cent of the goods vehicles of over six tons load and two-thirds of the buses, etc., but only 4 per cent of the goods vehicles of under six tons load. The last category accounted for 87 per cent of total commercial vehicle output.

however, this has not adversely affected the output or profits of the larger heavy vehicle firms.

3. TRACTORS

Tractor production is sometimes ignored in discussions of the motor industry, perhaps on the grounds that tractors are not primarily a form of transport and should more properly be classified as 'agricultural machinery'. The PEP Report on the Motor Vehicles Industry, for example, makes no mention of tractors throughout its extensive analysis. However, it is the car producer, not the maker of agricultural machinery, who accounts for the vast majority of the tractors produced in the UK, so that it is imperative to treat tractor production as part of the output of the motor vehicle industry.

This near-monopoly on the part of the car producers indicates that there are significant economies to be gained from the joint production of cars and tractors. Despite the obvious differences between these two products, considerable interchangeability of parts is possible, particularly in the case of engines and related mechanical components. It is common knowledge, for example, that the Standard Vanguard engine is made use of in the Ferguson tractor. In addition, since the basic techniques of production are very similar for both these products, the car firm can make more extensive use of its 'know-how' and its manufacturing facilities, as well as spread its general overheads over more units. These considerations also apply to the suppliers of parts and components for tractors, who, for the most part, are the same firms who supply the car and truck producers with their parts and components.

Tractor production is even more highly concentrated than the manufacture of cars and trucks. Standard, maker of the Ferguson tractor, is the largest producer, closely followed by Ford. Together these companies turned out over 80 per cent of the 133,000 agricultural tractors made in 1954. David Brown, BMC and International Harvester furnished another 15 per cent between them. The small remainder was widely scattered among another fifteen or twenty companies, some of which made use of engines and other components supplied by the principal manufacturers.

4. PARTS AND COMPONENTS

A striking characteristic of the UK motor industry, taken as a whole, is the very high percentage of the total cost of a vehicle that is represented by bought-out materials and components. One of the popular, volume-produced cars has a bought-out content of nearly 80 per cent, which indicates that even the larger firms may confine their manufacturing activities largely to final assembly and the machining of the engine and other major mechanical components. It follows that the role of the supplier is vitally important and that some analysis of who these suppliers are, and their relative importance to the final cost of the car, is essential.

A product as large as the motor car, with all its refinements and complexities, in addition to its thousands of separate parts,[1] offers ample scope for many different firms to participate in the various stages of its manufacture. There is, indeed, a very large number of companies who supply something toward the final product. The SMMT lists over 400 of its members as suppliers of car parts, components and accessories. However, it would be misleading to conclude from this that this section of the industry is composed of many small firms striving to supply the vehicle manufacturers under conditions resembling perfect competition. In such a mass-production industry where the final stage of production is highly concentrated, and where 'flow production' techniques are widely used, one would expect to find considerable specialization and concentration amongst suppliers.

Table 3 is an analysis of the bought-out content of a typical volume-produced car, which in this case amounts to 75 per cent of the total cost. It serves as a useful guide to the structure of the components section, and it highlights the relative importance of individual suppliers.

TABLE 3

Major Bought-out Components as Percentage of Total Expenditure on Bought-out Material in Typical Small Car—Company Y, 1954

1. Body	46.0
2. Electrical Equipment	9.3
3. Tyres and Wheels	8.2
4. Front Suspension Assembly	4.9
5. Castings	4.7
6. Brakes	3.2
7. Forgings	2.7
Total	79.0

Since the bulk of material expenditure is concentrated on a few items, it follows that the suppliers of these items are the ones that

[1] There are 2,500 totally different items in a motor car, most of them used in multiple, according to E. W. Hancock, Director and General Manager, Rootes Group. (*Machinist*, March 11, 1955, p. 407.)

matter from a cost standpoint. In this case they were responsible for nearly 60 per cent of the total cost of the car.

The car body is by far the most important single item of material expenditure. It may be supplied in the form of an unpainted body shell or, as in this case, trimmed and finished in every respect. The only independent volume producer of car bodies is the Pressed Steel Co. of Oxford, which makes upwards of 40 per cent of the entire output of the country. There are some fifteen other independent body firms, but their individual output is small, consisting of expensive, coach-built saloons, limousines, convertibles, estate cars and various other adaptations of standard models. Ford and Vauxhall make almost all their own bodies, Ford through its subsidiary, Briggs Motor Bodies. The British Motor Corporation obtains a large proportion of its requirements from its subsidiary, Fisher and Ludlow, but also relies heavily on Pressed Steel for other models. Rootes secures the bulk of its needs from Pressed Steel, with most of the remainder coming from its subsidiary, British Light Steel Pressings. The absorption of Fisher and Ludlow by BMC in 1953 left Standard in the position of being dependent on one of its rivals for its car bodies. Since that date Standard has transferred the production of the Vanguard bodies to Pressed Steel, and has entered into a long-term agreement with Mulliners Ltd. of Birmingham, with the aim of expanding the body-building capacity of the latter concern.[1] Pressed Steel remains, however, the only supplier capable of meeting the needs of the mass producer who has no body-building facilities of his own.

The second most important item of expenditure is electrical equipment; dynamos, starters, lamps, horns, wiring harness, etc. No vehicle manufacturer makes his own electrical equipment, and there is only one supplier of a complete range of such products for the whole industry, namely, Joseph Lucas Ltd. Having a virtual monopoly on a number of essential electrical items, the company is in a strong position to secure the original equipment business for other related products, such as batteries, ignition coils, distributors, windscreen wipers, etc., for which there is a certain amount of competition. But even if the vehicle manufacturers do not all buy the entire Lucas range, some 7 per cent to 10 per cent of the total cost of any popular-priced car made in Britain is represented by Lucas components.

Tyres and wheels are almost as significant a cost item as electrical

---

[1] Bodies for the Standard Eight and Ten continued to be supplied by Fisher and Ludlow. Later (1958) Standard acquired Mulliners.

equipment, with tyres absorbing the bulk of the outlay in this category. All the vehicle manufacturers buy their tyres outside rather than make them themselves. There are ten independent companies manufacturing tyres in the United Kingdom, but five of them account for almost all of the sales to car producers. Dunlop supplies more than two-thirds of all the car tyres sold as original equipment,[1] with the remaining third distributed amongst Avon, Firestone, Goodyear and Michelin. As for car wheels, the Ford Co., through its subsidiary, Kelsey-Hayes Wheel Co., is the only car firm to make its own; the other vehicle manufacturers obtain them from firms such as Dunlop, Rubery Owen, or Joseph Sankey (a member of the Guest, Keen & Nettlefolds Group). Unlike the situation with regard to car bodies or electrical equipment, there is a fairly wide choice of suppliers of tyres and wheels open to vehicle producers. Nevertheless, they have, in practice, tended to concentrate their purchases in the hands of a few companies.

For the front suspension, firms such as Alford & Alder and Rubery Owen supply the complete front axle assembly, while a fairly large number of companies specialize in producing front axles, shock absorbers, dampers, and other components of suspension systems. In the example given, one supplier furnished the complete assembly; but usually the larger car manufacturers make part of this equipment in their own plants, purchase certain specialized components from suppliers, and perform the assembly operations themselves.

Castings for cylinder blocks, cylinder heads, rear axle casings, etc., are an important outside purchase for the smaller car manufacturers who do not have their own foundry. Since the recent acquisition of Beans Industries Ltd. by Standard, the only member of the 'Big Five' without any foundry facilities is Vauxhall. But even the larger firms find it convenient to buy some types of castings outside. There are numerous foundries scattered throughout the country, catering to a wide variety of industries, which are capable of handling automotive business. Nevertheless, car producers have, to a large extent, centred their purchases of castings on the Birmid Group (Birmingham Aluminium Casting, Dartmouth Auto Castings, Midland Motor Cylinder, Sterling Metals) which has specialized in the motor trade.

The remaining items on the list, brakes and forgings, are almost entirely bought out by all the car manufacturers. In the case of brakes, their purchases are confined to two sources of supply—Auto-

[1] The Monopolies and Restrictive Practices Commission, *Report on the Supply and Export of Pneumatic Tyres*, 1955, p. 38.

motive Products and Girling Ltd. The latter company is a subsidiary of Joseph Lucas. For forgings, there are numerous companies supplying industry in general but, as in the case of castings, the car companies have tended to concentrate their business, in particular with Garringtons, another member of the Guest, Keen & Nettlefolds Group.

In concluding this examination of Company Y's material expenditure, it is evident that it is highly concentrated on a few major items and on a few firms. In fact, six suppliers were responsible for three-quarters of the expenditure. The remaining quarter was much more widely distributed amongst firms making products which, however essential they might be from the standpoint of the proper functioning of the car, are of minor importance when considered individually as costs. Very few of these items would cost the car manufacturer more than £2 each—none more than £5 each. Some goods in this category would be of a general nature—nuts, bolts, wire, metals, cloth, etc., but the bulk of the items would be highly specialized, proprietary components whose production is concentrated in a few companies whose output, with a few exceptions, is entirely devoted to the motor industry.

To illustrate this proprietary group of products, as far as the 'Big Five' are concerned, all the new cars are fitted with Champion sparking plugs, except Vauxhall which makes use of AC plugs made by another General Motors subsidiary. All steering gears come either from Burman & Sons or Cam Gears; all carburettors from Zenith or Solex (firms with a common ownership) or from SU Carburettors, a BMC subsidiary; all clutches from Borg & Beck (Automotive Products); all propeller shafts and universal joints from Hardy Spicer (Birfield Industries); all instruments from Smiths, again with the exception of Vauxhall which is supplied by AC; nearly all fuel pumps from AC; nearly all oil filters from AC and Automotive Products; most shock absorbers from Armstrong or Girling (Lucas). The list does not attempt to be complete, but serves to illustrate how very specialized firms in this group have become, and how one or two companies act as suppliers to the whole industry for their speciality.

It is difficult to sum up briefly the supplier situation for the industry as a whole, partly because of the considerable differences in the degree of integration existing between car manufacturers. No two producers are entirely alike in this respect, but Company Y's expenditure may be taken as representative of the non-integrated firm. The supply requirements of the highly integrated company, on the other hand, differ in important respects from this, and naturally involve some different supplying concerns. Table 4 provides a rough statistical picture of the contrast in the expenditure pattern between the two types of firms.

TABLE 4
Material Expenditure and Total Car Cost
(Per cent)

	Non-integrated firm	Integrated firm
Body (complete)	33	–
Tyres, wheels, brakes	9	9
Electrical equipment	7	7
Castings and forgings	6	2
Front suspension (complete)	4	–
Other proprietary components	10	12
Raw materials and non-proprietary	6	25
Total material	75	55
Share of car manufacturer	25	45
Total car cost	100	100

The integrated British firm makes its own bodies, but remains dependent on suppliers for such major items as electrical equipment and tyres. Nor does it attempt to make a whole host of smaller parts and components such as instruments, carburettors,[1] steering gears, fuel pumps, sparking plugs, locks, door handles, etc. On the other hand, the integrated firm, with its own body-building plant and foundry, performing as it does more manufacturing operations, naturally relies more heavily on suppliers of raw materials and non-proprietary products. This expenditure would be directed towards such items as steel, pig iron, brass, aluminium, bronze, copper, zinc, solder, rubber, wood, glass, leather, paint, insulating and upholstery materials. The Ford Company, with its own blast furnace, would add iron ore, coal and limestone to the list. The companies furnishing these basic materials to the car firms act as suppliers to industry in general, and hence cannot be considered as part of the motor industry.

With certain modifications, the supply structure for commercial vehicle and tractor production is very similar to that for cars. In general, the same suppliers are relied upon for electrical equipment,

[1] With the exception of BMC which makes part of its own requirements (SU Carburettors).

tyres, brakes, and the numerous smaller specialized parts and components. As far as heavy commercial vehicles are concerned, the main difference lies in the supply of bodies. Here the demand is often for small quantities, and a wide variety of shapes and sizes, designed, in many instances, to suit the individual requirements of customers. The techniques of mass-produced body pressings are obviously out of the question in this market, and Pressed Steel does no heavy commercial vehicle body work. Its place in this sphere is taken by over fifty small, independent concerns, turning out a largely hand-made product, in addition to the output of bodies made internally by the larger commercial vehicle producers such as Leyland and ACV.

5. THE MANUFACTURING INDUSTRY AS A WHOLE

In common with the other major vehicle producing countries, the British industry is highly concentrated. Five large-scale manufacturers produce over 90 per cent of the total output of cars, commercial vehicles and tractors. For some purposes it may be desirable to define the industry in terms of these big firms and the companies from whom they purchase their parts and components, and to treat the more numerous specialist car producers and the heavy vehicle producers as two separate, but related, branches of the main industry. Outstanding differences in product and in manufacturing techniques distinguish these producers from the 'Big Five'. There are similarities too, of course, and a certain amount of 'fringe' competition does take place between the firms in this group and the mass producers.

The extent of vertical integration varies considerably from firm to firm but, on the whole, the industry is not highly integrated in this direction. With such a structure the role of the suppliers is extremely important. Some of these, notably Pressed Steel, Joseph Lucas and Dunlop, are as large as the vehicle manufacturers themselves, and each one of them is responsible for a significant proportion of the total cost of all vehicles produced. Numerous other suppliers, varying greatly in size and in dependence on the motor industry, specialize in the mass production of the large number of essential bits and pieces needed by the vehicle producers. Individually, their share in the total cost of the vehicle is small, but much depends on the efficiency of their collective efforts.

The structure of the British industry is much less integrated, both horizontally and vertically, than that of the United States. There, three companies, instead of five, dominate a market many times the size of the British. These giant concerns make many more of the parts and components entering into the final product than do their British counterparts. This reflects historical factors, such as the insistence of the first Henry Ford that his company should produce everything that went into the car, including raw materials, and the merger policy of General Motors in its early years when numerous suppliers, as well as car manufacturers, were absorbed. But the underlying explanation lies in the huge volume of the American companies, a volume great enough to enable a single firm to gain most of the economies of scale at each stage of production, and thus to remove any cost advantages vertical disintegration may possess.

The Continental producers are also more integrated vertically than the British, but this is largely the result of necessity rather than choice. On the Continent, the growth of an independent components industry has lagged so far behind that of the vehicle manufacturers that the latter have had no alternative but to make a large proportion of their own parts and components.

A further feature of the British industry, not previously alluded to, is that a significant part of it is under the ownership and control of American interests. Vauxhall is a wholly-owned subsidiary of General Motors, and 55 per cent of the ordinary capital of the British Ford Company is owned by the parent concern in Detroit. In the parts and components section, one of the leading American manufacturers, the Borg Warner Corporation, is strongly represented, and is expanding rapidly as a producer here of automatic transmissions. Also American-owned are the Champion Sparking Plug Co., who supply most of the original equipment market for sparking plugs, AC Delco, a subsidiary of General Motors who make sparking plugs, instruments and a variety of small components such as air cleaners, fuel pumps, oil filters, etc., and the two tyre companies, Firestone and Goodyear.

Total employment in the manufacturing side of the industry is not easy to calculate. Approximately, however, vehicle manufacturers and suppliers concentrating on work for them together employed about 450,000 persons at the beginning of 1956. Employment in the industry was about 50 per cent higher than in 1939. The greatest concentration of employment was in the Midlands, where nearly one-half of the labour force was employed. The London area was next in importance, accounting for about one-fifth of the total labour force. Other important regions were Oxfordshire and Lancashire. The total labour force of the industry appears to have been almost equally divided between those manufacturing vehicles and bodies and those manufacturing other parts and components. In all, the manufacturing side of the motor industry accounted in 1956 for about 5 per cent of the total number employed in manufacturing industry, but a far higher proportion than this was of course dependent on the industry's fortunes.

6. THE RETAIL TRADE

Since vehicles are technical in character and need a good deal of attention and maintenance, it is important for manufacturers who wish to achieve a high level of sales to ensure that spares and service for their vehicles are widely available. For this reason, manufacturers take a great deal of interest in those who distribute their vehicles, and their normal practice is to link themselves closely to them by means of written agreements. These agreements typically contain provisions relating to the annual number of vehicle sales that the dealer is expected to make, to the amount of stocks of vehicles and spare parts that he is required to hold, the minimum amount of advertising he is to carry out, and so on. Agreements also require dealers to maintain adequate premises and staff,[1] to render certain specified free service to purchasers of vehicles, and to maintain the manufacturers' published list prices for their vehicles. The usual period of an agreement is one year in the United Kingdom,[2] but most agreements can be terminated by the manufacturer at comparatively short notice if there is a breach of the terms of the agreement. These agreements give manufacturers considerable power over their dealers, but in practice the relationship between manufacturers and their dealers is, generally speaking, a harmonious one and dealers continue to represent the same manufacturer indefinitely.

Car manufacturers usually have at least two grades of dealer: distributors and retail dealers, as they are often called. Most of the larger manufacturers have three grades of dealer—distributors, area dealers and retail dealers. Distributors are wholesalers, each covering an area of the country in which they are responsible for trade sales. They receive vehicles direct from the manufacturers and pass them

[1] Virtually all manufacturers require dealers to send their staff to courses in which they are given instruction in the servicing of the manufacturers' vehicles.
[2] There has been a trend recently in the United States for agreements to be for longer periods, e.g. three years.

on to area dealers or retail dealers. In addition, they sell vehicles to traders who do not deal regularly in that particular brand of vehicle, and they also sell direct to the public. Area dealers perform a similar role in a more limited geographical area. Retail dealers, as their name implies, only sell to the public. Distributors and dealers sell to the home market alone; export sales are handled directly by the vehicle manufacturers themselves.

The smaller car manufacturers have relatively few dealers. Heavy commercial vehicle manufacturers do not on the whole rely greatly on dealers and many carry out negotiations with their customers directly. Light vans and commercial vehicles, on the other hand, made principally by the 'Big Five' car manufacturers, go through distributors and dealers in the same way as cars. Commercial vehicles up to 15 cwt. made by car manufacturers are usually included in car agreements, but separate agreements are signed for the heavier commercial vehicles, and it is by no means always the case that all those dealing in the cars produced by a particular manufacturer deal also in his heavy commercial vehicles.

Distributors are naturally much larger in size on the average than dealers. They have more obligations, and in particular have to carry much larger stocks. In 1955 there were approximately 1,600 distributors compared with 5,800 area and retail dealers. The total number of 7,400 dealers was about 3 per cent less than it had been in 1937–8. The number of distributors was about 25 per cent higher, and the number of dealers about 10 per cent less. Total employment in all these firms was approximately 120,000.

In addition to distributors and dealers, there are a large number of other firms in the retail motor trade. In 1955, there were about 12,500 firms, employing some 75,000 persons, who did not regularly sell vehicles but were engaged on the repair of vehicles for the public and in the sale of fuel and accessories. A further 5,000 small firms sold only fuel and did no repair work. In all, employment in the garage trade must have mounted to well over 200,000 people in 1955.[1]

In recent years, oil companies have bought a few of the garages that sell their petrol and oils, but such acquisitions have not been common enough to suggest that there is any definite trend in this

---

[1] These figures have been based partly on trade estimates and partly on those given in the Census of Distribution and Other Services, 1950 (Vol. II, Retail and Services Trades) HMSO 1954. Allowance has been made for the fact that there was a response of only 84 per cent of the establishments, representing 88 per cent of total sales, in the motor vehicle group.

direction.[1] Such ownership links as there are in this sphere, however, are possibly more numerous than those between vehicle manufacturers and their appointed dealers. The only ownership connection of importance between vehicle manufacturers and dealers occurs in the case of Rootes, and this has an historical explanation—the Rootes organization began its existence by dealing in vehicles. Even in the Rootes' case, it is probable that only a small proportion of total home market sales are made through the firm's own retail outlets. In general, ownership links between vehicle manufacturers and their dealers are very weak. This does not mean, however, that the working links between them are not very powerful. Close collaboration is ensured not only by the system of annual agreements but also by frequent personal contacts at all levels between the staff of the manufacturing and the retail firms.

In one respect the links between manufacturers and dealers are less close than in the United States. Exclusive dealing has long been established in the American motor industry, although recent anti-trust decisions are causing some changes now,[2] but there is little insistence on it in Britain. The Ford Company is alone among the major British manufacturers in insisting on exclusive dealing, although there is nothing to stop Ford dealers and distributors from carrying on separate businesses to sell other makes of vehicle, and many in fact do so. Somewhat half-hearted attempts have been made by one or two of the other large car manufacturers to persuade their dealers to deal exclusively in their vehicles, but they have not been very successful. There is opposition to exclusive dealing on the part of the retail trade, which does not like to keep all its eggs in one basket. In addition, manufacturers themselves have been reluctant in recent years to push the notion of exclusive dealing too forcefully because of the atmosphere created by the restrictive practices legislation of 1948 and later years.[3] Apart from such considerations, however, the large manufacturers are aware of the fact that exclusive dealing would probably bring little real benefit to them. Although most of their dealers and distributors hold franchises for more than one make of

[1] There has, however, been a very marked trend towards exclusive dealing in the sale of petrol and oils. The large oil companies have offered strong inducements to garage owners to become exclusive dealers in their products, and it is the exception to find a 'free' garage which sells all the leading brands of petrol.

[2] *The Economist*, February 8, 1958, p. 520.

[3] It should be noted, in this connection, that exclusive dealing is never completely exclusive. Even when it is in force, dealers are permitted to make occasional sales of other makes of vehicle.

vehicle, it is rare for any but the largest retail firms to hold franchises for more than one 'Big Five' make. Their other franchises are usually for specialist makes of car which do not compete directly with the 'volume' makes of car produced by the 'Big Five'. These makes have by far the largest sales, and the business of most retailers is primarily based on them. Possibly the sales of the specialist makes of car produced by the 'Big Five' suffer from having to share the same showroom as such cars as Rover and Jaguar, but even for these cars the effect on sales is probably not great.

CHAPTER III

The Demand for Vehicles

THE outstanding feature of the market for vehicles has been its enormous expansion since the beginning of the century. At times the forces of expansion have been so strong that they have to a large extent counteracted the effects of trade depressions on vehicle sales. This happened in Great Britain in the early 1930s: at their worse (in 1931) new registrations of cars were only 16 per cent below their 1929 peak, and by 1933 they had surpassed it. In the United States, on the other hand, new registrations of cars fell by 75 per cent between 1929 and 1932 and did not recover to their 1929 level until after the outbreak of war. One of the main reasons for the different experiences of the two countries in these years was that in the United States the vast initial growth in demand that had followed the introduction of the motor car had, for the time being at least, exhausted itself. In the United Kingdom, however, the initial growth was still taking place.

In any study of the demand for vehicles an attempt must be made to distinguish the initial growth in demand that arose as consumers who could afford to buy motor vehicles heard of their existence and realized their value to them, from the type of demand that arises in a mature industry. One such attempt was made by de Wolff[1] who isolated a long-term trend in the 'demand for first purchase' of passenger cars, as he rather misleadingly called it. His calculations suggest that in the United States the growth in demand for first purchase was at its maximum in 1921. Whether this result is accepted or not[2], it is clear that by the late 1920s the factors having the greatest influence on the demand for vehicles in both the United States and Canada were other than those arising from the demand for a new

---

[1] P. de Wolff, 'Demand for Passenger Cars in the United States', *Econometrica*, 1938.

[2] de Wolff's study has been criticized on a number of grounds. See, for example, C. F. Roos and Victor von Szeliski, 'Factors governing changes in domestic automobile demand', in *The Dynamics of Automobile Demand*, General Motors Corporation (1939), p. 31.

product. The same can be said of the United Kingdom in the late 1930s. Today, this type of demand is of comparatively little importance in mature industrial countries.

A feature of American experience in the great depression which throws light on the factors affecting the demand for vehicles in 'mature' conditions, was that the great fall in the demand for new vehicles did not lead to a corresponding fall in the use of vehicles. In the United States, the number of cars on the road fell by only about 10 per cent between 1929 and 1933, and the number of commercial vehicles by only about 5 per cent. During the depression, the consumption of petrol in the United States was almost as stable as the consumption of bread.[1] The position of the United States in 1929 seems to have been that the average age of the vehicle fleet was rather low in that year because both private motorists and businessmen had replaced their vehicles during the boom. After 1929, when incomes fell disastrously, many motorists and businessmen went on using their existing vehicles, and the average age of the vehicle fleet rose. The experience of the United States in these years illustrates the fact that the basic demand is not a demand for new vehicles but a demand for vehicle ownership.[2] Potential buyers of new vehicles do not normally wait for their existing vehicles to fall to pieces before they replace them, and they are thus able to defer new purchases when times become bad. Ownership continues, but sales of new vehicles fall off.

The recognition of the fact that the basic demand for vehicles is a demand for ownership helps towards an understanding of the forces affecting the demand for second-hand as well as new vehicles. There is a very active second-hand market for vehicles, especially for cars. Many would-be owners of cars cannot afford to buy new cars, and have to content themselves with second-hand cars. A large number of those who become car owners for the first time do so by buying second-hand cars. In a mature consuming country, the number of car owners grows far less as a result of people buying new cars for the first time than as a result of their buying second-hand cars. Most pur-

[1] J. W. Scoville, 'Reasons for the fluctuations in automobile production', *Proceedings of the 1938 Ohio Conference of Statisticians*, p. 40.

[2] This is stressed by M. J. Farrell, 'The Demand for Motor Cars in the United States'. *Journal of the Royal Statistical Society*, Series A (General), Vol. 117, Part 2, 1954, p. 171.

For a general treatment of the demand for durable goods which emphasizes similar factors see Richard Stone and D. A. Rowe, 'The Market Demand for Durable Goods,' *Econometrica*, Vol. 25, No. 3, July 1957.

chasers of new cars are already car owners, so that their demand for new cars is a replacement demand. The cars they sell are usually only a few years old and have many useful years of life before them.[1] These cars enter the second-hand market and are eventually scrapped—not by their second owner probably, but by their fifth or sixth owner.

The market for cars is in effect, therefore, 'a set of interrelated markets for a series of close substitutes'. When prosperity increases, owners of very old cars become more ready to scrap them and buy newer cars. The sellers of these cars buy even newer cars, and so on up the chain of second-hand car owners. Strength in the second-hand market leads to high part-exchange allowances for those disposing of cars in exchange for new cars, and thus stimulates new car sales. This reinforces the stimulus already given by higher incomes generally. The converse occurs when prosperity decreases: scrapping is delayed, second-hand car prices fall, and new car purchases are put off.

A weakness of most of the statistical studies of the demand for cars that have been made in the past is that attention has been concentrated on factors affecting the demand for *new* cars. In Roos and von Szeliski's study,[2] for example, the price level of used cars was taken as given and not as a variable affected by the same forces as the demand for new cars. Farrell's study is exceptional in that it recognizes the interdependence of new and second-hand markets and attempts to deal with the demand for cars of all ages. All studies, however, whether they deal with the demand for new cars only, or with the demand for cars of all ages, are agreed that it is consumers' income that is the most important factor affecting the demand for cars. According to calculations made by the Office of Business Economics of the United States Department of Commerce'[3] each change of 1 per cent in the level of real disposable income in the United States was associated, in the period 1925–40, with a change of 2.5 per cent in the same direction in new car sales.[4] Calculations such

---

[1] In the United States in 1954, 86 per cent of new car buyers sold cars before acquiring their new cars. Two-thirds of the cars they sold had been bought within three years or less and over 90 per cent within five years. Only 58 per cent of used car buyers sold cars before acquiring their cars; presumably most of the remaining 42 per cent were buying cars for the first time. *Automobile Facts and Figures*, 1955, pp. 20 and 32.

[2] In *The Dynamics of Automobile Demand*, op. cit.

[3] *Survey of Current Business*, April 1952, pp. 19–21.

[4] This is an average figure. With durable commodities like motor cars it is to be expected that income elasticity of demand will vary over the trade cycle (see footnote to p. 41).

as these drive home the importance of the relationship between the level of income and the demand for cars, but even if such calculations had not been made it would still be very clear that the main reason for the catastrophic fall in new car sales in the United States between 1929 and 1932 was the steep fall in incomes brought about by the slump.

Another important factor affecting the demand for cars—although less important than the level of income—is the price of cars in relation to prices in general. The Office of Business Economics' estimate is that, in 1925–40, each 1 per cent increase in the ratio of the price of new cars to the index of consumer prices compiled by the US Department of Labour was associated with an average decrease of one and one-third per cent in new car sales.[1]

Many other factors do, of course, affect the demand for cars than consumers' income and car prices. The Office of Business Economics includes in its demand equation for new cars not only income and relative car prices, but also the number of households and the average scrapping age of cars. Roos and von Szeliski, while embodying similar factors to these in their equations, also include a number of others, notably consumers' stocks of cars. High stocks of cars in the hands of consumers (in relation to a calculated 'maximum ownership' level) will be a depressing influence on demand and low stocks a stimulant. High stocks are especially likely to depress demand if the average age of cars is low. A conjunction of high stocks and low average age is likely to be brought about by a boom. In a boom owners tend to replace their cars more speedily than they otherwise would, and the average age of the car fleet falls. If the boom in car sales is very strong, there is a danger of satiation and of a fall in new car sales even before any reduction in the general level of prosperity occurs. When the depression comes, consumers have a very big hump of 'unused mileage', as Scoville calls it,[2] to work off, and can therefore delay replacement for a very long time. The higher the level of sales in the preceding boom, the worse the slump in new car sales is likely to be.

---

[1] Estimates of this sort can only be regarded as a rough guide to the true position. This is illustrated by the fact that although Roos and von Szeliski's best estimate of price elasticity of demand in 1922–37 was 1.5, their calculations showed that it might be anywhere between 0.65 and 2.5. It is interesting to note that Roos and von Szeliski's estimates of income elasticity of demand over the years 1919–38 varied between 1.55 (in 1920) and 2.58 (in the saturated market conditions of 1938).

[2] 'Behaviour of the Automobile Industry in Depression.' Address delivered before the Econometric Society, New York, December 1935.

The factors affecting the demand for cars that have so far been mentioned by no means exhaust all those that are relevant. In a saturated market, one of the most important influences on new car sales is the stimulus given by the introduction of new models. New models have an effect both on the timing of sales and on their overall level. As far as timing is concerned, there is a definite falling off in sales when new models are anticipated, and a strong revival once they have been introduced. Roos and von Szeliski's calculations[1] suggest that in the USA, before the war, sales began to fall off significantly four months before the new model was introduced, and, in the final month before its introduction, were 38 per cent below average monthly sales. In the first months of the new model, on the other hand, sales were 28 per cent above average monthly sales, and the effect did not become negligible until four or five months later. Sometimes new models cast their shadow over the market for much longer periods than these: it was frequently asserted in the United States in 1956, for example, that one of the chief factors causing the slackening of car sales in that year was that revolutionary new models were to be introduced in the autumn. No doubt this view gave too much weight to the effect of the anticipated new models on sales, but it clearly was a factor of some importance.

Apart from seasonal variations in car sales associated with the introduction of new models, there are also seasonal variations in sales due to the weather: sales are normally at their highest in the spring and at their lowest in December and January. It is an important object of policy in the industry to counter the effect of the normal seasonal fluctuations by introducing new models at a time when the demand would otherwise be seasonally low. The British Motor Show, for example, at which new models are often introduced, takes place in October, a month when sales would otherwise be well below the average. Since the war the situation on the British home market has been subject to too many conflicting influences for the effect of seasonal fluctuations to be clearly distinguished. Before the war, holding the motor show in October had the effect of producing a revival of demand in the last quarter of the year.[2] As was seen earlier, however, the penalty of introducing new models at a time that is known in advance is that sales fell off considerably for months beforehand. It is no doubt partly for this reason that many British manufacturers have in recent years adopted the practice of announc-

[1] *Dynamics of Automobile Demand*, op. cit., p. 76.
[2] Political and Economic Planning, *Motor Vehicles*, p. 67.

ing their new models whenever they happen to be ready for large-scale production. Until 1956, however, the high level of demand for British cars made the question of the timing of new models a subsidiary one, and it would not be safe to predict that the abandonment of a conventional date for the introduction of new models represents a permanent change from the pre-war position. In the United States new models are still, in general, introduced towards the close of the year.

So far, only the effect of new models on the timing of sales has been considered. Much more important than this in market conditions where there is a constant threat of supply outrunning demand is the effect that new models have on the overall level of sales. In the United States, in particular, the truth has long been discovered that the way to increase sales of cars is to introduce new models which make the old models look old-fashioned. When the demand for new cars is largely a replacement demand, and when the cars replaced are not on the average very old, there is no doubt that one of the important influences affecting the speed of replacement is whether or not new models have been introduced. There is little doubt that an important contributory factor to the extremely high level of car sales in the United States in 1955 was the introduction by all the major companies of substantially re-styled models in late 1954. This was the date when the 'wrap-around' windscreen appeared on Ford, Chevrolet and Plymouth cars. Conversely, one of the factors contributing to lower sales in 1956 was probably the anticipation of new models later in the year. It might be argued, therefore, that all that happened in 1954–6 was that the new models of 1954 and 1956 induced a seasonal movement in sales extending over two years. To those familiar with the situation, however, this would not be a plausible hypothesis: they would have no doubt that during the whole period car sales were appreciably higher than they would have been if new models had not been introduced at the end of 1954. Unfortunately, it is not possible to give a convincing proof of this statement. Many of the statistical studies of demand that have been made incorporate factors which take account of the effect on demand of gradual improvements in the quality of vehicles, but make no allowance for substantial changes in quality. The type of analysis that Farrell has employed, however, could be used to show up the effect of substantial model changes on the gap between new and used car prices, and thus, by implication, the effect on the demand for new cars, but such an analysis has not been carried out for the period 1954–6.

A factor affecting the level of vehicle sales that has not been mentioned so far is the availability of credit for buying new and used vehicles and the terms on which it can be obtained. An appreciable proportion of vehicles are sold on hire purchase in the United Kingdom and a very large proportion in the United States. In the latter country, 62 per cent of the sales of new passenger cars in 1954 were financed by instalment credit or by other borrowing, and 63 per cent of used car sales. The proportion of sales financed by borrowing has gradually increased since the war: the comparable figures for 1949—the first year for which full statistics are available—are 43 per cent for new cars and 52 per cent for used cars.[1] Unfortunately, the corresponding statistics for this country are less comprehensive than in the United States since they only include borrowing under hire purchase agreements. Also, they have only been available since 1953.

TABLE 1
UK—Vehicles Subject to Hire Purchase Agreements

	1953	1954	1955	1956
New cars '000	26.5	52.8	85.3	69.7
Percentage of new car registrations	9	13	17	17
New commercial vehicles '000	13.5	21.5	37.8	39.4
Percentage of new commercial vehicle registrations	13	19	24	26
Used cars '000	167.6	253.5	339.8	333.8
Used commercial vehicles '000	26.2	35.4	44.2	44.8

As can be seen from the table, the proportion of new cars and commercial vehicles sold on hire purchase almost doubled between 1953 and 1955, although it scarcely rose in 1956, a year of low demand and stringent hire purchase restrictions.[2] It is clear that unless borrowing, other than under hire purchase agreements, is far more important than would seem likely, the proportion of new cars bought on credit of one sort or another is still much lower than in the United States. The table also brings out the fact that hire purchase agreements on used cars far exceed in number those on new cars, although the ratio of used to new car sales on hire purchase fell from approximately six

---

[1] *Automobile Facts and Figures*, 1955, p. 19. In 1955 and 1956 the proportion of sales financed by borrowing continued to rise, but it fell slightly in 1957.

[2] In the first eight months of 1957, when total sales revived, and hire purchase restrictions were less severe, the proportion of new cars sold on hire purchase rose to 21 per cent.

to one to four to one between 1953 and 1955. The proportion of used cars sold on hire purchase cannot be calculated because the total annual sales of used cars in the United Kingdom is not known. In the United States, the total annual sales of used cars are approximately double those of new cars.[1] It seems possible that in the mid-1950s the ratio was higher than this in this country. If one assumes it was three to one, then used cars sold on hire purchase would have accounted for approximately one-quarter of total used car sales in 1956.

In view of the steep upward trend in the proportion of new cars and commercial vehicles sold under hire purchase agreements during the period 1953–5, and in view also of the return of more or less normal market conditions by the mid-1950s, it seems reasonable to expect the proportion of sales on hire purchase to continue to grow, if allowed to do so. Even at present, however, hire purchase sales are of considerable importance, and variations in hire purchase terms can appreciably affect the demand for vehicles. Apparently some economists in the United States motor industry hold the view, or held it before the war, that when hire purchase terms are made easier this does not induce more people to buy cars so much as it induces those who were going to buy cars anyway to buy a more expensive car.[2] Presumably the converse would also hold true—harder terms induce people to buy cheaper cars. There may be a grain of truth in this view, but there seems no doubt, going by the experience of the last few years, that the imposition of more severe hire purchase restrictions can very effectively lower the total level of demand. It is difficult to isolate the effect of a tightening of hire purchase terms on demand, just as it is difficult to isolate the effect of changes in other variables, but there is little doubt in the minds of competent observers that much of the fall in Canadian demand for vehicles in 1951–2 was due to Government-imposed restrictions on instalment terms, and the same is true of British experience after February 1956, when the minimum deposit required on vehicles was raised to 50 per cent of their purchase price.[3]

Analogous to the effect of hire purchase controls on demand is the effect of tighter credit conditions generally, which reduce the ability

[1] *Automobile Facts and Figures*, 1955, p. 19.
[2] *Dynamics of Automobile Demand*, op. cit., p. 68.
[3] The minimum deposit on cars was reduced to 20 per cent in December 1956. Part of the recovery in car sales after this date can no doubt be attributed to this reduction. The minimum deposit was raised to 33⅓ per cent in May 1957, and at the same time the minimum deposit on heavy commercial vehicles was lowered from 50 to 33⅓ per cent.

of both private individuals and businesses to borrow from banks in order to finance the purchase of vehicles. In the case of businesses, the effect of tax allowances is also important—for example, the granting of investment allowances in the United Kingdom during the period 1954–6.

Among the factors affecting the demand for vehicles that have so far been ignored, the most important is the level of maintenance and running costs. Because of the great practical difficulties involved, none of the statistical studies of the demand for vehicles has taken these costs into account. Their level, however, affects both the total number of cars and commercial vehicles demanded and also the distribution of demand between different types of vehicles. Over the life of an average vehicle, they may amount to two or three times its original price.[1] In view of this, it is not surprising that many would-be private motorists are deterred by costs of upkeep rather than by the initial purchase price of cars, or that operators of commercial vehicles scrutinize running costs as carefully as they do.

So far, most of the discussion has been concerned with the demand for cars, and the tacit assumption has been made that cars are bought primarily by private motorists. In fact an appreciable proportion of car sales are made to business firms, local authorities, etc., so that these bodies are an important factor in the car market as well as being the only factor in the market for commercial vehicles. Businesses and other bodies may buy cars directly, they may help employees to buy cars for use in the business, or they may pay expenses to employees when their cars have been used on company business. Because of the variety of ways in which business demand for the services of cars manifests itself, it is virtually impossible to determine what proportion of new car sales can be attributed to demand by or on behalf of businesses. It was commonly said in the trade, in the first few years after the war, that some 80 per cent of new car sales were financed directly or indirectly by businesses, and some observers claimed that the figure was as high as 90 per cent. Whether figures of this magnitude were correct or not, the true figure was undoubtedly a high one because of the priority given to fleet users and other busi-

[1] For example, Scoville, *Reasons for the Fluctuation in Automobile Production*, op. cit., p. 54. Scoville's calculation, which was made for the United States in the 1930s, was that if an ordinary passenger car were operated for nine years, the original cost of the car would only amount to 32 per cent of the total cost of buying and operating it. A similar calculation for the United Kingdom would have yielded a figure as low as 25 per cent.

ness customers at that time. In recent years, the proportion of sales to businesses, or to those subsidized by businesses, has probably been lower, but it is still a very appreciable one.[1]

There is no doubt that the demand for commercial vehicles and for those cars which are paid for by businesses is affected by very much the same factors that affect the demand for private cars. Car and commercial vehicle registrations normally move very closely together, and it is clear that fluctuation in income is the main causal factor in both cases. Demand from businesses is influenced also by the size and age of their existing stock of vehicles, and by changes in taxation provisions. Price is almost certainly a subsidiary factor from the point of view of the number of vehicles bought, although it does, of course, affect the type of vehicles that are used. The fashion element in demand that raises the level of private car sales when new models are introduced is largely absent in the case of commercial vehicles, although its effect on business demand for cars is probably appreciable. Many businesses normally buy new cars, and they feel that it would reflect badly on their prestige if their models were to become too outdated. Businesses using numbers of vans and goods vehicles usually buy these new also, but the reason for this is much more closely connected with economy in running costs than with fashion considerations, and new models are appraised very largely in the light of the financial advantages that their purchase might entail.

VEHICLES IN USE

Differences in the level of income per head in different countries, together with differences in vehicle prices and in the weight of taxation (see below), help to account for the striking differences that are to be found in the level of vehicle use. Many other factors, such as the size of the country and the state of its roads, are clearly of importance also. In all these respects the United States has been particularly fortunate, and the result has been that the level of vehicle ownership in that country is unsurpassed anywhere else in the world. As early as 1929, there was a car for every six members of the population. The position did not alter much before the outbreak of war, but

---

[1] According to *The Economist*, 'well over half the new cars sold in Britain, in most post-war years, have also been reckoned as "business investment" '. September 7, 1957, p. 778. It was (very roughly) estimated by the Central Statistical Office that rather more than half of new cars registered in 1954 were bought by private consumers. *National Income Statistics* (CSO 1956) p. 125.

by the early 1950s the number of cars in use had risen so much that there was one for every three persons. The level of vehicle use is of course very high in the United Kingdom as compared with most other countries—taking cars and commercial vehicles together it is the highest in Europe—but it is well behind the United States. This can be seen by the figures of car ownership. There were in this country about 45 people per car in 1929, 25 per car in 1937, and rather less than 20 in the early 1950s. The corresponding figures for commercial vehicles show a big discrepancy between the two countries also, but it is only about half as great as in the case of cars and the relationship has not altered greatly since 1929. Relative to the position in the United States, the use of commercial vehicles was far more developed in this country in 1929 than the use of cars.

TAXATION AND DEMAND

In many countries, heavy taxation raises appreciably both the initial price of vehicles and their running costs. This is particularly true of the United Kingdom, where vehicle taxation is heavier than in most other countries. Calculations made by the Society of Motor Manu-Manufacturers and Traders[1] suggest that before the war the total amount payable on a 1,500 c.c. car, travelling 8,000 miles per annum, in the form of direct taxes, taxes on fuel and compulsory insurance, might have amounted to about £26 per annum in the United Kingdom, as compared with £6 10s in the United States, £5 10s in Canada, £19 in France, £15 in Germany, and £14 and £16 in South Africa and Australia respectively. None of the leading motoring countries had a level of taxation as high as that of the United Kingdom. This was true even when compulsory insurance was excluded from the computation. Since the war, the imposition of purchase tax in the United Kingdom has increased the weight of motor taxation relative to that of many other countries.[2] It has been calculated that on the basis of 1954 tax rates, taxation on a 1,500 c.c. car, travelling 8,000 miles per annum and with a life of eight years, amounted to about £86 per annum. This compared with £18 in the United States, £25 in South Africa and £30 in Australia. In 1954, however, Western Germany and Italy both had heavier tax burdens than the United

---

[1] Society of Motor Manufacturers and Traders, *The Motor Industry of Great Britain*, 1939, p. 141.
[2] Ibid., 1954, p. 298.

Kingdom, their taxes amounting to £92 and £104 per annum respectively.

British taxation on cars takes the form of a flat rate annual tax,[1] a petrol duty[2] and a purchase tax.[3] Third-party insurance is compulsory, and the premiums charged by insurance companies rise with the size of car engine. The annual tax on cars deserves particular mention. From 1910 to 1947, this tax was assessed on horse-power, which was calculated by means of a formula based on the piston diameter multiplied by the number of cylinders in the engine. Cars with engines of equal cubic capacity were therefore taxed more heavily the larger the piston area of their engines. The horse-power tax put a premium on small-bore, long-stroke engines, and it almost certainly influenced design in the direction of such engines. It also influenced design in the direction of small engines generally, and its effect reinforced that of the petrol tax and of the higher insurance premiums on larger cars. By itself, the horse-power tax, which was only 15*s* per horse-power per annum in the years immediately before the war, made very little difference to the cost of running cars which differed by only a few horse-power. As between running an 8 horse-power or a 12 horse-power car, for example, the difference due to the horse-power tax was only 1*s* 2*d* per week. It has been argued, however, that the horse-power tax had a greater effect on the pattern of demand than was warranted by its absolute size.[4] It was one of the factors that induced manufacturers to concentrate on small cars and to offer a wide range of models differing from each other by only a few horse-power. This had repercussions on British success in those important export markets where standardized large-engined American cars were very popular. There was, however, the counteracting advantage, from the British point of view, that the form of taxation helped to protect the domestic market against high-powered imported cars.

These arguments place a great deal of weight on the form of taxation, and particularly on the horse-power tax. It is doubtful, however, whether the tax was as important as these arguments imply. Given the general level of income in this country and the nature of

[1] In 1957 the tax was £9 on cars of 6 horse-power or less, £10 10*s* on cars of more than 6 horse-power but not exceeding 7 horse-power, and £12 10*s* on cars of over 7 horse-power (the great majority).
[2] 2*s* 6*d* per gallon in 1956, until December, when it was raised to 3*s* 6*d* following the blocking of the Suez Canal. It was lowered to 2*s* 6*d* again in April 1957.
[3] 60 per cent of the wholesale value in 1957.
[4] Political and Economic Planning, *Motor Vehicles*, p. 65.

the terrain, it is probable that home demand would in any event have been concentrated on medium-sized and small cars. The incidence of taxation may also have been a factor in encouraging a diversity of models, but here again other forces, such as the desire to attract motorists in a competitive market by offering a 'full line', were at work in the same direction. The form taken by taxation certainly played a part in giving the domestic industry protection from imports, but the import duty of 33⅓ per cent was probably more important here than domestic taxation. On balance, the truth may be that the form of motor taxation before the war imposed some bias towards low-powered cars, and hence some hardship on exports, but that other factors were more important. What is certainly true is that the overall weight of taxation reduced the level of demand below what it would otherwise have been. In so far as this prevented economies of scale from being realized, this was a factor tending to raise costs and hence to inhibit exports.

Agitation against the horse-power tax was considerable after the war,[1] and in 1947 it was replaced by an annual tax on cubic capacity. This was designed to remove the distorting effect of the horse-power tax on engine design, but it still penalized cars with large engines. It was replaced in the following year by a flat rate tax which was at first only made applicable to cars registered after 1946, but was later extended to all cars. The tax on fuel was raised to compensate for the loss of revenue from the annual tax, some of the burden thus being shifted to commercial vehicles. The effect of these changes in taxation is not easy to judge. Shortly after they were made a number of new car models were introduced, the first of wholly post-war design, which were higher-powered on the average than those they replaced. The main explanation of this change, however, was probably the increased dependence of the manufacturers on export markets rather than abolition of the horse-power tax. In any case, in more recent years, several manufacturers have concentrated again on small car production and the balance has swung back the other way. By 1955 the pattern of registrations had become very like that of 1938 and 1947.[2]

[1] For example, National Advisory Council for the Motor Manufacturing Industry, *Report on Proceedings* (1947).

[2] This was true of total production also. However, the production figures show a slightly lower proportion of small cars, because a rather lower proportion of small cars are exported than are sold to the home market. In 1954, for example, 74.5 per cent of total car production was of cars under 1,600 c.c. Of total car exports, 70.1 per cent were under 1,600 c.c. *v.* Society of Motor Manufacturers and Traders, *Motor Industry of Great Britain*, 1955, pp. 12–13.

TABLE 2
Percentage of Total Car Registrations in the UK

	1938*	1947*	1948	1955
Up to 1,000 c.c.	30	31	14	31
1,000–1,500 c.c.	48	46	41	48
1,500–2,500 c.c.	11	17	19	15
Over 2,500 c.c.	11	5	26	6

* The figures for 1938 and 1947 were calculated with respect to horse-power.

These figures suggest that the abolition of the horse-power tax has, in itself, not had any appreciable effect, although it may be that the increase in fuel taxation has influenced demand towards the less-highly-powered cars. On the whole, there seems little doubt that the level of British income, the size of British roads and the relatively short distances that have to be covered, are, together with the heavy overall weight of motor taxation, the predominant factors in determining the pattern of demand for cars. In one respect, however, the abolition of the horse-power tax does appear to have been important. There has been a trend towards 'squarer' engines in recent years; that is, engines with large bores and short strokes—a type which was definitely discouraged by the horse-power system of taxation.

Taxation has played a part in the development of commercial vehicles as well as in the development of cars. In 1928 the tax on petrol, which had been repealed in 1921, was reimposed. No duty was placed on heavy oil until 1933, and between that year and 1935 the duty on heavy oil was much lower than that on petrol. Since 1935 the rates of duty have been the same, but the initial difference in duties certainly provided some of the impetus for the development of the diesel engine which uses heavy oil as fuel. Diesel engines have now fully established themselves, and are used in Great Britain in virtually all heavy goods and passenger carrying vehicles, as well as in a large number of tractors. They are widely employed on the Continent also. In the United States, where fuel costs are much lower (one of the main advantages of the diesel engine is that it is economical in the use of fuel), diesel engines have been less widely adopted.

Several other legislative influences have affected the market for commercial vehicles in the United Kingdom. The most notable before the war were the Road and Rail Traffic Acts of 1930 and 1933, and the substantial increase of taxation[1] on commercial vehicles that

[1] Annual taxation on goods vehicles is based on unladen weight, and for passenger vehicles on seating capacity. For both categories the tax increases with vehicle size.

took effect in January 1934. At the same time the speed limit for lorries—20 miles per hour for vehicles exceeding 2½ tons unladen weight[1] and 30 miles per hour for vehicles under 2½ tons—was more strictly enforced. These measures almost certainly held back the expansion of the commercial vehicle fleet and encouraged operators to turn to lighter types of vehicle.

Since the war, the most notable legislative measures affecting commercial vehicles have been the nationalization of certain road-transport undertakings in 1947, and the partial de-nationalization of 1952. The effect of these measures on the demand for commercial vehicles is not easy to judge. Possibly the 1947 Act was an important factor in encouraging the rapid growth that has taken place since the war in the number of commercial vehicles run by businesses for their private use. Possibly also the greater freedom to fix their rates that was given to the railways in the 1952 Act will indirectly have some adverse effects on the demand for commercial vehicles. The effect of all these factors is likely to be of small importance, however, in comparison with that of such fundamental factors as changes in the general level of national income.

---

[1] The speed limit for heavy lorries was raised to 30 m.p.h. in 1957.

CHAPTER IV

Technique of Production

THE process of manufacturing motor vehicles is an extremely complex one. It has been said that the modern small car contains about 2,500 parts or assemblies of parts. If every nut and bolt is counted separately, the total number of parts is as high as 20,000. It follows from this complexity of the product that the process of vehicle manufacture must consist primarily of the working of raw materials in a great variety of ways in order to manufacture all the necessary component parts of the vehicle, and finally of the assembly of all these parts to form the complete vehicle. Most of the parts used are of metal. It has been estimated that the average private car contains 10 cwt. of sheet steel, 10 cwt. of other steel, and 400 lb. of cast iron.[1] This, together with much smaller quantities of brass, copper and lead, make up very nearly the whole weight of the car. The growing use of aluminium and plastics for body panels has so far had a negligible effect on the consumption of steel. Other important raw materials are rubber, wood, leather, plastic covered cloth, glass and textiles.[2]

The metals used in vehicle manufacture have first of all to be cast, forged, pressed or otherwise processed. The most important single casting is the cylinder block, and the crank shaft is among the most important of the forgings. Castings and forgings have to be machined before they are ready for assembly into the completed vehicle, and the engineering work involved is an extremely important part of the process of manufacture. In order to carry out all the necessary machining, the industry needs a vast quantity of machine tools: it does, indeed, use more machine tools than any other British industry.[3] It also uses more sheet steel than any other industry—taking approximately one-quarter of all deliveries to the home market. When it is producing at capacity (as in 1955), it has to rely on heavy imports as well

[1] PEP *Motor Vehicles*, p. 20.
[2] PEP, op. cit., p. 19.
[3] PEP, op. cit., p. 21.

as on home production. All this sheet steel is, of course, required primarily for vehicle bodies, but it is also employed in a number of other uses. The pressing of sheet steel into the appropriate shapes for bodies, etc., is another extremely important part of the process of vehicle manufacture.

The process of assembling the vehicle is in practice carried out in a number of stages. Some parts are assembled into components such as carburettors, dynamos and starter motors. Other parts are assembled directly into such 'sub-assemblies' as engines, vehicle bodies, gear boxes and rear axles. The engine sub-assembly is the most complex of all and comprises the cylinder block and head, the crankshaft, the pistons, etc., together with such components as the carburettor and the dynamo. Before the war, it was the common practice, in the case of most popular cars, for the various sub-assemblies to be brought together with the chassis frame to form the chassis[1] of the vehicle, and then for the completed body to be added in the final assembly stage. It is now the common practice in this country, although not in the United States, for the body shell and chassis frame to be built as a single unit.[2] The practice of unitary construction in the British industry has altered the final assembly process to a certain extent, but it is still essentially the same. This final assembly of the completed vehicle is, of course, always carried out by the vehicle manufacturer himself, but those activities that precede the final assembly are, as has been seen in Chapter II, carried out partly by the vehicle manufacturer and partly by a large number of other firms. These include firms in the iron and steel industry, component manufacturers, engineering firms, and so on.

For export purposes, it is becoming increasingly the practice to ship completed vehicles in unassembled form. This cuts down the amount of shipping space required, it reduces the value of the vehicles and therefore attracts less duty in the importing country, and it fits in with the desire of some importing countries to build up assembly industries of their own. Many of the assembly plants in these countries, e.g. Australia and South Africa, are owned by British vehicle manufacturers. When vehicles are exported in this way, they are only partially assembled in the parent factory and then crated in a form suitable for export. In 1956, just over 40 per cent of

[1] i.e., all the working parts, excluding the body.
[2] The great size of most American cars is one of the factors militating against the adoption of unitary construction in the United States industry. For a discussion of this question v. *Automobile Engineer*, February 1957, p. 41.

cars exported complete were in this 'c.k.d.'[1] form. Not all cars are exported complete, however, In particular, cars exported to Australia are often sent without bodies (in 1956 the proportion was 50 per cent). This is because Australia has encouraged the growth of an extensive body-building industry of her own.

The manufacture of spare parts for vehicles is normally carried out at the same time as the manufacture of those parts which are to be embodied in the vehicles themselves. This is clearly the most economical way of producing spare parts, and the practice is to turn out a sufficient number of engine 'sets' per week, for example, to enable the scheduled number of vehicles to be built and to leave over a sufficient number of sets to be distributed to the retail motor trade at home and abroad and to be retained in the manufacturers' own stores. Manufacturers have in some cases been forced to set up special factories to provide spare parts for models no longer in production, but this has to some extent been forced upon them by the continued existence of large numbers of pre-war cars.

It will be clear from what has been said about the technique of producing vehicles that many different types of process are involved. Among the most important of these are the machining of cast and forged iron and steel, the pressing of steel, and the assembly of parts to form components, sub-assemblies and, finally, completed vehicles. The choice of technique to be adopted in each of these processes is flexible to a considerable extent. In particular, different techniques are appropriate to different scales of output. As the scale of output of any standardized product grows, costs can be reduced by altering techniques in two main ways.[2] First and most important increasing mechanization becomes worth while. This is because it is possible to leave machines on one task for a very long time. One step that can be taken is to fit standard engineering machines with devices to make their operations more automatic. Another, which is only economical at very large scales of output, is to employ machines which have been

[1] i.e., 'completely knocked down'. In fact, practically no car is ever built up before export. With heavy commercial vehicles on the other hand, which are often tailor-made to suit customer's requirements, a vehicle exported c.k.d. may actually have been fully assembled and then 'knocked down' again before export —this is to ensure that no parts have been forgotten.

[2] The rest of this section has been written mainly with machining processes in mind, but the general principles are applicable to most other processes carried out in the industry. It should be remembered, however, that automatic methods (discussed below) are less applicable at present to the assembly line than they are to the machine shop or the press shop.

specially designed for the particular work they have to do. Such 'special-purpose' machines do not have the virtues of flexibility, but they are often able to work much faster than general-purpose machines, to perform several operations at once—they may thus replace several general-purpose machines—or to do work which could not be done at all on ordinary machines. Since many special-purpose machines are specific to one particular set of operations on a particular part of the vehicle, they have to be scrapped when the design of that part of the vehicle is changed. They therefore have to pay for themselves over the life of the part concerned, possibly in as short a period as two or three years, and this explains why it is only worth while to introduce them at very large scales of output.

The second way in which the technique of production is altered as the scale of output changes is that 'flow production' methods supersede 'batch production' methods. When the volume of output is very large and the product standardized, it becomes worth while to adopt flow production, i.e. to arrange machines in sequence, so that a whole series of operations can be carried out one after the other. At smaller scales of output, it would not pay to do this, as it would be necessary to rearrange the machines when the type of work to be carried out was changed, and this would have to be done at frequent intervals. Batch production has therefore to be employed.[1] Flow production has many advantages over batch production.[2] It reduces greatly the quantity of working stocks required, it cuts out wasteful work handling from one part of the factory to another, and it greatly increases the possibility of mechanical handling. The adoption of flow production need not in itself lead to a reduction in the direct labour force, but it is likely to do so at volumes high enough to warrant the incorporation into the line of conveyor belts and other mechanical handling devices. At very large scales of output, it pays to introduce special-purpose machines into the line, and to mechanize extensively. The logical outcome of this is the automatic transfer machine, the principal form which 'automation' takes in the motor industry. Machines of this type are, in effect, automatic flow production lines. They work to a time cycle, and incorporate arrangements

[1] With batch production, a number of parts is processed on one machine, then moved to another machine for the next process, and so on. Each machine needs a batch of parts to work on and one worker per machine is usually needed also. Machines do not generally perform the same operation all the time. They are adapted from time to time to perform different operations.

[2] F. G. Woollard, *Principles of Mass and Flow Production* (1954), pp. 15 *et seq.*

for automatically transferring the part to be processed from one 'station' to the next one, when the machines at each station have carried out their work on the part. The obvious advantage of machines of this type is that they save labour, but they bring with them several other important advantages.

'The justification for the investment of capital in automation is not the mere elimination or reduction of the labour force. . . . The advantage is found in the reduction of the time expended in handling, conveying, loading and unloading the work and the consequent increase in the rate of production. Many machines have necessarily been operated in the past at considerably less than designed speeds as their cycle times were determined by loading and unloading operations. The compounding of reduced handling time and increased operating speed results in a much higher rate of utilization of costly machines. Other advantages accruing are better utilization of shop space, as room is no longer required for stacking work between machines, and less damage to work by eliminating setting down and picking up between operations.'[1]

Another commentator, after stressing the fact that the use of automatic transfer machines generally results in higher quality owing to the closer control that is essential on tool life, work location, and machine consistency, suggests orders of magnitude for the savings involved.[2]

'The adoption of transfer machines against individual special-purpose machines can result in a reduction in area of approximately 25 per cent, and in work-in-progress of between 10 per cent and 15 per cent. The reduction in operating labour is, of course, dependent on the number of stations in each transfer machine, but, generally speaking, it has been working out as a saving of 60 per cent to 80 per cent of labour required by previous methods. The fourth economic advantage, machine utilization, has the greatest single promise of savings, and this is especially true in concerns not operating on large quantities. With the adoption of transfer machines in the motor industry, machine tool utilization rose roughly to 85 per cent or 90 per cent, a probable gain of about 15 per cent. Automatic control of machines can raise utilization in the general engineering shop from an average of 40 per cent to approaching 60 per cent or more. This represents a gain of 50 per cent which would have a profound effect on manufacturing costs generally.'

[1] *Automobile Engineer*, February 1957, pp. 54–5.
[2] E. Cars, in *Metalworking Production*, January 27, 1956, p. 147.

Although an attempt was made to introduce automatic transfer machinery in the engines branch of Morris Motors in 1923-4, techniques were not far enough advanced for the attempt to be successful, and the first really large scale developments were made after the Second World War in the American motor industry. It was said in 1956 that the Ford Motor Company probably had the nearest approach to the automatic factory with their engine plant at Cleveland, Ohio, but that Austin, Rootes, Vauxhall, Standard and Ford in this country were moving towards the Cleveland example.[1] The first machines used in the large American motor plants, as also in the British plants, were built specially for the job in hand. They were, in effect, huge special-purpose machines which had to be scrapped when the life of the model on which they were designed to work came to an end. Such inflexible machines might justify themselves from a cost point of view in the American motor industry, with its huge scale of production, but could only do so in isolated cases in motor industries like the British, the French or the German: hence the comparative slowness with which automatic methods were at first introduced into these industries. In recent years, however, there has been an increasing emphasis in Europe on automatic transfer lines built up of standard units—'building block' machine tools as they have been called. The machine heads used and the equipment employed for transferring work between stations have been standardized—so that they can themselves be produced in quantity—and it is possible to adapt these standard units to be used again when a model change occurs. An even less ambitious way of obtaining automatic production is to link standard general-purpose machines together with automatic cycles to form automatic production lines, incorporating automatic loading and unloading devices. This, it is said, is the way that many of the German machine tool makers thought, in 1955 at least, that the pattern of automation was likely to develop in Europe.[2] Even the Americans began to have second thoughts, in the mid-1950s, about the cost and inflexibility of their highly integrated production lines, and there was a significant trend at the 1955 Chicago Machine Tool Show towards the automation of individual machines and towards automatic lines incorporating standard types of machine.[3] It was said in 1956 that the American Ford Company was proposing to adopt a policy of using standard unit machines, so that the major

[1] E. Cars, op. cit., p. 146.
[2] *Metalworking Production*, September 23, 1955, p. 1662
[3] Ibid., September 16, 1955, p. 1638.

units of a machine could be rearranged if desired, and that, in addition, they wanted machines to be of standard physical dimensions so that they could fit in where needed and one make could be substituted for another.[1]

On the Continent, the Renault Company was a pioneer in the adoption of standard unit machines to form an automatic transfer line. In this country, an interesting example of an automatic transfer line of this type is to be found in the Austin works at Longbridge. Austins were the pioneers in this field, although Ford and Vauxhall were the first firms to adopt automatic transfer machines.[2] The Austin case has been much quoted, mainly because the company has released figures showing the comparative costs of the new transfer-machine for making cylinder blocks and the thirteen equivalent standard machines which it replaced. As might have been expected, there was a saving of floor space when the transfer machine was introduced and also a very considerable saving in labour costs. Taking into account the increased output of the transfer machine, the floor space saved was 26 per cent and the saving in direct labour costs was nearly 85 per cent. What was less expected was that the new machine was cheaper than the machines it replaced: machine costs per unit of output were 30 per cent less.[3] Too much weight must not be placed on this example alone. Other cases of automation could certainly be found which use more capital than conventional methods, but the Austin example does at least indicate that the capital cost of automatic transfer machinery in the motor industry need not be exceptionally high. In order to install their new line, incidentally, Austins found it necessary to establish shops to build the machine heads and also to set up a department to produce electronic devices. The machine tool firm of James Archdale, which built the first automatic transfer machine for Morris Motors in 1923–4, supplied bases and transfer mechanism. Archdales were the only machine tool manufacturers that Austins could find who were really interested in sharing the work of manufacture with them. According to an expert in the field,

'The machine tool companies making this special equipment are all too few, but the credit for blazing the trail must be given to James Archdale and Company Ltd. There is, as far as I know, only one

[1] *Metalworking Production*, August 24, 1956, p. 1325.
[2] Ibid., June 10, 1955, p. 1035.
[3] F. Griffith, 'Why Austin developed Unit Construction Transfer Machines,' *The Machinist*, January 21, 1955, pp. 107–113.

concern in this country specializing in inter-operation transfer devices, although there are several who make individual pneumatic, hydraulic, electric and electronic devices.'[1]

It might be thought that complicated automatic transfer lines of the Austin or the Renault type involve very heavy maintenance costs to offset, to some extent at least, the savings in direct labour that they bring about. It is certainly true that very careful attention has to be paid to maintenance, and all machine tools, etc., must be inspected and, if necessary, changed at regular intervals. The Renault experience, however, is that the standardization of the special machine elements has allowed considerably increased production in their workshops without a proportionate increase in maintenance staff. Renault have estimated that if they were to replace 200 special-purpose machines in a particular department by the 1,000 standard machines that would be needed to take their place, the maintenance staff on these machines would have to be increased in number by 130 per cent.[2] The American Ford Company, on the other hand, found that maintenance costs were greatly increased when they first introduced automatic transfer machinery. In time, however, they found, like Renault, that maintenance costs could be reduced.[3]

It is evident that recent developments in automatic transfer machinery and in other aspects of automation such as automatic process control,[4] have brought such methods of production and control well within the reach of such large vehicle producers as Austins. From time to time statements have been made about the possibility of these methods being economical for smaller producers also. A special technical committee, set up in 1955 by the Production Engineering Research Association to undertake operational research into automation, decided to concentrate on the ways in which smaller firms, producing in small and medium batch quantities, could make use of

---

[1] F. G. Woollard, 'Machines in the Service of Men', in *The Automatic Factory —What does it mean?* Institution of Production Engineers, Report of the conference held at Margate, June 16–19, 1955, p. 204. Perhaps there is encouragement in the fact that Ford in the USA, when they pioneered automation in the motor industry, made similar complaints. Within a few years there was a mushroom growth of firms directly occupied in this sort of work. (*Metalworking Production*, June 10, 1955, p. 1021.)

[2] P. Bezier, 'Automatic Transfer Machines' in *The Automatic Factory—What does it mean?*, op. cit., p. 90.

[3] *Metalworking Production*, June 10, 1955, p. 1075.

[4] DSIR *Automation* (HMSO, 1956), Chapter II, B.

automatic methods.[1] It is particularly interesting from the point of view of the motor industry that in planning the production of a new diesel engine in 1955, AEC, the heavy vehicle manufacturers, took the opportunity of changing from batch to flow line methods in the machining of engine casings and cylinder heads, and introduced flexible automatic transfer machinery. The quantities involved were very small—three casings and six heads per hour—and did not justify a high degree of automation, but nevertheless the new cylinder head line included batteries of machines with automatic transfer of the components between them. These batteries comprised a number of individual Archdale machines, linked by a transfer mechanism. A new method of holding the work in place greatly simplified the construction of the machines and made it economically feasible to use the transfer system on relatively small quantities. The new layout resulted in five to six times the output of cylinder heads and three times the output of engine casings per man, and considerable savings were made in floor space and in stocks.[2]

If the AEC experience can be taken as a guide, it is clear that it is now possible for some, at least, of the benefits of automation to be reaped by medium-sized firms. As techniques in this field develop, small and medium firms should gain increasing benefits. However, it should not be forgotten that the term 'automation', like the term 'flow production', is a very loose one. Many degrees of automation are possible, and it is certain that the cost-saving possibilities of automatic machinery can only be fully realized at very large scales of production. Even the largest British motor manufacturers are too small for it to be profitable for them to adopt generally methods as highly automatic as those now being introduced into the American motor industry.

---

[1] *Metalworking Production*, October 7, 1955, p. 1728.
[2] *Ibid.*, November 11, 1955, p. 1931.

CHAPTER V

The Structure of Costs

IT is widely known that one of the outstanding characteristics of the motor industry is the high 'bought-out' content contained in the total cost of vehicles. The car manufacturers are not unique in this respect, however, for makers of radios, television sets, refrigerators and various household appliances often have similar cost structures, and manufacturers of tyres and chocolates have an even higher 'materials' expenditure expressed as a percentage of total cost than do the car producers. But although the share of materials expenditure for all car makers is high compared to, say, the average general engineering firm, there are great differences between companies in this respect, even amongst the 'Big Five'. Table 1 presents a comparison of the cost breakdown of two similar, medium-priced cars made by two of the major producers.

TABLE 1
Analysis of Total Cost of a Typical Car, 1954
(Percentages at Standard Volume
=80 per cent of capacity)

	Firm A	Firm B
Materials	60.5	79.6
Direct labour	9.5	5.1
Variable indirect costs	10.4	} 6.5
Variable commercial expense	1.1	
Total variable	81.5	91.2
Development expenses	2.8	
Special tools	3.2	} 8.8
Fixed expense—factory	9.5	
Fixed—commercial	3.0	
Total fixed	18.5	8.8

The above table illustrates the danger of generalizing about cost structures. There is no 'typical' cost structure although these two probably represent the extremes for the major producers as far as car production alone is concerned. A comparison of 'unit' cost structures for Firms A and B would appreciably narrow the gap, for materials expenditure on medium/heavy trucks is proportionately greater than on cars, and the labour content is proportionately less. Firm A's 'bought-out' content in this case is 68.6 per cent. But eliminating dissimilarities in product or product 'mix', the explanation of differences in cost structures between firms lies, of course, in varying degrees of integration. Some companies make more of the parts of a car than others—in this instance, Firm A makes its own bodies, Firm B does not. Other factors which might explain why cost structures differ, such as differences in capacity utilization, in allocation of costs, or in efficiency are comparatively unimportant. The cost significance of the car body, and the relative importance of the other major parts of a car are shown in the following table.

TABLE 2
Unit Factory Cost of a Mass Produced Car,* 1954
(Percentages)

Body†	38.4
Engine and clutch	14.6
Suspension	9.2
Chassis—sheet metal†	7.1
Chassis—electrical	6.1
Wheels and tyres	5.6
Final assembly	5.0
Transmission and controls	4.0
Brakes	3.5
Steering	2.0
Radiator	2.0
Development, etc.	1.5
Petrol tank and exhaust	1.0
Total	100.0

* Total cost of Firm A (as in Table 1) *less* commercial expenses. Labour costs and all factory overheads have been allocated to the various items.
† Includes special tools.

Once the cost structure is known, and the proportion of capacity working on which it is based, the behaviour of the various cost categories (see Table 1) as volume changes is such that it is not difficult to work out how costs per unit of output change in the short-period as output changes. The content and the behaviour of each of the cost categories included in Table 1 is as follows:

Materials. Includes all raw, semi-finished and finished components bought out which enter into the finished product. These costs tend to remain constant per unit as volume changes. Only if a cut-back in production were drastic and lengthy would suppliers feel forced to review their prices because of the reduction in quantities. Ordinarily, car manufacturers do not expect their suppliers to raise prices when volume is reduced—in fact they would press for price decreases.

Direct Labour. Labour directly engaged in fabricating or assembling the product. These costs are approximately constant over a wide range of output. Technically it is usually no problem to change the number of men on a flow line. If production is to be cut by one-half, half the men are laid off, with the remainder left tending more machines or 'stations', and the speed of the line slowed accordingly.

Variable Indirect Costs. Variable costs arising out of the employment of direct labour, such as operating supplies, fuel, power, maintenance and other indirect labour. About one-quarter is made up of the costs of indirect labour. Theoretically, the unit cost of variable indirect costs should remain stable at all levels of volume within a reasonable range of 'standard' volume (see below). In practice, the operation of certain policies, such as the 'Guaranteed Week' or 'Continuity of Employment' will usually result in a *slight* increase in this element as redundant direct labour is moved over to the indirect labour category and employed in painting, sweeping and other general housekeeping work.

Development Expense and Special Tools. The costs of bringing a new model into existence, and the special-purpose equipment required to produce it in large quantities. Dies for body pressings are, by far, the most costly of the special tools required. Such overhead costs are treated separately from fixed expense, and policies vary as to the methods of writing them off.

Fixed Expense. All establishment charges and other expenses not considered directly variable with production. About one-third of fixed expense is made up of depreciation charges, rent and insurance of plant and buildings. All fixed expense will, of course, increase per unit as production is reduced.

Table 3 provides a concrete example of the short-run behaviour of costs as volume changes, and represents the actual experience of Firm A for the twelve months of 1954. The months have been arranged in descending volume order to bring out the relationship between costs and volume. Fixed overheads in the table do not include development expense and special tools. For cost accounting purposes, these charges have been kept separate on the grounds that they are fixed for a much longer period than most other categories of fixed costs. Standard Volume represents 80 per cent of capacity.[1]

TABLE 3
Costs and Volume. Firm A, 1954

Volume as per cent of Standard	Cost Variance from Standard due to under- or over-absorption of Fixed Overheads (£'000)	Per cent Increase/decrease in actual unit cost
117.7	− 35.0	− 1.4
106.0	− 9.4	− 0.3
104.1	− 6.0	− 0.15
104.0	− 6.7	− 0.25
102.9	− 1.3	− 0.05
95.8	+ 10.8	+ 0.4
93.7	+ 14.6	+ 0.6
91.5	+ 18.1	+ 0.7
84.3	+ 33.8	+ 1.3
78.3	+ 46.2	+ 2.5
77.8	+ 48.0	+ 2.1
65.4*	+ 73.5	+ 3.0

* Holiday month.

The precise mathematical result of the spreading of fixed overheads as volume rises or falls is distorted somewhat by reason of seasonal and other factors affecting actual costs. But the pattern is plain, as is the extent of the effect on unit cost. During this period, unit costs of material and labour were only negligibly affected, while variable indirect costs registered a 'slight' tendency to increase per unit when output declined. Ignoring for the moment 'development expense and special tools', this means that variations in volume of the order of 20 per cent from Standard will increase or decrease unit cost about 2 per cent. Reckoned in terms of capacity, this suggests that a large UK car firm, whether operating at 100 per cent capacity or 60 per cent capacity, is within some 2–3 per cent of its planned cost level on which its long-term price policy is based.

[1] 'Capacity' is not, of course, a precise term. In this context, it means that volume of output, given the degree of shift-working, etc., which is normally considered appropriate at times of high demand, beyond which sharply diminishing returns would shortly set in.

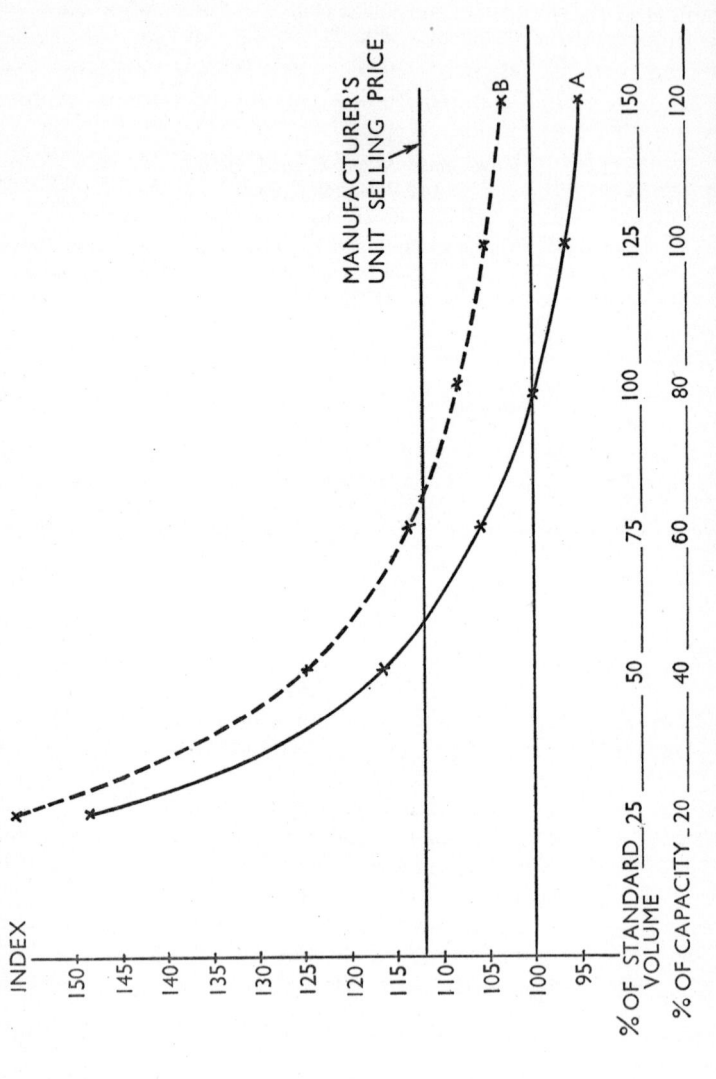

FIGURE 1 SHORT PERIOD UNIT COST CURVE 1954 LARGE SCALE VEHICLE MANUFACTURER

Just how much this figure underestimates the effect on unit cost of changes in the volume of output depends on the amount spent on development expense and special tools, all of which must be included in fixed costs for this purpose. When this is done, using the cost structure given in Table 1 for Firm A, the effect is more noticeable; for a 25 per cent fluctuation either way from Standard, the range would be of the order of 4 to 6 per cent. However, this must be regarded as the outside limit, as it is based on a single car model, and one with a relatively high development and special tool expense. If the firm's entire output is taken into consideration, then the inclusion of commercial vehicle production (with its greater per unit expenditure on materials and its smaller per unit expenditure on development and special tools) would damp down these fluctuations somewhat. This is reflected in Table 4 where the 'unit' represents a weighted average of cars, vans and trucks, but which excludes other business such as spare parts, engine reconditioning, etc.

TABLE 4
Firm A—Unit Cost Analysis, 1954

	Standard Volume		Capacity (125 per cent of Standard)	
	£	%	£	%
Material	267	68.6	267	70.8
Labour	26	6.7	26	6.9
Variable indirect costs	34	8.6	34	9.0
Total variable cost	327	83.9	327	86.7
Fixed expense*	63	16.1	50	13.3
Total cost	390	100.0	377	100.0

* Including development expense and special tools.

Figure 1 is derived from the data given in Table 4. It assumes that all variable costs, including variable indirect costs, remain constant as volume changes. Curve A represents the given costs, curve B the position after a 10 per cent increase in variable costs. The diagram illustrates one of the basic and elementary features of the economics of mass production, yet a feature which is often overlooked, or perhaps not fully realized; namely, that *at the level at which production is planned, only variable costs seem to matter.* Mass production ensures that, despite the huge outlays in capital equipment—the rows of transfer machines, the great presses, the moving assembly lines, etc.—fixed expense *per unit* is a small proportion of total cost. In short, the fixed cost of mass producing nothing is tremendous; the fixed cost of producing *one unit* at the level of volume at which all the expensive equipment is designed to operate is relatively slight.

The following quotation from the *National Advisory Council for the Motor Manufacturing Industry, Report on Proceedings*[1] serves as a useful illustration of this principle, and also of the popular misconception concerning it.

'Of the total cost of motor-car production an abnormally large part consists of costs which, in total, vary hardly at all with the number of units made. Thus, for instance, the total cost of tooling up for production of a given model may easily amount to as much as £1,000,000; and these are only part of the costs which must be recovered from the sale of a single model (or close variants of that model).'

There is no denying that it costs a great deal to tool up to mass produce a new model, and that £1,000,000 is an impressive figure. Yet it simply does not follow that because £1,000,000 is a lot of money that fixed costs constitute an 'abnormally large part' of the total cost of motor car production at planned levels of output. It is the usual practice to spread these tooling costs over the life of the model which, under post-war conditions, has tended to be about five years. A number of popular models have achieved production rates in the neighbourhood of 100,000 units per year, so that these special tooling charges are spread over 400/500,000 units, making tooling costs *per unit* £2 or £2 10s if total tooling costs are £1,000,000.[2] Admittedly, this is only part of the fixed cost which must be recovered on a particular model, but, as earlier tables have indicated, the share of fixed cost for the UK volume producer would not be much over 10–15 per cent, the precise figure depending largely upon the degree of integration.

It follows from this that fixed costs can exert relatively little influence on total cost at 'going volumes'. Of course, at small outputs, say, under 40 per cent capacity, the influence of the heavy investment in plant and equipment becomes increasingly stronger. Lengthy continuation at any level well below capacity would call for drastic action which would result, among other things, in a new set of cost curves.

[1] HMSO, 1947, p. 23.
[2] In 1947, when the National Advisory Council's Report was written, £1,000,000 would not have been an unreasonable figure in the UK for the tooling costs of a mass-produced car. The figure is now very considerably higher than this.

However, as the diagram shows, output can fluctuate in the wide range from 20 per cent above capacity down to 60 per cent of capacity without decreasing or increasing total cost more than 5 per cent from standard cost. And, under normal conditions, these variations in output will tend to balance out, so that the effect of short-period volume changes on costs can almost be ignored.[1]

On the other hand, as curve B shows, an increase in variable cost (10 per cent in this case) is a much more serious matter. Not only does total standard cost rise by over 8 per cent but also there is (in post-war conditions) every likelihood that such a rise, if it took place, would be sustained. In short, a 10 per cent increase in variable cost has the same effect on costs as a $33\frac{1}{3}$ per cent reduction in volume from standard *that is permanent*. Such a rise in variable costs would call for major policy decisions.

COSTS AND PRICES IN THE SHORT PERIOD

In a competitive industry in the short period, costs do not exert the decisive influence on prices that they do in the long run. Nevertheless, the cost/volume/profit relationships of Fig. 1 indicate that the price movements open to the vehicle manufacturer in the short period are limited to a narrow range. With constant input prices, these relationships, coupled with the mass-production techniques used which make it impossible to change a model in much less than two years, impose a strong tendency for vehicle prices to remain stable in the short run. As will be seen, short-period price cutting is very unlikely to lead to increased profits.

The unit selling price in Fig. 1 represents 1954 turnover of Firm A, less revenue from sales of spares, reconditioned engines, etc. (in this case one-sixth of total revenue) divided by unit sales of vehicles; the amount being expressed as a per cent of unit standard cost. Thus the figure stands for an average of car, van and truck prices, both foreign and domestic and, in this instance, reflects an overall profit margin on vehicle sales of 16 per cent at capacity volumes.

The break-even point (the point on the diagram where unit cost= price, i.e. at approximately 45 per cent capacity) can be used to demonstrate how great the increase in volume must be to offset a given price cut. By assuming that the company is operating at its break-even point, the effect of a 10 per cent price cut can easily be seen on the diagram by dropping the price line to 101 on the index. This

[1] The effect on *profits* may be important, however; see Chapter IX below.

raises the break-even point from 45 per cent to 75 per cent of capacity, an increase of nearly 70 per cent. In other words, in order to warrant a 10 per cent reduction in price, the company must expect *at least* a two-thirds increase in volume. Any increase smaller than that would mean that the company would be worse off than it was before it made the reduction in price. Moreover, given the cost curve and the break-even point indicated by the diagram, it does not matter what the initial position on the curve is before the price cut—a two-thirds increase in volume is needed to restore total profits (or losses) to their previous level. For example, a 10 per cent price cut at a time when the company is operating at 60 per cent of capacity would require output to be raised to 100 per cent of capacity before any increase in profits would take place.

With a different break-even point (either because the cost structure or the profit margin is not the same as in the diagram) the elasticity of demand required to offset any given price cut will, of course, also be different. What happens when the proportion of fixed costs at capacity and the margin of profit at capacity are both smaller is revealed in an interesting American study published in 1939 by General Motors.[1] This presents a number of break-even charts derived from the published figures of one of the major car companies. These charts are based on a cost structure in which fixed costs constitute only 7 per cent of total cost, and on a profit margin of less than 10 per cent, both taken at capacity.[2] Under these conditions, a price reduction of 10 per cent requires an increase in output and sales of nearly 200 per cent before the firm shows any improvement on its former profits (or losses). With further growth, the UK industry can be expected to approach this situation, and larger and larger volume increases will be needed to offset short-period price cuts. Whatever the exact position of individual British firms at the moment in this respect, it seems fair to conclude that, for any practically conceivable structure of costs and margin of profit, the elasticity of demand needs to be extremely large, possibly well over 7, before a short-period price cut can be expected to increase profits.

Even assuming that the elasticity required is no higher than 7, then

---

[1] General Motors Corporation, *The Dynamics of Automobile Demand* (New York, 1939).

[2] The difference between cost structure in the UK and the US can largely be explained by the huge difference in the scale of production. As scale increases, the expansion of fixed investment is normally less than proportionate to output (given no increase in the degree of integration). See Chapter VI below.

as far as short-period profits are concerned, this two-thirds increase in volume rules out any price cuts when the company is operating at levels higher than Standard Volume, for an increase of that size would take output well beyond its capacity with existing plant and equipment. While it is true that the term 'capacity' has no precise meaning, it is assumed here that any output beyond 120 per cent of capacity (or 150 per cent of Standard Volume) would run into sharply 'diminishing returns'. As long as the company is operating at Standard Volume or better, it will in any event have little incentive to introduce price cuts, nor will it have the ability to do so without reducing its total profits.[1]

Over the range of outputs where it *is* physically possible to obtain a two-thirds increase in volume without expansion of plant and equipment, demand conditions are likely to be unfavourable. Relatively small downward departures from Standard Volume due to seasonal or other factors believed to be temporary, will, of course, be ignored by the firm as far as its pricing policy is concerned. On the other hand, a large drop in sales leading to a lengthy period of low-volume operations would have to be met by a basic policy change. Such a situation could only arise because of a slump, which would affect all manufacturers of similarly priced cars more or less equally, or because the company's current models had failed to meet with popular approval, and a sizeable share of the market had been lost to competitors. In either event, the position of the firm is unlikely to be improved by reducing the prices of existing models. A price elasticity of demand of 7 (which is probably a minimum estimate) for the products of a firm is extremely high, even when trade is booming; this kind of response from consumers of durable goods such as cars, in the middle of a slump, would almost certainly be out of the question, even if no other car producer cut his prices. Even such a great believer in the influence of prices on car sales as Paul Hoffman, former head of the Studebaker Corporation, admitted as much when he testified before a US Senate Committee in 1939 that, in a depressed market, although

[1] It might be asked why firms do not *raise* prices in these circumstances. With a cost structure that greatly discourages price cuts, considerable increases in profits could be made by price rises. The answer to this is that some firms *do* maintain higher prices than their rivals for comparable cars—at least for a period. If, however, they attempted to raise prices substantially, they would find that the elasticity of demand for their cars would become extremely high, since consumers would buy rivals' cars instead. As regards a *general* price rise in the industry, this seems to be ruled out by considerations of long-run competition. *v.* Chapters VII and VIII below for a further discussion of price policy.

'every dollar up or down has some effect on demand, some effect on volume—every dollar, whether times are good or times are bad', and a $25 reduction in the price of a car would have an effect, it 'would certainly not have enough effect to justify making a reduction'.[1] And if the decline in sales has come, not from a generally depressed market, but from unpopular models, outclassed by competitors, it is very doubtful whether price reductions, even of the order of 10 per cent, would be sufficient to alter consumer tastes to any great extent. In the highly imperfect market which exists for cars, consumers become attached to particular makes, intense likes and dislikes are generated which are difficult to change, not less so because they are often irrational. No company could afford price cuts of sufficient magnitude necessary to overcome strongly held consumer prejudices against a particular model.

Hence, whatever the cause of the decline in sales, a company will not ordinarily attempt to recover its position by means of price reductions.[2] If a general slump is responsible, all car manufacturers will normally cut back production and will probably decide to wait until total demand improves. Many of them will be able to reduce output to 50 per cent of capacity and still make *some* profit. On the other hand, if the trouble stems from unpopular models which have been technically outdistanced or made to look 'old-fashioned' by the efforts of competitors, then the answer lies in product change rather than in price change. A new model can be made with the 'new look', incorporating all the latest technical innovations, and perhaps initiating some original developments. Furthermore, it can be made to sell at the price required, namely, at the price which meets that of the most successful models in its class made by competitors. But it takes time to make a new model, usually about two years—and therefore price changes are normally long-period events, sparked by product change and economies of scale.

This does not mean, of course, that the prices of existing models are *never* reduced. Obviously, the wider the profit margin to begin with, the more room for manoeuvre there is open to the manufacturer. A wide profit margin means that more weight can be given to the state of demand and the degree of competition, and less to cost considerations, in deciding upon price changes. The more expensive,

[1] TNEC *Hearings*, Part 21, December 6, 1939, p. 11199.
[2] The situation would almost certainly be different if the motor industry were not an oligopolistic one. If there were a large number of firms, 'some fool would cut'. See Chapters VII and VIII below for a further discussion.

high-quality cars produced in relatively small volume often have large profit margins during a period of buoyant demand. As a result, prices of cars in this class are often reduced when a buyers' market reappears. Examples of this can be found, even in the inflationary post-war years, notably in the period from the spring of 1953 to the end of 1954. During this time, the price of almost every car selling for more than £600 basic was appreciably reduced, while prices of cars below that figure remained unaltered almost without exception. The narrower profit margin associated with the popular, mass-produced cars usually ensures that reductions of this nature will not normally be extended to the cheaper models. Profit margins on the latter are narrower partly because they are smaller on mass-produced products to begin with (although total profits are very much greater), and partly because the manufacturer would rather lengthen his order book than endanger his long-run mass market by charging 'what the market will bear' for his popular makes.

The famous £100 Ford Eight provides an outstanding example of the rare case of a manufacturer reducing the price of an existing popular-priced model in a market where total demand was expanding relatively slowly.[1] During 1935 there were two price cuts, starting from an initial price of £120; one of £5 in January (which apparently was too small to affect sales significantly) and another in October 1935, this time of £15. As far as can be determined from the annual sales figures of this model, production roughly doubled under the stimulus of the price changes, indicating a price elasticity of demand of approximately 6. If we assume that the Company had a short-period cost curve and a profit margin before the price cut similar to that of Fig. 1, then the increase in sales was not quite sufficient to compensate for the price decreases, and the firm, in the short run, was probably somewhat worse off than before as far as this model was concerned.[2]

Lacking any detailed cost information, this conclusion must necessarily be conjecture. However, it is supported indirectly by the Company's financial results for the period. For 1936, the first full year after the price cut, the firm had a total increase in car sales of

[1] Other firms, producing newer models, did not cut their prices. This case is further discussed in Chapter VII from the standpoint of the competitive behaviour of firms.

[2] If sales of the Ford Eight had continued to expand in the years following 1936, the reduction would have been amply justified *in the long run* by the resulting economies of scale flowing from the use of more efficient techniques and machines at higher volumes.

nearly 50 per cent, as compared with an increase in the industry as a whole of about 12 per cent. Ford trading profits, however, went up by less than 10 per cent. Profits per vehicle fell very considerably. By its subsequent policy (see Chapter VII below) Ford seemed to admit tacitly that the attempt to compete by cutting prices had not been altogether successful.

All that has been said so far concerning costs and prices has assumed constant input prices, and has been restricted to short-period considerations. Obviously, in an industry where variable costs represent some 85 per cent of total cost, changes in the prices of materials and labour will exert an immediate and decisive effect on costs. The broken line B, in Fig. 1, demonstrates the drastic effect of a 10 per cent increase in variable costs on total costs and profits, the latter being reduced by two-thirds at Standard Volume. Since all car manufacturers are affected roughly alike by such changes, it is to be expected that the resultant cost increases or decreases will be reflected in prices, to an extent which depends on the state of demand and the degree of competition. As is seen in Chapter VII, most short-period price changes come about in this way; indeed, were it not for fluctuations in prime costs, car prices would be remarkably stable.

When long-period considerations are introduced, two new factors appear which are capable of causing major shifts in existing cost curves, and hence they provide the manufacturer with the ability to alter prices in a way that is quite impossible in the short period. These are the factors which explain the historical downward trend in car prices in real terms. They are changes in product, which enable the manufacturer to produce at practically any price that he believes demand and competitive conditions require, and the growth of output by firms and by the industry, which gives rise to considerable economies of large scale production—perhaps more appreciable in the motor industry than in any other. These factors will be considered in the chapters that follow.

CHAPTER VI

Economies of Large-scale Production

1. THE TECHNICAL OPTIMUM

IT was pointed out in Chapter IV that, as the scale of output grows, costs can be reduced in two main ways: by increasing mechanization and by adopting 'flow' production. In this section, the question is raised as to whether there is any end to these economies, whether there is some optimum volume in the production of a single model beyond which no further technical savings are realized. How great does the annual output of one model have to be in order to justify, from a cost standpoint, the use of the most efficient techniques known? The importance of establishing whether there is such a thing as an optimum, and of gaining some idea of its level, can hardly be exaggerated. Any company producing below the technical optimum must necessarily be at *some* cost disadvantage as compared to its larger competitors if the products are roughly similar. This has obvious implications in any discussion of competition in the industry, either at home or in overseas markets.

The search for an optimum is an impossible task, according to the National Advisory Council for the Motor Manufacturing Industry, who expressed the view that the gains from increasing volume are endless.

It is not possible to select a figure of, say, 50,000 or 100,000 as the optimum scale for mass production, i.e. the point at which further mass production ceases to give substantial economies in cost. Increasing volume efficiently produced will, other things being equal, always lead to diminishing cost. It is clear that mass production as it exists in this country is still very far short of the stage where increasing mass production would cease to yield substantial and worthwhile economies.[1]

There can be no disputing the final sentence of the quotation, for the maximum annual output of any one model before the war was about

[1] Report on Proceedings, HMSO, 1947.

50,000, and at the present time is little more than double that figure. Expansion should continue to yield economies for some time to come, but there is considerable evidence to indicate that, under the existing techniques, there is a limit to these gains.

The qualification concerning techniques is important, for the optimum is not a static concept; it changes as techniques alter. Although the introduction of more efficient methods of production may lower the optimum as well as raise it, the historical trend has strongly favoured the use of more and more costly equipment, requiring ever-increasing volume before the benefits of its greater efficiency can be realized. The optimum has been rising with the growth of the industry, and will in all probability, be higher in ten or twenty years than it is now.

In addition to the effect of technological change on the optimum, it must also be borne in mind that the optimum necessarily varies with the type of work being performed, that it will be higher for some operations or processes than for others. The optimum for a group of processes will be the best possible balance, or lowest common denominator, of the separate optima. If, for example, there are only two different operations to be performed to make a particular product, and machine A turns out 25,000 per annum to feed machine B, which has a capacity of 50,000, then the best balance is two of type A and one of type B, and the optimum is 50,000.

Duplication of equipment has no effect on unit cost,[1] and is a sure sign that the optimum has been exceeded.[2] In the above example, type A machine must be duplicated to produce the final product at the optimum level of 50,000. Expansion beyond 50,000 means duplicating type B machine, as well as A, and will bring no savings in unit-cost. Any firm operating at the optimum level would have cost advantages over a smaller rival with an output of 25,000, but the advantages would be derived solely from process B. In process A, the smaller company would be using the same equipment as its competitor, and using it just as efficiently. In process B, however, it cannot afford to use the same equipment since the equipment would be idle half the time and unit costs would be prohibitively high. Hence it is forced to use 'simpler' techniques, which result in the lowest unit cost for its own level of output but which, nevertheless, are less effi-

[1] In real life duplication does result in *some* savings because a perfect balance never exists; hence not *all* machines need to be duplicated to double output.

[2] i.e., that the flat portion of the long-run cost curve has been reached: further increases in scale do not lead to savings in costs.

cient than those of the larger company. The latter concern, on the other hand, when it is producing at the optimum figure, would be at no cost disadvantage as against still larger competitors whose volumes exceed 50,000.

In applying this approach to the motor industry, the hundreds of different operations required to produce a vehicle can be conveniently grouped together under four basic processes performed by nearly all major car manufacturers, namely, casting, machining, pressing, and assembling. There is abundant proof that the optimum varies widely between these different major processes and that in all of them the optimum has been exceeded—in America, if not elsewhere.

The process usually associated with the motor industry in the public mind is that of final assembly. The picture of men working in a long line of slowly moving cars in various stages of completion, with miles of conveyors feeding in parts and components, is a very familiar one. Impressive as this stage of final assembly undoubtedly is, it is a *relatively* small scale operation, one which is duplicated many times by large companies. In America, General Motors has twenty-three assembly plants, Ford and Chrysler fifteen each; and the capacity of the average plant is about 100,000 units per annum. The OEEC has reported that the average annual production in all assembly plants in the United States is 74,000 vehicles.[1] This wide decentralization of plants must mean that economies of scale beyond, say, 100,000, are less than the difference in transport costs between shipping an unassembled car and one all in one piece. Comparable assembly facilities exist in this country, although the unimportance of transport costs in the small area of the domestic market has permitted each company to concentrate its assembly operations in one place. However, within each plant, there is much duplication of equipment, for all the major companies have more than one assembly line. There can be no doubt that the larger UK companies are big enough to use the most efficient techniques known for the final assembly of cars, and that their individual total production is in excess of the optimum for this operation, which probably lies in the neighbourhood of 100,000 cars per annum.

Such a relatively low optimum does not mean that economies of scale in assembly are not important, for the change from batch production to completely mechanical flow production brings very great

[1] OEEC. *Some Aspects of the Motor Vehicle Industry in the USA* (Paris, 1952), p. 18.

savings indeed. Some idea of the extent of these savings is given in the early history of the Ford Motor Company. Shortly before the First World War, Henry Ford introduced what is believed to be the first installation of progressive assembly on a moving conveyor in the industry. It was used to produce flywheel magnetos, and it reduced the assembly time from twenty minutes to five minutes. The same technique was applied to many other small parts and finally to the car itself. 'The net result of conveyorizing at Ford was a reduction over a five-year period of 50 per cent in the production cost of the model T'.[1] Factory cost savings at the Ford plant must have been tremendous, for the bought-out content of the car was then high compared to later periods.

Similarly today, the switch from batch production to flow production brings very great savings. Unfortunately, it is not possible to name any particular volume as the minimum level at which this changeover may take place. This is primarily because flow production—like automation—is a very loose and rather vague term used to describe a general technique which can be utilized with widely different degrees of specialization and mechanization. When Ford first tried assembling chassis in a street alongside the factory by pulling them along a 250-foot route past stockpiles of parts spaced at regular intervals—that was flow production; and it reduced chassis assembly time from fourteen hours to six. Production was further speeded up by mounting the wheels on the chassis and rolling the chassis down a track from one station to the next. The introduction of the moving chain conveyor eliminated the need for pushing the chassis, and overhead conveyors were added later which brought the various parts and components to the main assembly line, which further reduced handling changes and saved floor space. The complete application of the principle can be seen in any large company in Europe as well as in the United States. Flow production has been used to describe all these stages, and it is because it is a technique that can be used with more or less mechanization that no set level of output need be attained before it may be adopted. Relatively small companies can, and do, use flow production techniques, just as they may benefit from automation—but in both cases the gains are limited to some extent by their low volume of output. It appears that, in car assembly, to make the extensive use of the flow

[1] *Automation and Technological Change.* Hearings before the Sub-Committee on Economic Stabilization of the Joint Committee on the Economic Report, Congress of the United States (October 1955), p. 52.

production techniques that are necessary to secure most of the economies of scale in this process, an annual volume of around 60,000 units is required. This need not be all of one model. Most of the equipment used in assembly is really general-purpose equipment. Several different models may be moved down the final assembly line at the same time if necessary and overhead conveyors can just as easily carry a pair of door panels as an engine. Variety and model change is not the costly headache in assembly that it is in machining or pressing, although frequent changeover must reduce efficiency to some extent.

These conclusions would generally apply to the various sub-assembly lines, e.g. body, engines, gear box, rear axles, etc., as well as to final assembly. Of these the body assembly line with its related processes is by far the most important. Here the various steel pressings are electrically welded to form the body shell, which is then painted, dried, fitted, upholstered and trimmed. This calls for an impressive array of conveyors, jigs, painting and drying facilities, etc. With the exception of the jigs, this is largely general-purpose equipment, for the painting and drying facilities are not restricted to any one model any more than are the conveyors. The duplication of this equipment that exists in the industry suggests an optimum similar to that for final assembly. There are for example, ten Fisher body plants assembling Chevrolet bodies alongside the ten widely dispersed Chevrolet assembly plants.

To sum up: the adoption of flow production methods in car assembly results in very great economies. While these methods can be utilized at fairly low volumes, the efficient use of the best assembly techniques calls for a volume of roughly 60,000 units per annum, which need not be all of one model. There are probably further smaller gains at higher volumes, but the significant economies in car assembly appear to be exhausted at about a volume of 100,000 units. This relatively low figure stems from the complexity of the product, the importance of direct labour, and the non-specific nature of most of the equipment, the use of which is normally limited solely by the length of its physical life.

The significance of this conclusion is heightened by the importance of assembly for the car manufacturer. While it is true that *final* assembly represents only about 5 per cent of the total cost of a car, it amounts to some 15 or 20 per cent of the average car manufacturer's factory cost in the UK. When all the costs of the sub-assembly processes performed by him are added, it would not be far wrong to conclude that upwards of one-third of the factory cost of the car lies in assembly.

Turning now from assembly operations to those which take place in the foundry, it can be seen that although the process is entirely different the same general argument applies. As in assembly, manpower is important, and the equipment is mostly general purpose—rails, conveyors and furnaces. Such equipment can be used with a wide variety of shapes and sizes of castings and can be used until it is worn out. The survival of so many foundries is in itself a strong indication that economies of scale are not important beyond relatively low volumes. There are over twenty foundries supplying iron castings to the UK motor industry alone, and of the major car manufacturers, only Vauxhall has no foundry of its own. In America, the foundries of the big car companies are, it is true, many times the size of those here. Although they are more highly mechanized, much of the difference consists in duplicated equipment. The US foundries are concentrated and huge because major machining operations are concentrated (Chevrolet has only two engine plants, for example, and Ford has three), and transport costs are high.

As in the case of assembly, a certain minimum production must be assured to enable the costly foundry equipment to be worked efficiently, and beyond this volume economies of scale are not of great importance. Whatever the exact figure may be, it seems well within the range of the major UK producers, indeed it appears that any car producer who has exceeded 100,000 units per annum is not under any serious competitive handicap as far as assembly and foundry operations are concerned, provided he can afford the heavy initial cost of the equipment. However, his position is very different when it comes to the machining of major components and the manufacture of large steel pressings. Here the most efficient techniques require extremely expensive equipment which is more or less tied to the particular model for which it is used, hence it requires very large annual volumes to justify its use.

It was recently reported[1] that the highest US output from a cylinder block line was 100 blocks per hour, or roughly twice that of any British producer. Working two eight-hour shifts for five days a week (the customary practice in machine shops), this indicates that the best annual output from one line in the US is 400,000 units per annum. This suggests that, for popular makes such as Chevrolet and Ford with annual outputs of well over one million vehicles, the opti-

[1] *Automobile Engineer*, November 1955, p. 1.

Economies of Large-scale Production

mum has been exceeded since duplicate lines are being used. However, it may be that the optimum is appreciably higher than 400,000. An OEEC Mission mentions an hourly production rate of 144 six-cylinder Ford engines at the new Cleveland plant.[1] This is supported by testimony of Mr J. D. Davis, Vice-President of the US Ford Motor Company, given before a Congressional Committee in 1955. After discussing at length the money the company had spent on automating a particular transfer machine line, Mr Davis referred to 'a cylinder block line producing 140 units an hour at 80 per cent efficiency . . .'[2] Such an output implies an optimum of over half a million units per annum, which is some two-and-a-half to three times the annual capacity of the best UK equipment. The latter, even at the relatively low capacity of 200,000, still exceeds the annual output of the most popular models, which is little more than 100,000 each; so that if the capacity of this equipment is to be fully taken up, the same engine must be used for more than one model.

Thus, although there is some duplication of the machinery used on major car components in the US, it takes place at very high volumes, probably at around the half-million level. Unlike conveyors or furnaces, this is special-purpose equipment: it can be used for only one basic engine. With an output of perhaps one-fifth of the optimum it is clear that UK firms cannot afford to use such equipment. Its heavy capital cost and the huge volume needed to amortize it in the necessary time was commented on by Sir Rowland Smith, Chairman of the Ford Motor Company, in a recent speech to the Machine Tool Trades Association[3], and he concluded:

I do not think that we shall see any of these huge units such as they have in the USA for a long time in this country. . . . Novelty is always seductive. It is the wise man who thinks of the housekeeping and makes that the arbiter of what he buys.

The same conclusions would apply, with even greater force, to the equipment and techniques used in the larger American press shops, for body tooling provides the outstanding example of the advantage of size in the manufacture of cars. The savings from volume here do not spring primarily from the giant presses used or even from the mechanical handling between presses. This equipment has a long life and can be used with different dies and models. The gains come

[1] OEEC, op. cit., p. 17.
[2] *Automation and Technological Change*, op. cit., p. 62.
[3] *Machinist*, April 1, 1955, p. 608.

F

mainly from the continuous operation of the presses on a single task, and the extremely large number of pressings obtained from the very expensive dies in such a short time. On this point the previously-mentioned OEEC Mission comments:[1]

Production lines in these plants are specialized, e.g. they make only roof panels or doors or body panels, etc. Basic production figures were as high as 4,000 pressings per day. It should be emphasized that even the larger manufacturers in the United States are cautious about installing equipment on this scale; it is difficult to see, therefore, how it would ever become possible for European manufacturers to do so.

Such a volume implies an optimum for large pressings of some 1,000,000 units per annum. The big European body plants use basically the same techniques, but since the largest annual output of any single model is around 300,000 units, continuous operation of this equipment is impossible, and the tremendous cost of the two or three thousand dies[2] needed per model must be spread over fewer units. The huge presses can be used. Even mechanical handling of pressings is possible; but the much lower annual volume means that frequent changeover of dies is unavoidable, and this is a costly, time-consuming operation.[3]

It is the press shop which sets the overall optimum for car production—probably in the region of 1,000,000 units per annum. This is much larger than the optimum for other operations, so that such a volume requires much duplication of assembly and foundry facilities, and some in machinery. Put the other way round in terms of the long-period cost curve—as volume increases to 100,000 units per annum, economies of scale are very great in all departments, but particularly so in assembly. Beyond this point important economies continue to come from machining and pressing as volume grows. These savings cease for machining at roughly the half-million mark, and finally taper off for major pressings at roughly one million. If there are significant economies of scale at still higher levels of output they are not likely to be technical.

Once again it must be said that the optimum is not a static concept, that changes in techniques and product are always being made which influence it. The overall effect of automation has been to increase greatly the optimum level of production, primarily by mak-

[1] OEEC, op. cit., p. 18.
[2] These last indefinitely if properly maintained.
[3] It takes approximately eight hours to change a big die.

ing possible an extraordinary speeding up of machinery and pressing operations. Some idea of the pre-war optimum is given in the testimony of Paul Hoffman, then President of the Studebaker Company, in hearings before the TNEC. After commenting that a company had to spend annually about $2,000,000 to keep up to date, and that this was the cost of one set of tools, he went on to say, in reference to large companies,

They, of course, have to have several sets of tools to build a million cars. One set of tools might be good for 250,000 cars, but when you go beyond that you get into duplicate sets of toolings.[1]

At that time, Mr Hoffman felt that 'if we could get our production up to 100,000 cars a year or more, we would be in a position to compete successfully and on even terms with the Big Three'.[1] Yet so changed were production conditions in the post-war period that volumes of much more than 100,000[2] were not enough to enable Studebaker or the other three remaining independents to survive without mergers.[3] A dramatic illustration of these changed production conditions is contained in a description of the new Ford engine plant at Cleveland by Mr Walter Reuther, President of the CIO,[4]

Some years back, we made the first engine block in 24 hours, from a rough casting to the finished block. To machine a rough casting to the finished motor block in 24 hours was hailed as an unprecedented technological achievement. Then we got it down to nine hours; the old equipment in the Rouge Ford plant did it in nine hours.

We jumped to 14.6 minutes. That is just the beginning, because they have drawings on the engineering drawing boards now that will do it in less time than 14.6 minutes.

The complete application of automation to foundry operations, which Mr Reuther suggests has now been made at the Ford foundry, may already have raised the optimum higher than previously indicated. Although there seems to be little prospect of automation in car assembly because of the technical problems associated with such

[1] TNEC *Hearings*, op. cit., p. 11218.
[2] For Studebaker, Hudson and Nash. Packard production was about 70,000 annually in the early 1950s.
[3] The Studebaker-Packard Corporation was formed in 1954, and the American Motors Corporation was formed in the same year by the merger of the Nash and Hudson Companies.
[4] *Automation and Technological Change*, op. cit., pp. 123–4.

a complex and changing product, the greatest opportunity for gains in productivity lies here where the optimum is relatively so low. Should it come it will have appreciable effects on competition and the industry structure.

Nothing so far has been said of the optimum in the production of parts and components commonly bought out by the car manufacturers. However, where no heavy pressings are involved and where the basic techniques are similar to those used by the car manufacturers themselves (as it is in most cases), there is no reason to suppose that the optimum is very different, or that it is in excess of half a million units per annum. Obviously the optimum will vary considerably between components. The reluctance of UK car firms to undertake the production of their own electrical equipment, plus the extreme concentration of its production both here and in the US suggests that the optimum may be high for such components. Lucas supplies almost all of the UK electrical equipment; in America, General Motors makes all of its own, Ford some of its own, with the remainder of the industry being supplied by the Auto-Lite Co. The efforts of Lucas to standardize dynamos and starters for the entire UK car industry on three main sizes of the former and two of the latter also suggests a high optimum—but not necessarily one in excess of the figure mentioned. Drop forgings and heavy pressings, such as bumpers, also appear to have a higher optimum than most parts and components, but even here the supplier's economies of scale are not likely to be significant beyond 500,000.

With an overall optimum figure of the order of 1,000,000 units, it is clear that no European car manufacturer is producing anywhere near the optimum. How serious a handicap is this, and are there any compensating factors?

The handicap is greatly reduced when it is realized that this optimum only applies to the press department. The extensive duplication of assembly and foundry facilities suggests that there is no real problem there. An optimum as high as 500,000 for machining major components is a disadvantage which can really only be overcome by growth. If each company standardized on one basic engine, obviously this would help matters (if one ignores its effect on sales) but even this extreme would only bring one British company, BMC, within the optimum range. Vertical disintegration is clearly not a solution, for an outside supplier could only get the necessary volume by standardizing an engine for several manufacturers and no major manufacturer could afford to have the same engine as his competitors. There remains the possibility of offsetting the higher American *annual* volumes to some extent by using the special-purpose equipment for a longer *total* period so that the cost of the machinery is amortized over the same number of engines.[1] The long life of basic American engines effectively blocks this alternative.

There is no present indication of major engine changes. . . . The expense of designing, testing, and tooling up for a brand new engine is so great that the engine is intended to be used for ten years. So we shall probably have the V-8s for the next decade. . . .[2]

Recent developments in the US motor industry suggest that engines may now be expected to have a considerably shorter life than ten years, but even so not very significantly shorter than the life of mass-produced British engines. With engine life about the same, only a higher volume of output in European countries can remove the advantages of US producers which come quite simply from the more efficient equipment used.

The situation is somewhat different in the case of body pressings. The advantages of the US companies come from two main sources: continuous operation of the giant presses, and the spreading of body tooling costs over more units. Again, further standardization would help European producers to achieve more of the possible economies under both headings—but even if each company produced only one model it would be very far from the optimum. Only an *annual* volume of a single model of the order of 1,000,000 could bring the gains from the continuous operation of the body presses. This is clearly out of the question for European companies for many years, unless considerable further concentration of production should occur over the next decade.

The US advantages under the second category can be reduced by extending the life of the model over a longer period. Dies and body tools are physically the same anywhere. The annual volume of production is not all-important to the type of dies and tools employed. In America, it has been customary in the post-war period for complete body changes to take place every two years. UK firms appear to have settled down to a basic change every five years or so.

[1] Since the type of machinery used depends to some extent on the *annual* volume of production, the American advantage could not be completely offset by producing for a longer period.

[2] Harold Blanchard, Editor of *Motor* magazine, New York, quoted in *Motor Critic*, August 1954, p. 15.

The dies and tools needed for efficient volume production are so costly that it is necessary to spread the initial expense over some such period of time [5–7 years.][1]

The new design must be capable of living for probably some five years in its basic form.[2]

In round numbers the effect of the longer life of UK car bodies is as follows:

	Annual Volume	Total Volume
UK	100,000	500,000
US	1,000,000	2,000,000

In other words, the US advantage is reduced from 10:1 to 4:1. It still remains formidable, and no amount of lengthening model life that is at all feasible under modern competitive conditions can alter the fact. Only an increase in the annual volume of production of one model can remove the handicap, although it needs to be only to 400,000–500,000 if the present difference in model life is maintained. This would not, of course, bring all the economies to be derived from the continuous operation of heavy press equipment, which can only be achieved at the optimum.

In summary it can certainly be said that the scale of production of American car firms still gives them considerable savings denied to their European competitors. It would be extremely rash to attempt to estimate the extent of these cost advantages, mitigated as they are by much lower labour costs in Europe. A tentative attempt to assess how far American costs compare with those in the United Kingdom has been made in Appendix B.

2. ECONOMIES OF SCALE: THE FIRM

As has been seen in Chapter II, the production of a car is shared between a large number of producers, and car manufacturers themselves account for a relatively small proportion of the total cost of a car. An extremely important consequence of this is that in applying the theoretical conclusions of the preceding section to a particular firm or industry, account must be taken of the existing structure of

---

[1] Maurice Platt, Director and Chief Engineer, Vauxhall Motors, *Motor*, May 18, 1955, p. 600.

[2] B. B. Winter, Director of Engineering and Design, Rootes Group, ibid., May 18, 1955, p. 604.

the industry. For the economies of scale open to the firm depend to some extent on how integrated it is, and the savings from the expansion of a single firm may be quite different from those obtained when the whole industry becomes larger. The purpose of this section is to analyse what happens to the costs of a single firm as its output grows.

With the broad general conclusions of the analysis in the preceding section of this chapter, there would probably be widespread agreement. No one seriously objects to the notion that there are increasing returns in the manufacture of motor cars, or that such savings continue to be obtained until very high volumes are reached. That these economies of scale are sizeable is a verdict amply supported by statements emanating from the industry itself, an outstanding example being provided by a group of British car manufacturers in 1947 when they enthusiastically concluded that:

In respect of two characteristics, elasticity of demand and production under a law of sharply increasing returns . . . the use and production of motor cars are believed to constitute a case almost without parallel among the major economic activities.[1]

However, when further details are sought as to the extent of these economies, and their significance over different ranges of output, this unanimity is shattered.

The explanation of the wide differences of opinion that have emerged at this point lies primarily in the astonishingly small amount of published quantitative evidence pertaining to such an important question as that of economies of scale. The meagreness of the available data stems partly from the controversial nature of the subject, coupled with the natural reluctance of manufacturers to disclose cost information, and partly from the difficulties inherent in attempts to obtain empirical evidence of the relationship between volume and cost in any industry. There is no need to dwell at length here on these well-known obstacles: the 'industry' that is so hard to define and which is always altering its structure, the techniques that never do remain constant, the ever-changing prices of inputs, and the arbitrary cost allocations of the multi-product firm together with the little homogeneous product that isn't there. These difficulties are formidable, and they account in large part for the vague and conflicting shapes that have been ascribed to that, perhaps, shyest and most retiring of all economic concepts—the long-run average cost curve.

[1] National Advisory Council Report, op. cit., p. 23.

In this section (and in the Appendix to this chapter), the small amount of available quantitative evidence is assembled and discussed, together with some new material supplied by one of the major UK car firms. The latter was obtained in response to the question, 'What, in general terms, would be the effect on unit costs of increasing volume from 100,000 to 200,000, 300,000 and 400,000 vehicles per annum?' Our informants were careful to point out that their estimates were based solely on an opinion—that it would require a major study and take up to six months to answer the question with any degree of accuracy. Nevertheless, we have no doubt that such an opinion, based on past experience and a first-hand knowledge of the behaviour of costs in the industry, is worth serious consideration. Table 1 is derived from these data.

TABLE 1
Cost/Volume Relationship—Company X, 1954

Volume (units)	100,000	200,000	300,000	400,000
Total fixed investment (index)	100	140	180	240
Unit cost (index)				
Material	100	96	94	92
Labour (direct)	100	92	85	76
Variable indirect costs	100	100	100	100
Fixed overhead	100	70	60	60
Total unit cost	100	92	89	87
Unit factory cost (total cost *less* materials)	100	85	78	76

The unit used in the table is a 'product mix', consisting of several models of cars, vans and trucks, with varying degrees of interchangeability between them. The composition of the output is assumed to remain unchanged as production expands.

According to these data, the economies of scale to be expected by the firm over this range of output (the range which most UK companies face today when considering further expansion) are moderate: 8 per cent with the first doubling, 5 per cent with the second. The savings in unit *factory* cost are more impressive, being approximately twice the above figures. In other words, a manufacturer envisaging a fourfold increase in volume from a base of 100,000 units per annum can anticipate that the costs directly under his control may be reduced by nearly one quarter and that the total cost of the car may fall by roughly 15 per cent.

This difference between factory cost and total cost savings is simply a reflection of the fact that as the car manufacturer expands his output, his suppliers' costs (and prices) do not, in general, fall in proportion to his own. This variation in cost behaviour, and the overwhelming importance of bought-out materials and components (over 70 per cent of total cost in this case) are primarily responsible for the moderate economies of scale indicated by the table. Materials expenditure per unit shows some savings, of course; 4 per cent with each doubling of output. The economies that accrue from larger orders and the better utilization of materials are reflected here. The big buyer of sheet metal, for example, benefits from being able to get the exact size he requires from the steel producer so that there is no wastage. But such savings are not of the same order of magnitude as those taking place inside the car plant as volume grows. Assuming that suppliers are as efficient as the car manufacturers, there are two possible explanations for this difference: smaller economies of scale for the supplier, or sufficient monopoly power on the part of some suppliers to enable them to retain their gains from expansion.

Suppliers' economies of scale may be smaller either because the processes they perform are not subject to such gains (at least in the range under consideration), or because the suppliers' scale of operations in units is considerably larger than that of the firm, hence a doubling of the firm's output may perhaps represent only a 20 per cent increase in volume for the supplier. The variety of processes performed by suppliers is so great that clearly no blanket generalization can be made on the former point. For bought-out finished components one would expect that the conditions of production would resemble that of the car manufacturer himself, and the gains to be roughly similar if the scale of operations is similar. However, the scale of the supplier in producing his particular part will generally be much larger than that of the car manufacturer. This is partly because he may be supplying an item, more than one of which is required per car (springs, shock absorbers, tyres, replacements for consumers, etc.), or because he is providing other car manufacturers with the same part. Of course, if the supplier's output of a part is completely non-standardized as between car manufacturers, his scale will be no greater than that of his largest customer, as far as technical economies are concerned. But normally this is not the case: as a general rule, up to 50 per cent of a part or component is said by suppliers to consist of a standard 'base or core' to which is added the special requirements of each customer. Hence the scale of the supplier of finished components is normally much larger than that of the car manufacturer, so that the expansion of one of his customers will mean a proportionately smaller increase in volume for himself, and thus smaller savings.

The same argument would apply with even greater force to suppliers of semi-finished parts and raw materials, for manufacturers of items such as castings, forgings, sheet steel, metal bars and strips, paint, leather, glass, textiles, rubber, fuel and power, supply these products to other industries besides motor vehicles. In addition, many of the processes and techniques involved are very different from those normally performed by the car manufacturers, so that the shape of the relevant long-run cost curves are dissimilar. Some of these suppliers perhaps cease to obtain significant economies of scale at relatively low outputs, a condition that is probably true of foundry operations. The reverse may be true for other products such as sheet steel. Extremely high volumes are required to support a continuous strip mill, and it was the huge demand of the entire American vehicle industry that first made this cost-saving technique possible.[1] However, there can be no numerical correlation between these discontinuous economies at high volumes and the expansion of a single firm. They come with the growth not only of the car industry, but of industry in general.

There are therefore sufficient economic causes for the discrepancy noted in Table 1 between the savings in factory cost and in total cost on the part of a single expanding firm without invoking the second reason previously cited—monopoly power on the part of suppliers, which would enable them to pocket all or part of the gains from larger volumes. Indeed, relations with suppliers and relative bargaining strength is such that few, if any, suppliers are likely to possess this power, especially in the long run.[2]

The changes in total fixed investment and in fixed overhead per unit indicated in Table 1 reveal the familiar pattern of mass-production, i.e. the heavy increase in capital investment accompanying expansion together with a fall in fixed expense per unit. But this relationship between fixed investment and expansion is far from being uniform. In the example given, the first doubling is achieved by a 40 per cent increase in fixed expense; the second doubling requires 70 per cent more. In fact, fixed expense per unit notably fails to decline at all in the range from 300,000 to 400,000 units. At certain levels of output, particularly costly equipment is needed, or even a whole new plant and a complete change of layout may be necessary,

[1] TNEC *Hearings,* Part 21, op. cit., p. 11193.
[2] See the discussion of this point in Chapter VIII.

resulting in a reorganization which will not only cope with the immediate needs of expansion, but which will also lay the groundwork for meeting a future enlargement of demands. A similar situation arises in the jump from small-scale production to the 50,000 level, for to produce 50,000 units efficiently requires similar techniques and much of the fixed investment, especially in assembly facilities, of double that amount. It is a characteristic feature of this investment that it results in the introduction of new (but usually already largely known) techniques which become worth-while at the higher levels of output. No firm would consider a major expansion in terms of its existing techniques and equipment, although there would be exceptions for some processes and for particular machines.

The higher levels of mechanization which accompany growth are, of course, reflected in the significant savings in direct labour cost per unit. Indirect labour costs, however, in the form of supervision and maintenance charges may increase with greater mechanization, and there may be greater losses arising from possible breakdowns when production is made more interdependent. On the other hand, there may be savings arising out of a better balance and the use of better systems of control which become possible at higher outputs. It is assumed in Table 1 that these conflicting tendencies offset each other, so that variable indirect costs per unit remain constant as scale increases.[1]

In assessing the extent of the economies of scale indicated by these data, there is no reason to think that they are *less* than the amount shown. What little published quantitative evidence there is suggests that they may be greater.[2] Support for this view comes from the reports by the Austin and Renault Companies, in connection with their recent experience with unit automatic transfer machines that have already been mentioned in Chapter IV. The Austin Company's extremely interesting comparison—of costs of a 13-station transfer machine, chosen at random, compared with the existing equivalent standard machines performing the same operations on the A-40 cylinder block—shows clearly that not only does the new equipment reduce cost per unit very greatly, but that it is also cheaper to buy, and to operate per hour, than the machines it replaces.[3] A drastic

[1] Later discussions with the firm have suggested that, with tight controls, a unit decrease in variable overheads of perhaps 2 per cent would be possible with a doubling of output from, say, 50,000, 100,000 or 200,000. Beyond this point it is believed that these economies would cease or that there might be diseconomies.
[2] See the Appendix to this chapter.
[3] F. Griffith, Chief Project Planning Engineer, Austin Motor Company, *The Machinist*, January 21, 1955, pp. 107–113.

reduction of direct labour costs of over 80 per cent has been achieved, and repair costs have been reduced by 16 per cent. Startling increases in *machine* productivity have been reported from America, using machines which actually cost less than the old ones they replace.[1] And from the Renault Company in France comes the remarkable claim that they have found maintenance charges for special machines to be 70 per cent *less* than for standard equipment.[2]

All these examples come from the process of machining, and this has special significance for the large UK firms because the possibility of the major gains from economies of scale for them lies here. They have passed the optimum for assembly, and they cannot hope to achieve the volume necessary to justify the continuous production of major pressings. If these are not isolated cases, it may be that Table 1 understates the savings available in the range of output from 100,000 to 400,000 vehicles per annum. It is not for a moment suggested that all, or even the majority of future fixed investment in machining will be capital-saving, but it may be that Table 1 overestimates the capital required for expansion. And perhaps also it understates the effect of automation on direct labour costs, and is too pessimistic about maintenance expenses, both for the car firm itself and its suppliers. Whether this is so or not, it seems highly unlikely that Table 1 exaggerates the importance of economies of scale in the 100,000 to 400,000 range.

For savings at smaller outputs, there is an estimate by the National Advisory Council for the Motor Manufacturing Industry[3] which states that, for a firm using flow production, a volume increase from 50,000 to 100,000 units may bring savings of 15–20 per cent per unit. These are considerably greater than the economies shown in Table 1, but this is as one would expect, for more scope for savings exists with smaller outputs, especially in assembly. The Council also gives an estimate of savings using batch production, which suggests, together with other evidence, that costs fall rapidly over the range up to 50,000.

At the other end of the scale, *The Economist* has done some calculations from American data which imply that unit costs continue to fall beyond 400,000, but at a slower rate.[4] No optimum is indicated,

[1] The Cincinnati Milling Machine Company replaced six machines installed in 1949 for machining cylinder heads with one new machine in 1954. Output was the same in both cases; the new machine had a 4 per cent lower original cost and a 15 per cent lower replacement cost than the earlier equipment.
[2] *Automobile Engineer*, December 1954, p. 534.
[3] Report 1947, op. cit., p. 23 (HMSO).
[4] *v.* Appendix to this chapter.

but *The Economist's* conclusions are based on *price* per pound comparisons of different makes, which reflect selling and other non-technical economies of scale, as well as differences in profit margins between makes. Hence the figures are not necessarily inconsistent with the conclusion of the preceding section that all the *technical* economies appear to be exhausted at about the 1,000,000 mark, and they provide a rough and ready confirmation of the levelling off of unit costs at high volumes.

Figure 2 draws together the quantitative evidence in an attempt to picture the long-period average total cost curve of the firm.[1] A rough, general idea of the shape of the curve is all that such a diagram can reasonably hope to achieve; nevertheless, it is believed to be sufficiently close to reality to enable certain important conclusions to be drawn.

As one would expect, economies for the firm appear to be very great in the early stages of expansion. Something like a 40 per cent reduction in costs can be expected as production increases from 1,000 to 50,000 units per annum. Doubling volume to 100,000 units should lower costs by 15 per cent; while a further doubling to 200,000 should achieve another 10 per cent in savings. The jump to 400,000 yields an additional 5 per cent, and expansion beyond this point results in progressively smaller savings for each additional 100,000, the gains tapering off at a level of about 1,000,000.

There is little likelihood that the firm's economies are *less* than this; they may be more. Even on this conservative basis, the estimates show the possibilities of significant savings from expansion for the major UK manufacturers, most of whose popular models are now being produced in the 50,000 to 100,000 units per annum range. On the other hand, so huge is the absolute increase in output required to get significant economies beyond, say, 250,000, that no British producer is likely to be in a position to secure them for very many years to come.

3. ECONOMIES OF SCALE: THE INDUSTRY

Further reductions in the cost of producing cars can be expected when the industry, as well as the firm, grows, that is, when the production of materials for the motor industry by suppliers is doubled or trebled to match that of car producers as a whole. The extent of

[1] Given the present structure of the British industry and a relatively high degree of vertical disintegration.

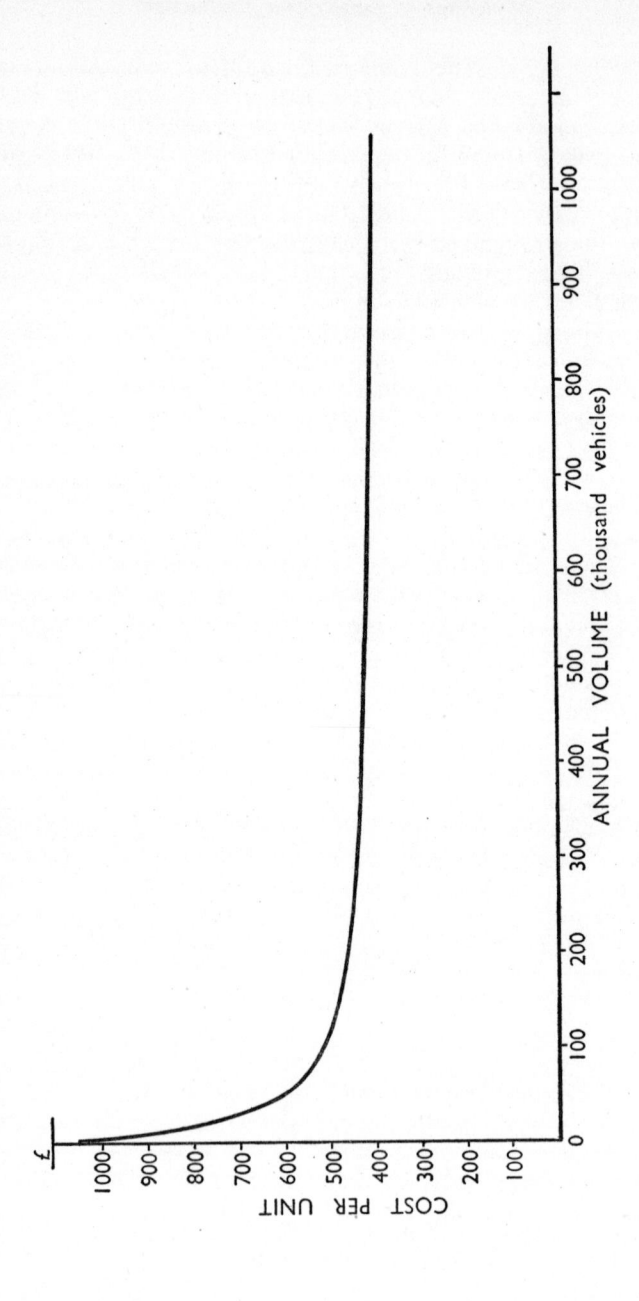

FIGURE 2   THE FIRM'S TECHNICAL ECONOMIES OF SCALE

these savings (which will be reflected in a further reduction in materials expenditure per unit on the part of car firms) will depend primarily on the initial scale of operations of suppliers, the shape of their cost curves, and how much of their production is allocated to the motor industry. For a highly industrialized country such as the UK, with a mature motor industry possessed of a well-developed parts and components section, there are reasons for believing that the economies of scale open to suppliers are considerably less than those available to car manufacturers.

For industries such as steel or chemicals, who are suppliers of many industries other than the motor industry, the increase in volume would still be far from proportionate, i.e. a doubling of the car industry might involve only a 10 or 20 per cent increase in volume for such suppliers, and consequently would lead to smaller savings for them. On the other hand, basic industries such as steel are subject to major economies at very high levels of output with the adoption of entirely new techniques, and a huge increase in demand from the motor industry might be sufficient by itself to bring about such a fundamental change—for example, the introduction of the continuous wide-strip mill. But obviously such changes are not a frequent occurrence. It is more important in assessing the expected economies to study the existing scale of operations of parts and components makers whose technical problems may be assumed to be similar to those of the car manufacturers. Many of these industry suppliers are producing at volumes well in excess of the individual car producer; a few may have already reached the optimum with some items. Hence further growth will bring these producers smaller economies, or perhaps none at all. This is not something to be deplored. It merely means that by vertical disintegration and standardization the industry has secured most of the economies of scale in these items sooner than would otherwise be the case, and that the savings are already incorporated in the cost structure of the industry.

Nevertheless, an industry increase certainly should bring some gains for the firm in addition to those discussed in the last section. Any serious attempt to estimate the extent of these savings would be an extremely hazardous and lengthy operation. However, a rough idea can be obtained by taking two plausible extremes for a four-fold expansion. If it is assumed that the average supplier's factory cost and materials cost are reduced by the same percentage as those of the car firm in Table 1 (24 per cent and 8 per cent respectively), and that there is a 50–50 ratio of factory cost to materials cost for suppliers, then suppliers' costs will come down by 16 per cent. For the other extreme, assume that suppliers' costs come down by only half these percentages, in other words by 8 per cent. If it is assumed that these savings are additional to the 8 per cent savings in material costs taken into account in Table 1, then the car firm in Table 1 (with a materials expenditure of 71 per cent of total costs to start with) can be expected to reduce its materials costs by 15–25 per cent and his unit total costs by between roughly one-fifth and one-quarter with a four-fold industry expansion.

This figure is considerably lower than the 40 per cent suggested by the National Advisory Council.[1] There are a number of possible reasons for the higher estimate given by the Council. In the first place, they were presenting a case for a reduction in motor car taxation, and having based their argument on the economies of scale that would accrue from a large home market they may have been over-zealous—in what must have been merely an informed guess based on their intimate knowledge of the industry—in stating the amount of these savings. Secondly, they wrote in 1946–47, when the industry was reorganizing for peace-time production. Output was below a rate of 500,000 cars and commercial vehicles per annum, and there was considerable excess capacity. One would expect potential gains to be greater under such conditions than when making an estimate on the basis of an output of over 1,000,000 vehicles per annum and full capacity utilization. Lastly, the Council may have taken into account the consequences of further standardization: the possible gains from standardization were very much in the minds of the Government and industry at that time. On the other hand, it may be that, as suggested earlier, Table 1 underestimates the firm's economies of scale, in which case the industry estimate of savings derived from it is also understated. There can be no certainty in such matters, but it seems safe to conclude that a four-fold industry expansion would reduce costs by not less than one-fifth to one-quarter.

Such a huge expansion in the UK industry is highly unlikely for many years to come, but an annual output of 2,000,000 cars is considered a distinct possibility in the not-too-distant future. This would mean roughly doubling output from present levels and should bring more than half the gains from a four-fold expansion. As a conservative estimate, something in the region of a 15 per cent reduction in costs seems indicated.

No account of economies of scale in the motor industry would be

[1] Report, p. 23.

complete without some mention of the vital importance of technological change. The durable nature of the product and the demand conditions facing a mature industry call for the continued stimulation of replacement demand with new ideas and better quality, often for the same money or less. This puts a premium on innovations, product improvement and improvement in production methods[1]: it is precisely here that absolute size is extremely important—size of the firm, the industry, and the whole economy. Only the giants can undertake the vast research and development programmes required to maintain progress in the long run in the modern world. Even when they do not make the original inventions, their huge resources enable them to introduce innovations much more speedily than smaller firms. Hence, the final reward for growth, one which continues to bestow competitive advantages when perhaps all the technical economies of scale are exhausted, is what might be termed 'the economies of technological progress'.

The dynamic characteristics of the motor industry are of particular relevance as regards the position of suppliers. Their contribution to technological progress, as well as being extremely important to car producers, may well be the basic explanation of their survival in many fields. In a sense, the laboratory of the specialist supplier is his insurance against redundancy. American suppliers who do nothing more than make parts to blue-prints supplied by their customers have been described as 'merely parasites on the industry'.[2] But these are the exceptions; the importance to themselves and to the industry of the heavy specialized research expenditure of large suppliers can hardly be overrated. The US motor industry owes its leading position today, partly to its own size, and partly to the fact that it is flanked by other giant industries—steel, chemicals, oil, metals, machine tools, etc., each capable of supporting tremendous research programmes which directly or indirectly benefit car production. In other words, it has the good fortune to be in the most highly developed industrial economy in the world.

---

[1] As productive methods change so, of course, may the extent of economies of large-scale production. In ten years' time, the estimates contained in this chapter may need considerable alteration. It is difficult to believe, however, that economies of large-scale production will not continue to be of very great importance.

[2] OEEC. *Some Aspects of the Motor Vehicle Industry in the USA*, op. cit., p. 34.

APPENDIX TO CHAPTER VI

Economies of Scale

Source	Volume Increase Units per annum	Increase in output %	Cost Reduction %
1. *The Economist*			
(a) 1954	125,000–175,000	40	5–6
(b) 1952–53		25	8
(c) 1954 (USA)	300,000–1,200,000	300	17
2. G. Wansbrough			
(a) 1950–54 (Industry–UK)	903,000–1,172,000	30	20
(b) 1955–	130,000–260,000	100	20
3. Joe S. Bain USA	60,000–300,000	400	'substantial'
	150,000–300,000	100	'moderate'
	300,000–600,000	100	'probable added advantages'

Notes:

1. *The Economist*, October 23, 1954. Motoring Supplement. 'Volume and Costs', pp. 7–11
   (a) Derived from graphs presented in a paper to Société des Ingénieurs de l'Automobile by M. Picard, head of Renault's design bureau.
   (b) Derived from Ford (UK) published turnover and profit figures for both years, roughly adjusted for price and cost changes. 'These figures are admittedly crude, but a general knowledge of engineering costs at high production rates makes them seem reasonable.'
   (c) Based on price per pound and output comparisons of various makes.
2. *Lloyds Bank Review*, October 1955. 'Automobiles: The Mass Market'.
   (a) Based on actual volume change (total of cars, trucks and tractors) and the estimated change in actual costs inferred from a price rise of only 10 per cent per pound during a period when wages and raw material prices increased by about 33 per cent.
   (b) Guess 'on the basis of past experience' as to the savings per unit when the current expansion is completed.
3. *Barriers to New Competition*, Harvard University Press, Cambridge, Mass., 1956.
   These estimates are derived from questionnaire data. The author states that 'it has been impossible to obtain quantitative estimates of what a moderate cost disadvantage is; the firms of the automobile industry seem generally uninterested in publicizing their plant and firm scales'.

CHAPTER VII

Competition in the Car Market, 1929-1956

1. 1929–1939

BY the end of 1929, two firms—Morris and Austin—dominated car production, accounting for 60 per cent of the output of the industry. The only other concern producing more than 10,000 cars per year was Singer, whose share was about 15 per cent of the market. The concentration of some 75 per cent of car production in the hands of these manufacturers, and the elimination of many small producers during the 1920s, had been brought about by the competitive pressure exerted by a few rapidly expanding companies benefiting from the economies of scale that accompanied the introduction of elementary mass-production techniques. For this, the relatively long production runs of two highly successful models were mainly responsible: the Morris-Cowley, which first appeared in 1915, and the Austin Seven, which was introduced in 1922. As a result of these developments, the outline of the present structure of the industry had already emerged, i.e. a few 'mass producers' of cars and a larger number of 'specialists'. Within this framework the situation remained fluid as far as the position of the individual firms was concerned. Neither Morris nor Austin had an average output in the late 'twenties of much more than 50,000 cars a year, and the gap between the large and small producer was not yet great enough to prohibit a small company from climbing into the front rank. The competition of the 1930s was to decide who the present-day contestants for the mass market were to be. The purpose of the first part of this chapter is to analyse that competition; to examine the forms it took and the effects it had on the product, the structure of the industry, and Britain's position in overseas markets.

On the whole the 1930s represent as good a period as one could expect for a study of competition in the industry. The output of the British motor industry, unlike that of the American, was only slightly curtailed during the depression in the early 1930s, and in the closing years of the decade production was twice that of the 1929 peak. The competitive emphasis was on retaining one's share in an expanding market, which is still a characteristic attitude in the motor industry. During this time production conditions were 'normal' in the sense that there were no shortages of steel or other essential supplies, and no strikes or other barriers to production of any consequence. Improved techniques were continually being introduced, but there were no sudden or drastic effects on the competitive situation on this score. Rising output led to economies of scale, but, as we shall see, the advantages accruing to the larger companies from expansion tended to be offset by a trend towards greater variety—more models and more frequent model changes. However, the changes in the product that this implied were gradual, like the improvements in technique. No shattering innovations in design or performance appeared which completely altered the relative standing of the competitors.

Probably the most significant external force at work affecting the fortunes of individual firms was the major shift in demand which took place in this period. This was the very rapid growth in the demand for small cars; a trend greatly reinforced by the effects of the depression and the heavy taxation on motoring which discriminated against the ownership of large cars. In 1928 a quarter of all cars sold were 10 h.p. or under. Only five years later the proportion had risen to 60 per cent, and it remained at that high figure throughout the rest of the 'thirties. It was necessary for any large-scale manufacturer, actual or potential, to produce a small car. In practice, he usually produced two different types of small car, because the 60 per cent was fairly evenly divided between the 8 h.p. and 10 h.p. classes. The remarkable popularity of the 'Ten' was probably the first real proof the industry had had of the willingness of the public to pay a little more for a 'de luxe' version of a standard model.

In the detailed analysis of price changes which follows, attention is concentrated on the small car market in the belief that this reflects the behaviour of the industry as a whole. It also centres on the price and model changes of the 'Big Six'—Austin, Ford, Hillman (Rootes), Morris, Standard and Vauxhall—for the same reason. Chart I is a visual price history of the 'Big Six' models in the 7–8 h.p. class.

It is evident that price changes in the popular car market were few and far between, and almost invariably were small in amount. The number of such changes averaged less than one a year per model, and most of them were of less than 5 per cent. The vast majority of the price changes that did take place were associated either with changing input prices or with product changes made before the annual motor shows. Morris, for example, only made three price alterations in this

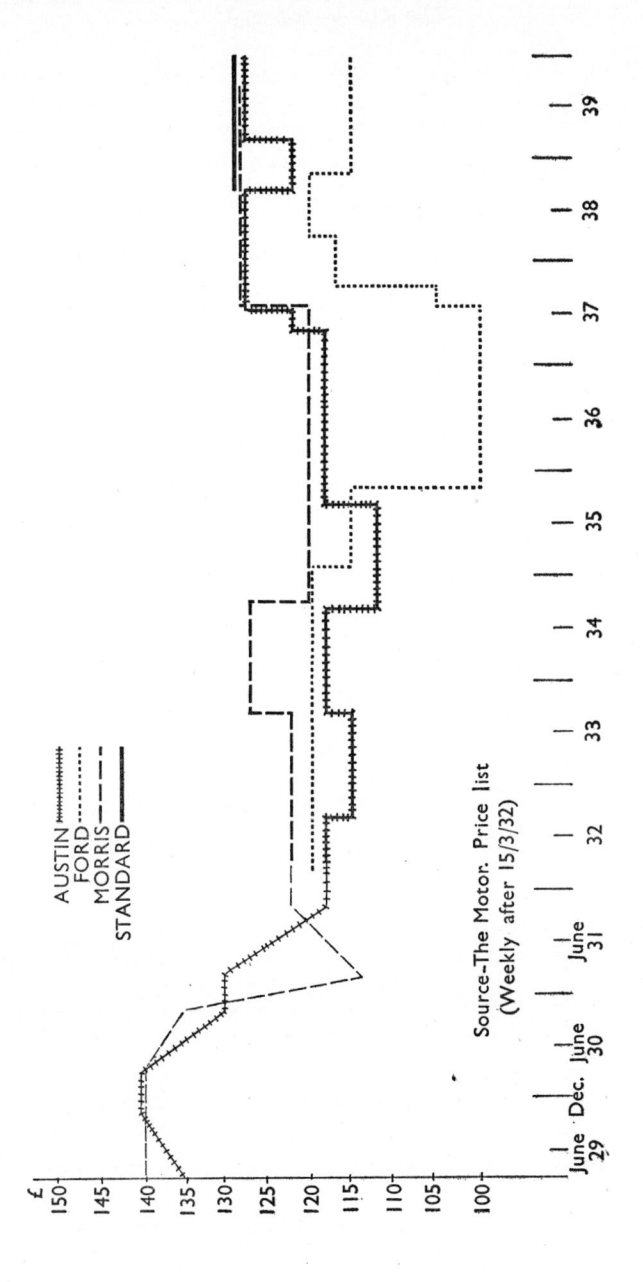

CHART I   PRICES OF 'BIG SIX' 7–8 H.P. MODELS 1929–39

class in nine years, two of which (1933 and 1937) were a reflection of rising prime costs. The third (1934) coincided with the introduction of an entirely new model. With one major exception, competition between firms did not take the form of price changes in existing models, but was confined to questions of style, quality and service.

This one exception was the 13 per cent reduction in the price of the current model of the Ford Eight in October 1935, which then sold for almost two years at £100, some 20 per cent cheaper than its rivals. This experiment in pricing is extremely interesting from a number of economic standpoints. It has already been discussed briefly in Chapter V.

TABLE 1
Domestic Car Sales, 8 h.p. and under

Year	Total UK New Car Registrations— 8 h.p. and under	Domestic Sales Ford 8 h.p.	Ford Share (%)
1934	50,283	27,000	54
1935	80,856	17,000	22
1936	80,381	33,000	41
1937	86,824	37,000	43
1938	82,796	28,000	34

Table 1 shows the market situation prevailing at the time of the price cut, and suggests the motive behind it. The Ford Eight, introduced in the latter part of 1931, had been extremely successful, and had captured well over half the market by 1934. However, in the following year, sales fell off by nearly 40 per cent in spite of a sharp increase in total demand, so that there was a drastic fall in the Ford share of the market. This fall seems mainly attributable to the new Morris Eight model which came on the market towards the end of 1934, and which had been completely redesigned to fit the new production methods adopted at that time by Morris.[1] This Morris became the most successful car ever sold in the UK before the last war. Ford chose to meet this competition by lowering price rather than by the usual course of bringing out a new model. Hence the move appears to have been one of retaliation rather than part of an aggressive drive for sales based on economies of scale.

In arriving at their decision to cut prices, the Ford management must have concluded that in all probability their competitors would

---

[1] *v.* Andrews and Brunner, *The Life of Lord Nuffield*, p. 197. Sales of the Ford Eight may also have been affected by the introduction of the Ford Ten, which appeared at this time.

not retaliate, at least in the short run. They may have banked on the fact that, given the structure of costs in the industry (*v.* Chapter V above) other firms would hesitate before running the risk of a price war. In any event, rival prices did in fact remain constant. The total demand for 8 h.p. cars also remained constant, but Ford sales of their 8 h.p. model nearly doubled. From the standpoint of stimulating unit sales the move was, therefore, a highly successful one, and it enabled Ford to recapture a good part of the share of the market it had lost in the preceding year. From the point of view of profits, however, the move was not so successful. Although the total sales of Ford vehicles rose by a third, there was an overall increase in trading profits of only 10 per cent for the year 1936, the first full year of the price cut. The increase in sales was little more than enough to offset the fall in profits per vehicle caused by the reduction in price. This drop in profit margins came at a time when other competitors, such as Morris, were sharply increasing theirs. In the following year, all prices rose, but the price of the Ford 8 rose relatively to the others, so that its price became 10 per cent cheaper than the rest rather than 20 per cent: tacit admission that the attempt to plumb a new mass market had not been altogether successful. Although the Ford remained the cheapest car in each class, the Ford management had apparently joined the other companies in a policy of 'a better car for the same money' rather than 'the same car for less money'.

Had sales of the Ford Eight continued to expand strongly in 1937 and 1938 as a result of the price cut, instead of levelling off after 1936, the reduction would have been amply justified by the economies of scale that could have been secured. In the long run, given a rapid and sustained increase in demand, short-run cost considerations no longer apply and the impossible becomes possible. Henry Ford demonstrated this in the early days of the industry. His car production in America in 1911 was some 40,000 units—about the same as that of the UK Ford company almost a quarter of a century later. Within six years, volume had increased twentyfold. The 'snowballing' of Ford sales on the groundswell of American demand led to spectacular reductions in price. Morris repeated the performance on a much smaller scale in the early 1920s. It was extremely unlikely, however, that these early successes could be repeated in the 1930s under quite different supply and demand conditions. They had come at a time when cars were new, simple in design and construction, and when the gap between the general level of engineering efficiency and the new mass production methods was extremely wide.

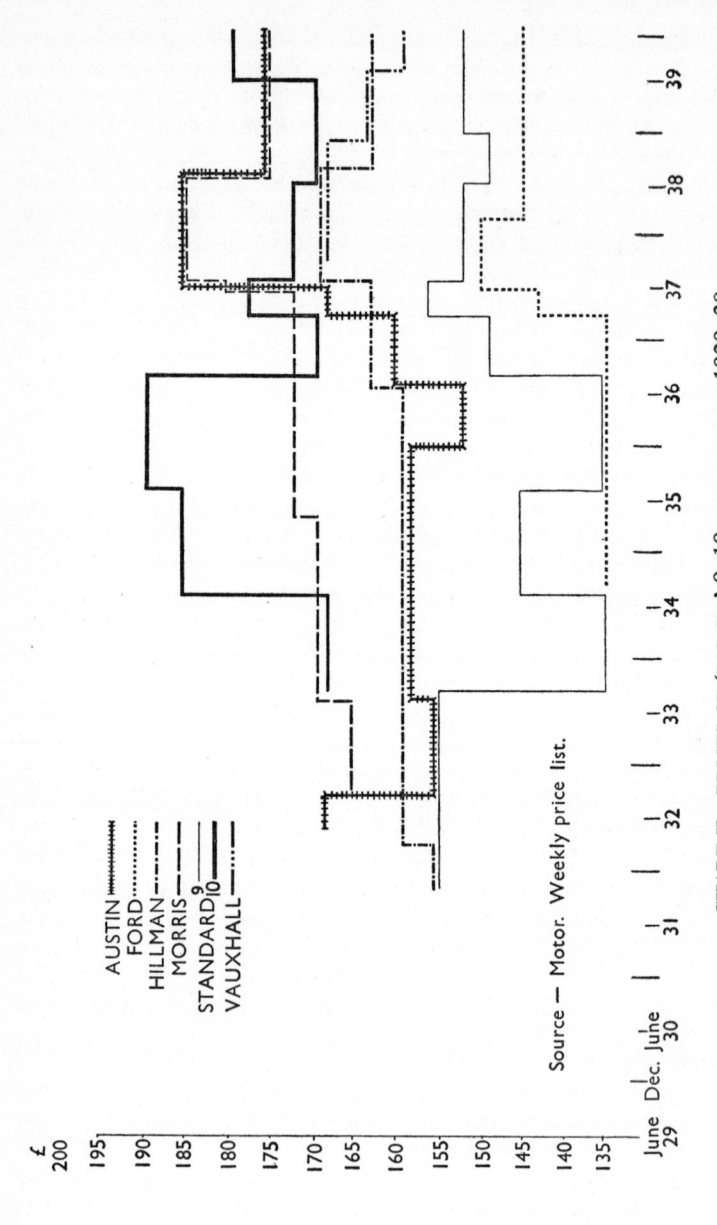

CHART II   PRICES OF 'BIG SIX' 9–10 H.P. MODELS 1929–39

Source — Motor. Weekly price list.

Chart II records 'Big Six' price changes in the 9 and 10 h.p. class.

Excluding for the moment the somewhat erratic price movements of the two Standard cars, the price pattern is very similar to that of the cheaper models. Price changes are few and far between, usually small in amount, and associated with model changes or with changing prime costs affecting all companies alike. Although Standard's price changes were not much more frequent than the rest, and the two largest price changes in the 9 h.p. car marked the introduction of new models, this company appears to have followed a different policy from the others at times. This is especially true of the 10 h.p. model whose price fluctuations suggest 'charging what the traffic will bear'.

Certain general conclusions emerge from this historical survey regarding the related questions of price competition, price leadership and price agreements. Competition in the 1930s seldom took the form of short-period price competition. Car prices tended to remain stable unless there was a quality change, or unless input prices altered. The structure of costs in the industry helps to explain this price stability. In addition, such a policy appeals to consumers and dealers; both groups might be antagonized by frequent fluctuations in prices.

The lack of short-period price competition carried with it certain implications regarding price leadership and price agreements. Stability of prices left little scope for the exercise of price leadership,[1] and reduced any incentive there might have been for price agreements. The timing of the price changes that did take place—over two-thirds in the summer months preceding the annual Motor Show—makes it difficult to infer anything about price leadership. Obviously, any number of *post hoc propter hoc* arguments are possible. It might be maintained, for example, that Morris followed Austin's lead from 1937–1939, or that all the manufacturers cut prices in 1938 in response to Ford's move in this direction, but such contentions would be hard to prove. With one exception, the timing of price changes provides no evidence for any sort of agreement between firms. The exception was in July 1937 when Austin, Ford and Morris announced price increases, on account of rising wages and material costs, on the same day. Even in this case, there was probably agreement on the timing of the price change only. In general, the picture is one of complete independence of action on the part of each company in the setting and changing of its prices.

The foregoing conclusions apply only to competition by means of

[1] In the sense that one firm habitually initiates price changes.

short-period price changes. In the long run, a much more active form of competition was taking place. This form of competition, connected with the introduction of new models, might be called 'model-price' competition. For the manufacturer, price was the starting point in all his strategic calculations. Having decided on the price, he proceeded to build the best (or the most appealing) car that he could at that price. His selection of the price was usually determined by assessing the market in terms of the more successful models. The highly popular model often became a 'price leader'—using the term now in a different sense—and set the price around which other firms tended to cluster.[1] The Hillman Minx was such a price leader in the 10 h.p. class. The Austin 'Seven' undoubtedly set the pace for the smaller cars until the middle of the 'thirties, when Morris took over from Austin with the new Morris Eight. The £100 Ford, on the other hand, failed to become a price leader. It was the price of the Morris Eight that became the price of the new Standard and the new Austin models introduced in the 1938–39 seasons. Success came to those firms whose models, selling at the conventional price for their class, made the greatest appeal to the public.

It was this long-run model-price competition that was responsible for the elimination of one-third of the firms in the industry in the 'thirties, and for the major changes that took place in the share of the market held by those firms that remained. As might be expected, the competition was most severe in the popular priced market. Many companies attempted to compete in the small car class who were either forced out of business or back up the price ladder into the 'specialist' category. In the 8 h.p. class, Jowett, Singer, Swift and Triumph had entries at the beginning of the period. Rover made an attempt to break in with the Scarab in 1931, a two-cylinder, air-cooled, rear-engined car, seating four and selling for as little as £89. It remained on the market for less than a year. By 1939 Jowett was the only independent producer making an 8 h.p. car. However, the Jowett was no longer competitive in price with the 'Big Six' products, selling as it did at some 30 per cent more. In the 10 h.p. class, over fifteen independent companies attempted to compete, but by 1939 only Jowett and Singer remained in a field pre-empted by the 'Big Six'.

Along with this elimination of small competitors, went major changes in the shares of the 'Big Six' themselves. This is shown in Table 2.

[1] Vance. TNEC *Hearings*, Part 21, December 6, 1939, p. 11214.

TABLE 2
Percentage of Total 'Big Six' Car Production
1929–1939

	Vauxhall	Standard	Rootes	Ford	Nuffield	Austin
1929	1.1	4.9	n.a.	5.7	51.0	37.3
1930	5.9	5.1	5.6	7.0	39.3	37.1
1931	6.4	10.6	6.8	3.5	38.5	34.2
1932	5.6	12.7	8.0	7.5	36.8	29.4
1933	7.1	8.9	9.1	18.9	27.2	28.8
1934	8.7	8.6	8.7	15.5	29.4	29.1
1935	8.6	7.8	8.3	17.4	33.6	24.3
1936	6.3	9.6	9.3	22.1	29.6	23.1
1937	8.1	9.7	9.5	22.3	27.6	22.8
1938	11.3	10.8	11.1	19.0	25.6	22.2
1939	10.4	12.8	10.9	14.7	26.9	24.3

The outstanding change is the great reduction in the share of the market held by Austin and Morris, so that the period ended with six major producers instead of two. The apparent inability of the two largest firms to consolidate the dominant position they held in 1929 is one of the most interesting questions in the history of the industry. Most of the relative setbacks suffered by Austin and Morris occurred in the early 'thirties, in the four year period 1930–1933. The timing of the change suggests that the following factors were mainly responsible:

1. The shift in demand to small horse-power models.
2. Increased competition, especially from the American companies, Ford and Vauxhall.
3. The emphasis on rapid model change and a wide range of models.
4. Management difficulties.

The shift in demand has already been referred to, the most notable feature during these years being the increase in the share of the 9 and 10 h.p. cars from 10 per cent in 1929 to 34 per cent in 1933. Together with the 8 h.p. groups, these cars accounted for 60 per cent of the total in 1933. Obviously Austin and Morris, as the two largest companies, had to be represented in both these categories. However, their early attempts to meet the shift in demand by bringing out new models were not particularly successful, and it was not until the mid-1930s that they produced new 8 and 10 h.p. models which were as popular as those of their competitors. Austin was more fortunate in that, with the 'Seven', it was already firmly established in the 'baby' class before the shift in demand came. Probably it was this more than anything else that was responsible for the smaller decline in Austin's share as compared with that of Morris.

Other firms benefited from the shift to small cars, especially in the 8 and 10 h.p. class where there were no 'established' models. Two companies, Hillman and Standard, probably owed their success to the shift in demand. Whether by accident or design, they were the first of the larger companies in the 9–10 h.p. field, with the result that Standard's share more than doubled in two years, and the Hillman Minx became the mainstay of the Rootes Group, a position which it still enjoys to the present day. Competition from the American companies did not come at first in the new 10 h.p. class[1] but in the two extremes of the horse-power range. The Ford Eight introduced in August 1931 was, more than any other single model, responsible for the relative decline in the fortunes of Austin and Morris. It is worth noting that Ford's successful entrance into the small car field was achieved through quality competition rather than price competition. The company chose to produce the best car it could at the 'going price' rather than to attempt to undersell its rivals. Towards the other end of the horse-power scale, the heavier Fords were joined by the six-cylinder Vauxhall Cadet (20 h.p. and 26 h.p. models) which were successful in capturing a large share of a class which was becoming relatively less important. The Cadet was the first new model to be produced since General Motors took over the Vauxhall company, and it reflected a complete change of policy: some 50 per cent cheaper than the old Vauxhall, it represented a move into an entirely new price class, and a bid to make Vauxhall a volume producer of cars. There is no doubt that both American companies, although their volume was at first small compared with that of their main British competitors, possessed certain scale advantages denied to Austin and Morris. As subsidiaries of General Motors and Ford in Detroit, they naturally shared in the technical knowledge and in the research and development programmes of the parent companies, and could make use of their world-wide network of assembly plants and sales agents for their overseas sales.

The shift in demand and the increase in competition were met by Austin and Morris with a multiplicity of models which tended to dissipate their scale advantages. In their pamphlet issued to the public in 1955 called 'Austin, 50 Years of Car Progress' the Company stated:

[1] The Ford Ten was not introduced until 1934 and the Vauxhall Ten until 1937.

The range now [1927] comprised twenty-four distinct models. In 1929 the number had increased to twenty-eight.... The elaboration of the Austin range continued until by 1934 there was a choice of forty-four separate models based on nine alternative chassis. If one takes into account the wide range of colours and equipment offered then a grand total of three hundred and thirty-three different cars were listed!

One must not, of course, take this 'sales talk' too literally with regard to models. Obviously there must have been considerable interchangeability of parts between the forty-four 'separate' models. However, there can be no doubt that the trend was away from standardization, and a large number of variations on each of nine chassis sizes seems an inordinate amount of variety for a company averaging around 50,000 cars per year.

Discussing the same question with regard to Morris Motors, Lord Nuffield's biographers comment:[1]

The company had developed five new models between 1926 and 1929 —a very rapid pace for a business whose mainstay had continued to be the 11.9 Cowley ... four more cars were developed between 1929 and 1932 ... the 1933 season's catalogue offered a range of 8, 10, 12, 14, 16, 18 and 25 h.p. cars (each car being offered in saloon and coupé versions, and all except the 16 as tourers also). This preoccupation with new models was one reason for Morris Motors' poorer financial results during the depression. For one thing, quite promising models were not necessarily in production long enough to recover all their initial costs.

Morris and Austin were, of course, not alone in the trend towards greater variety, although, in general, their competitors resisted the temptation to produce a successful model in every horse-power class throughout the wide range of consumer demand. By the end of the period, however, all six of the larger firms were producing 10 h.p. models, and in 1938 Standard joined Austin, Ford and Morris with an 8 h.p. model. Rootes and Standard, despite a considerable number of models, were probably saved from the penalties of too much variety by the success of the Hillman Minx and the Standard Nine. Ford and Vauxhall, geared to produce the larger American-type cars, reluctantly brought out smaller models to meet the shift in demand.

The final factor contributing to the changes in market shares—management difficulties—pertains to Morris Motors. Lord Nuffield's biographers refer to 'uncertainty in management' and 'some internal

[1] Andrews and Brunner, *The Life of Lord Nuffield*, pp. 194, 195.

strife' during this period.[1] It culminated in the departure of several key directors, and the arrival of Mr L. P. (now Sir Leonard) Lord in 1933 to plan the complete reorganization of the Cowley works. This reorganization, and the introduction of the successful new models that followed it, enabled Morris Motors to hold their own for the remainder of the 'thirties.

By the end of 1933, the basic shift in the relative positions of the major producers had taken place, During the remainder of the 'thirties there were changes in relative shares, but none of fundamental importance. The 'Big Six' companies all grew in size with the increase in total output and, to a lesser extent, with the decline in importance of the 'specialists'. Temporary and limited gains in shares were made at each other's expense, particularly when one or other produced a successful new model. In general, market shares were relatively unaffected by price changes, except in the Ford case already discussed.

The form that competition took during the 1930s prevented economies of scale from being grasped as fully as they might have been. Greater variety meant shorter runs of individual models and this resulted, for reasons explained in Chapter VI, in higher costs of production than might otherwise have been achieved. Commenting on this question in 1938, *The Economist* stated[2] that the 'Big Six' car manufacturers produced between them

'no less than 40 different types of engine and even larger numbers of chassis and body types. In the United States, however, the three largest manufacturers (General Motors, Ford and Chrysler) accounted last year [1937] for about 90 per cent of a total output of no fewer than 3,915,000 units, but actually had fewer models in production than the six British manufacturers. . . . It was estimated last year that 26 out of 40 [British] models achieved sales of less than 5,000 units. And so small an output in the "popular" class is uneconomic.'

According to the National Advisory Council for the Motor Manufacturing Industry,[3] the entire Chevrolet output of 900,000 cars in 1937 was spread over one basic engine and chassis. The Ford output of nearly 800,000 cars was spread over two basic engines and chassis, while nearly half a million Plymouths were produced by the Chrysler Corporation, all with the same basic engine and chassis.

[1] Andrews and Brunner, *The Life of Lord Nuffield*, pp. 195–6.
[2] April 16, 1938, pp. 131–2.
[3] *Report on Proceedings*, HMSO, 1947.

It appears that about 60 per cent of the output of the three largest firms in the United States was accounted for by their three best-selling models in 1937, while in the United Kingdom the three best-selling models of the three largest firms accounted for only about 40 per cent of their total production. Variety and frequent change were characteristics of the American industry as well as the British, but the American industry was a good deal more successful in marrying variety with standardization.

The great contrast between the scale of the British and American industries, together with the greater standardization to be found in the American industry, helps to explain why the USA was so much more successful than the UK as an exporter of cars during the 1930s. The situation is illustrated by the following quotation, dealing with the production of the Ford V-8 at Dagenham, which is taken from the PEP report on the motor industry:[1]

'. . .the Dagenham factory was unable to market the Ford V-8 on the Continent at competitive prices. The same car made in Detroit could be delivered in France at a price some 30 per cent lower. The reason for this is not entirely clear . . .'

In fact, the reason could hardly be clearer. About half a million Ford V-8s were produced in Detroit in 1938: the Dagenham factory turned out 3,677! And Dagenham's English suppliers were furnishing parts and components for an industry only one-tenth the size of the American industry, and one turning out 30 makes of cars, with 136 basic models and 299 body variations. This was at a time when over 50 per cent of the huge American output was accounted for by only three models, while the three best-selling British models accounted for only 27 per cent of output.[2]

The inability, in general, of the British industry to compete with foreign, particularly US producers, is reflected in the overall statistics of production and exports. In 1938, 44,000 private cars were exported and of these three-quarters were sold in Imperial Preference markets. Over 85 per cent of the total production of 341,000 cars was disposed of in the home market, sheltered behind a 33⅓ *ad valorem* tax on all imports of motor vehicles. Some 97 per cent of all the cars produced in Britain in 1938 were therefore sold in protected markets.

[1] *Motor Vehicles. A Report on the Industry*, 1950, p. 29.
[2] Ibid., p. 129.

2. 1946–1956

The economic conditions existing after the war, when the production of private cars was resumed, were entirely different from those prevailing in the 'thirties. Manufacturers faced a world so starved for cars, both at home and abroad, that there was a sellers' market throughout most of the period, and the major difficulties confronting the industry lay on the side of supply. Production was continually plagued by shortages of materials and skilled labour, with steel being the worst bottleneck. During the early post-war years, the scarcity of steel forced plants to operate well below capacity, and delayed the return to pre-war levels of output until 1949. The demand of rearmament on steel and other materials forced a cut-back in car production of 10–15 per cent in 1951–52. In addition to various shortages of materials, there were restrictions on capital expenditure and on the import of machine tools which naturally hampered the expansion plans of the industry. All this, of course, was merely the reflection, in one particular sphere of manufacturing, of the economic problems of the nation as a whole—in particular the twin problems of inflation and the balance of payments. In common with many other manufacturers, the car makers had to cope with more or less continually rising costs for labour and materials and the need to expand export markets at a time of unprecedented demand at home. Prices rose, domestic waiting lists lengthened, and competition took the form of a production race rather than a sales contest. As a result, the emphasis on new models, so characteristic of the 'thirties, was replaced by the more pressing need to increase output.

An outline of the post-war competitive situation as regards the major models and their price history is given in Charts III and IV. By far the cheapest car on the market during the period was the Ford Popular, which was introduced under this name in 1953 and which sold at a basic price of £275 at the end of 1956. The Popular excepted, the cars sold by the big manufacturers fell into two principal price classes (October 1956, basic prices).

Class I (£360–£401)	Class II (£498–£535)[1]
Austin A30–A35	Austin A40–A50–(A90–A95 Westminster)
Ford Anglia	Hillman Minx (—)
Standard Eight	Ford Consul (Zephyr)
Morris Minor	Morris Cowley (Isis)
	Vauxhall Wyvern (Velox)

[1] The Triumph Mayflower (produced by Standard) competed in this class but was discontinued in 1953.

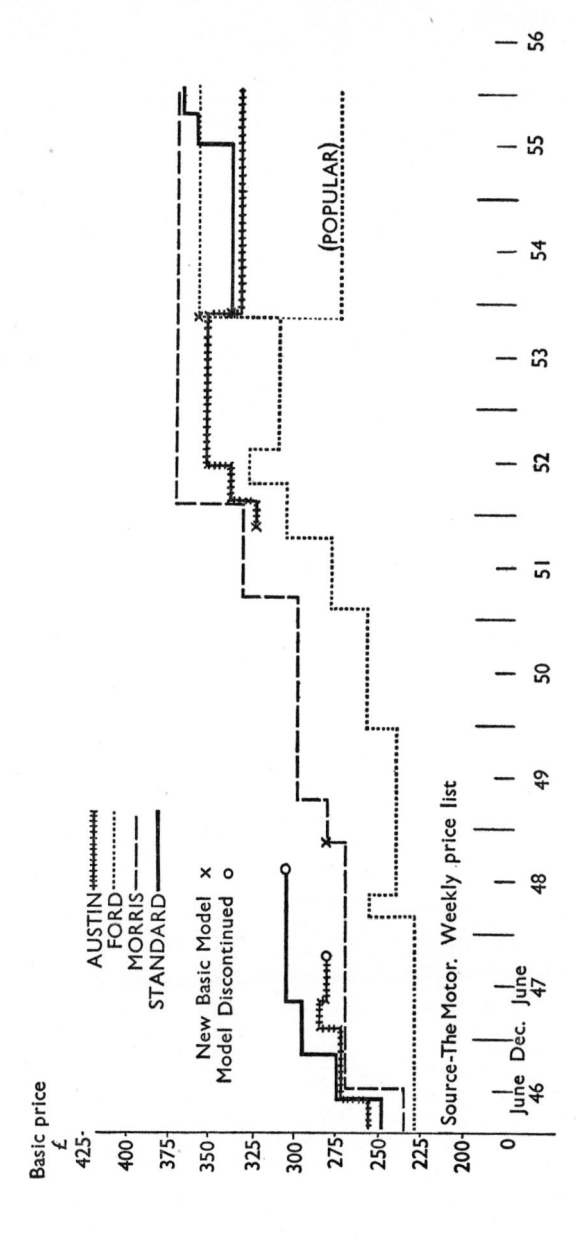

CHART III PRICES OF CLASS I (£360–£401 BASIC) MODELS, 'BIG FIVE' 1946–55

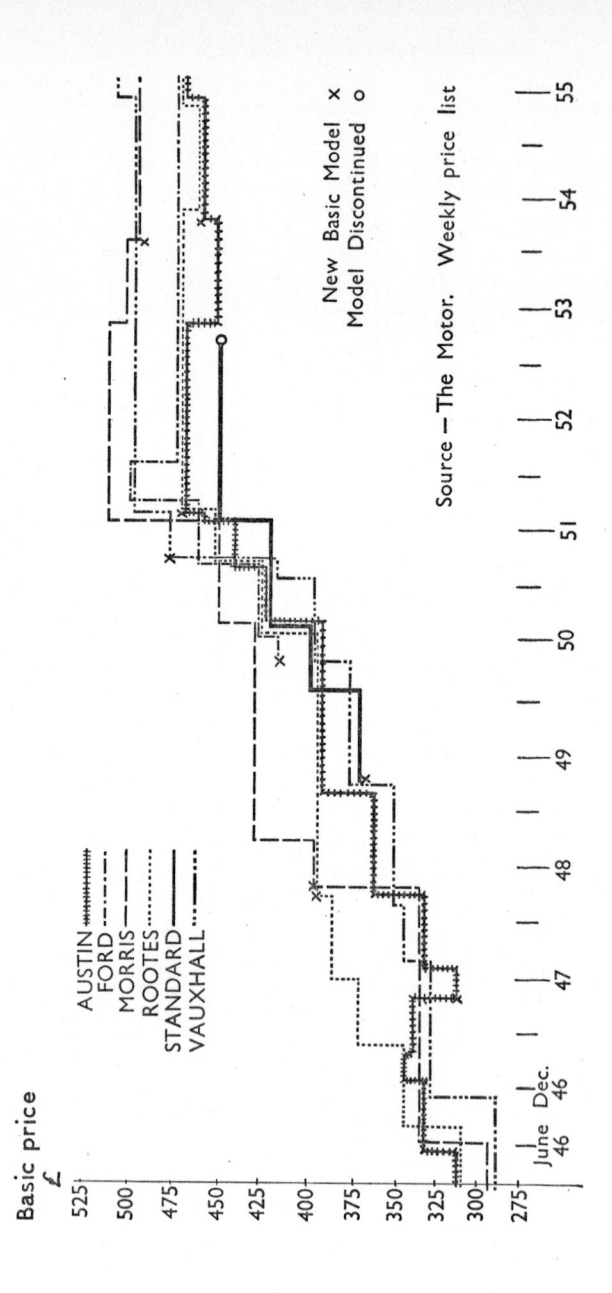

CHART IV PRICES OF CLASS II (£498–£535 BASIS) MODELS, 'BIG FIVE' 1946–55

Competition in the Car Market, 1929–1956

The gap between these classes was filled with various 'de luxe' versions of the Class I models. At the top of the scale, ranging up to £665, were the six-cylinder versions of the Class II models (in brackets). Competition for the mass market took place largely in these two categories, and no manufacturer could hope to survive as a major producer without a successful model in at least one of them.

Competition since the war has not taken the form of short-period price competition any more than it did in the 1930s. Indeed, there has been little change in price policy despite the vastly different economic framework in which post-war competition has been conducted. As in 1929–39, the price changes that occurred between 1946 and 1956 reflected changes in labour and material costs and, to a lesser extent, model changes, rather than competitive manoeuvres in a battle for sales. The almost continuous inflation caused price changes to be slightly more frequent and somewhat greater in extent than before the war, and less likely to take place just before the annual Motor Show. Each company must have made its price adjustments with a careful eye on the extent and timing of similar moves on the part of its rivals, but there was no sign of any industry agreements to raise prices, or of any settled pattern of leadership in the upward surge of prices. Certainly on the few occasions when price reductions were made on existing models, there was no attempt made on the part of rivals to retaliate. The Ford reduction in 1948 and 1952 went unchallenged,[1] as did those of Austin in 1953 and Hillman in 1954. Nor did anyone contest the unique position of the Ford Popular, a pre-war model admittedly, but nevertheless a car selling at a price nearly 20 per cent cheaper than any other make. In brief, short-period price competition was as conspicuously absent as in the pre-war period.

Long-period price competition continued to be characteristic of the industry in the form of what has been called model-price competition. The sellers' market caused it to be much less prominent in the early post-war period, its appearance being largely confined to the changeover from pre-war models. In 1954 and the years immediately following, however, a second round of new models was introduced—models which had been designed and brought into production in the expectation of an early end to the sellers' market.

For the cars in Class I, the Morris Minor appears to have acted as

[1] A curious feature of these Ford price cuts is that they were preceded, by only a few months, by larger price increases, so that the net result of the two moves was an increase in price.

'price leader' in this long-term price competition. Three years after the Minor was placed on the market, the Austin A30 made its appearance, at a price £8 cheaper. The new Ford Anglia, which arrived in 1953, was safely priced between its two competitors, while the new Standard Eight, introduced in the same year, undercut the Morris price by nearly £40 and enjoyed a brief period as the cheapest postwar car on the market. Austin swiftly retaliated and stole the title with a two-door A30 selling for £4 less. When the flurry of new models subsided, price competition ceased. The only further changes were two price increases for the Standard Eight, which suggests that the volume of sales may not have been high enough to sustain the initial price. The result was that by the end of 1956, all the new models were priced within 10 per cent of that of the Morris, the Morris (£401) being the most expensive, the Anglia and A30 the cheapest (£360) and the Standard right in the middle (£379).

The somewhat special case of the Ford Popular is of considerable interest from the point of view of price policy in the motor industry. Here was an example of that rare event, particularly in the case of the smaller cars: a major price reduction in what might reasonably be regarded as an existing model (in fact one that had existed since the early 1930s). Up to a point, the Ford Company repeated their prewar experiment, this time with a 12 per cent cut in price which took the Popular nearly 20 per cent below that of its nearest competitor. The main difference from the situation in 1935 was that then the Ford Eight had been much more like its competitors in type than the Ford Popular was in 1953. In 1953, Ford lowered the price of an old-fashioned car—the only one of its type left on the market. This essay into price competition led to no retaliation from rival companies. Had the Popular proved to be an unmistakable 'winner', the history of the industry suggests that the prices of existing models would not be reduced to meet it, but that there would be model-price competition, i.e. new cars would appear in the long run specifically designed to compete at that level—cars rather more austere than the Morris Minor, say, or cars rather smaller in size. So far this has not happened in the case of the Popular. Although there can be no doubt that it was a success from the standpoint of the Ford Company (some 75,000 Populars were sold in two years) some of that success depended on the swollen demand conditions prevailing at the time, and the feeling in the industry seemed to be that there was room for only one such car.

In Class II model-price competition, there were more contestants and no obvious price leader, and uncertainty prevailed in the early post-war years in the pricing of these models. During the price increases which reflected the effect of the inflation, prices were brought closer together. The introduction of the Ford Consul at the 'going price' in 1950, and the Austin pricing of new models since then at about the Consul-Hillman price level suggest that this is the centre of gravity for prices in this category. The new Vauxhall Victor, introduced early in 1957, was at first very competitively priced at appreciably below the Hillman-Austin level, but a price increase in July brought it closer to that level, although still below it. Clearly, the Victor—which was a four-seater, not a five-seater like its rivals—was intended to offer a model-price challenge of some magnitude.

The outcome of the competition for the mass market in the first decade after the Second World War is shown in Table 3.

TABLE 3
Estimated Share of Total Production of Private Cars, 1946–55
%

Year	Austin-Nuffield[1] (BMC)	Ford	Rootes	Standard	Vauxhall	Independents
1946	43.4	14.4	10.7	11.6	9.0	11.0
1947	39.3	14.8	10.5	12.9	10.6	12.0
1948	40.2	19.8	10.3	11.2	11.8	6.7
1949	39.4	18.7	13.3	11.1	11.0	6.5
1950	39.4	19.2	13.5	11.1	9.0	7.8
1951	40.3	18.9	12.3	12.6	7.4	8.4
1952	39.4	21.1	13.0	10.6	8.1	7.8
1953	35.2	27.0	12.8	8.6	10.4	6.0
1954	37.9	26.5	11.0	10.6	9.4	4.6
1955	38.9	27.0	11.4	9.8	8.5	4.4

The most significant change is the increase in the share of Ford, which was partly at the expense of the Independents and partly (in 1952–3) at the expense of BMC. The shares of the other members of the 'Big Five' tended to remain fairly stable, regardless of the introduction of new models or changes in relative prices in the home market.

The Ford gains cannot be ascribed to a multiplicity of models or to frequent model change. The new post-war range was confined to two

[1] Data not available for Nuffield and Austin separately prior to the formation of BMC in 1952.

basic models, and these continued unaltered until 1956, when the larger model was changed. Nor can it be held that it was the result of aggressive price competition for, as far as the new models were concerned, the Ford Company accepted the 'going price' and abandoned its pre-war policy of having the cheapest car in each major price class. The explanation may lie on the side of production rather than sales, and it may be simply that the Ford Company won the production race that characterized post-war competition until 1956. Perhaps the layout and facilities inherited at Dagenham at the end of the war were such as to make expansion easier there than elsewhere.

This is not to dismiss model changes or price policy as being unimportant in this period. The production gains could not have been sustained had not Ford cars met with a large measure of public approval. Quality and price must always affect the competitive position of a company, and it can be argued that although Ford prices were not the lowest, the value for money offered by Ford was as great as that offered by any other company, and greater than that offered by many. However, in periods of excessive demand the effect of offering better value for money is postponed, and in the period in question this does not appear to have been the immediate cause of the increases in the Ford share which came in two particular years, 1948 and 1953. At the earlier date, Morris introduced the Morris Minor, and this model changeover may have slowed up the rate of expansion of Ford's only competitor in the small car field at that time. At any rate, Ford's output went up 60 per cent as against a rise of 20 per cent for 'BMC'.[1] The notable increase in share in 1953 seems mainly ascribable to highly efficient organization which enabled production to be greatly increased when there was a general easing of the supply situation for the whole industry. The merger with Briggs, and the introduction of the new Anglia-Prefect together with the Popular in the autumn, whatever their long-run benefits to production and sales, could scarcely have explained a 70 per cent increase in the output of cars, together with a small rise in the output of commercial vehicles, in the year in which they took place.

The main losers in this production race were the Independents. Being less integrated, they were more dependent on suppliers, and, in a time of general shortage of materials and components, their necessarily small orders placed them at a disadvantage compared to the big buyers. The scramble for car bodies and the absorption of

[1] The Ford expansion in cars was not made at the expense of commercial vehicle or tractor production, both of which remained fairly constant at that time.

much of the body-building capacity by the financially stronger manufacturers was a particular handicap. The old-established Jowett Company claimed to have been forced out of business because of its inability to obtain bodies. But production troubles were not the whole story in the case of Jowett or of the other Independents. The Independents were meeting more intense competition from the 'Big Five' in sports cars and in the more expensive saloon models whose prices reflected partial standardization with mass-produced cars. Singer, which was acquired by Rootes in 1955, was an example of a company which produced cars very comparable to the higher quality cars made by the 'Big Five' but which did not have the volume to compete on price. Furthermore, the inevitable price gap between the small-volume, high quality, specialist products and their mass-produced competitors was made much greater in absolute terms by the purchase tax. The Lea-Francis Company, another old-established firm, considered that this tax imposed an impossible handicap on them and, in the early 1950s, decided to cease production of cars until it was removed. Altogether, the post-war period proved to be a difficult time for the Independents, despite the great demand for cars.

One feature of post-war competition in cars that does show a significant change from the position in the 1930s is that there has been a good deal less emphasis on variety and on frequent model change. This has already been remarked in the case of Ford, but it is true of the other large producers also. Unfortunately, it is not possible to carry out a direct comparison between the two periods because great difficulties arise when it is attempted to obtain agreement on how many different models are being produced at any one time and when a model change occurs. No two cars in a company's range of models are completely different—there is some interchangeability of parts, even if only of nuts and bolts. On the other hand, some models may differ only in the amount of accessories offered. It is not easy to draw the line between 'basically different' models, and to apply the same standard to all companies so that comparisons are meaningful and the total for the industry makes sense. Similarly with model changes. Rarely, if ever, is a car completely altered from bumper to rear light when a new model is announced. On the other hand, minor modifications or 'face lifts' are made from year to year, some of them extremely costly. When is the change a 'basic' one? Again, it is not easy to draw the line, and to apply the same criterion throughout the industry.

In addition, the whole issue is distorted if the output of the 'specialists' is included with that of the mass producers. In looking at the number of models produced and at the frequency of model changes, one has to bear in mind that great variety and frequent change increase the general level of costs and prices in the industry, and tend to make British products non-competitive in overseas markets. From this point of view the cars produced by the 'Big Five', representing as they do 95 per cent of production, are far more important than those produced by the Independents. The interesting question is how far the 'Big Five' have cut down variety since before the war and how far they have adopted a policy of less frequent model change.

There remains, however, the problem of definition referred to earlier. Fortunately this is not too difficult to deal with for the post-war period. The sellers' market, the large increase in output, and the considerable publicity given to the whole question of standardization have not only helped to bring about more standardization, but also more willingness on the part of manufacturers to admit it in reference to their own models. As far as model changes are concerned, there can be no dispute over the replacement in the early post-war years of essentially pre-war models by post-war designs—these were definitely 'basic changes'. With a few exceptions, these new models continued unchanged, except for the customary 'face lifts' until the end of 1955. The next round of major changes took place in 1956–7. Table 4 summarizes the position at the end of 1956. There may be grounds for

TABLE 4
Saloon Models Selling at under £665 Basic—October 1956

British Motor Corporation (7 models)
  Austin A.35
       A.50
       A.95
  Morris Minor
    Cowley ⎫
    Oxford ⎬
    Isis
  Wolseley Fifteen Fifty

Ford (3 models)
  Popular
  Anglia ⎫
  Prefect ⎬
  Consul ⎫
  Zephyr ⎬
  Zodiac ⎭

Rootes (3 models)
  Hillman Minx
  Humber Hawk
  Singer Gazelle

Standard (2 models)
  Eight ⎫
  Ten ⎬
  Vanguard

Vauxhall (1 model)
  Wyvern ⎫
  Velox ⎬
  Cresta ⎭

argument concerning the classification in one or two individual cases, but it is believed that the table gives a substantially correct impression.

It is noteworthy that by 1956 only the 'Big Five' were competing in the 'popular' market; no other British company produced a normal saloon car selling for less than £665 basic. The table indicates that sixteen basically different models were produced to cater to this market, and that nearly half of these were made by one company— the British Motor Corporation. The criterion used for a 'basically different model' was a major difference in the body shell *or* in the engine[1] from any other model. This exaggerates the variety since considerable standardization existed between some of these models, especially in mechanical parts. BMC, for example, produced only three basic engines for its seven models. In body pressings, too, there was some interchangeability among models listed above as separate, notably in the case of the Hillman Minx and the Singer Gazelle. Making allowance for this partial standardization, it would be fair to say that the British industry was turning out, at the end of 1956, something like a dozen fundamentally different models to compete in the mass market. This number was very considerably less than was being produced in the 1930s.[2] As far as model changes are concerned, the situation was also quite different. In the 1930s, when the volume of production of most models was very small, and when supply tended to outrun demand, the rate of model turnover was high. But in the post-war years, the major companies, with only three basic changes in thirteen years,[3] can scarcely be accused of changing models too frequently. Higher volumes and the use of more specialized equipment made such changes more costly, and the strong sellers' market before 1956 made them largely unnecessary. The larger companies like to achieve a total production run of 400/500,000 units over which to spread the cost of special tools and equipment associated with a particular model. This implies a life of five years or more for a model. In the post-war period, the major companies have in most cases been able to achieve this. Whether they will be able to keep on doing as well as this remains to be seen. The frequency of

[1] Four- and six-cylinder engines with many common dimensions, e.g. Ford Consul and Zephyr, have been counted as one.

[2] It is very difficult to make a detailed comparison for the reasons given earlier, but the quotation from *The Economist* on page 110 above makes it clear that there was far greater variety before the war.

[3] This includes the new models introduced by firms like Ford and Vauxhall in 1957. Before these models are replaced, an average life of about five years per basic model will have been achieved.

model change in the United Kingdom has, it should be noted, been very much less since the war than in the United States, where competition between themselves has driven the 'Big Three' to introduce completely new bodies for their cars every two or three years. Their scale of production has enabled them to afford this. The Independents, producing on a much smaller scale, have had to adopt a policy of much less frequent change.

3. SUMMARY

It has been seen that, in the periods 1929–39 and 1946–56, competition in the car market rarely took the form of short-period price competition. Such behaviour made for a high degree of short-period price stability, although it is not true that prices were never cut unless there had been a prior drop in wages or material costs. The main example of a price cut largely unrelated to changes in material costs is that made by Ford in 1935. Occasionally also, manufacturers lowered their prices to 'clear the decks' for a new model, e.g. Austin in 1938 when the original 'Seven' was discontinued. But ordinarily, the price of a model tended to remain unchanged, even in the face of a change in rival prices. It was more normal for manufacturers to compete by changing their product than by changing their price. To change product takes time, so that price competition was a long-run affair, tied in with model change and the problem of growth.

At the end of a model run, the manufacturer is no longer tied to a particular cost structure. He is free to change his prices, to alter his scale of operations, and to make major technical and design changes in his product. At this point he may choose to make a startling innovation or to strike out in a new price range. Or he may move to counter the successful new model of a rival with a model at a similar price, matching any innovations or improvements which it might possess. These decisions, on which the ultimate survival of the firm depends, are necessarily competitive decisions, and it is at this point that competition is most apparent—not in day-to-day pricing in the market place. Apart from the perpetual struggle to produce, sell and service the product more efficiently than competitors, a struggle which is a feature of most industries, competition in the motor industry primarily takes the long-range form of model-price competition.

The extent (but not necessarily the severity) of this model-price competition depends primarily upon the state of demand and the scale of production. In the 'thirties, both factors favoured a multiplicity of models and frequent model change. Demand was never in excess of supply, and manufacturers had seen again and again that new models justified themselves in terms of higher sales figures. On the other hand the scale of production of any particular model was low; few, if any, achieved a rate of production of 25,000 units a year. The rate for most models was a good deal less than this, so that hardly any models involved a sizeable investment in special-purpose machines and equipment. In short, changing a model stimulated sales, and the short-run cost to the individual manufacturer was not great. In the long run, however, such a policy meant that costs, and therefore prices, were higher than they might have been because potential economies of scale were sacrificed, so that the cost of such competition to the public was far from negligible.

In the post-war period, conditions were such that model-price competition was subordinated to other considerations. Model variety and change was not needed to stimulate the sales of the individual manufacturer, and the output of mass-produced models was reaching the point where it cost a great deal to make a change. With nothing to gain on the side of sales, and much to lose on the side of costs, it is not surprising that model-price competition was kept to a minimum. This does not mean that the industry became less competitive, but that the major consideration was the need to expand, to grow rapidly enough to retain one's share of the market. The company that did not grow could not hope to compete in the mass market when the post-war boom was over. Model change and variety would have hampered growth at a time when sales were virtually guaranteed.

In the early 1950s the indications were that a return to more normal demand-supply conditions was bringing with it more model-price competition. However, the excesses of the 'thirties have not yet been repeated and are not likely to be in the foreseeable future. Volumes are certainly high enough to ensure that the lesson of increasing returns is unmistakably clear, but not so high as to encourage imitation of the US practice of frequent model change. The sales advantage may be greater for the firm which keeps its costs and prices down rather than for the one that relies on variety and frequent change at the expense of higher costs and prices.

Where prices tend to be stable there obviously is only a limited scope for price leadership in the short run, although it may appear when general prices move upwards or downwards in response to changes in labour and material costs. The timing of such price changes in the past does not suggest any settled pattern of price leadership. In the long run, however, companies with highly successful models tended to act as price leaders in the sense that the success of their models induced competing models to appear at about the same price. A feature of the 1930s, in particular, was that throughout the period there was little change in the price of successful models. Prices became in effect conventional, but the models sold at these prices increased steadily in quality.

As far as price agreements are concerned, there is no evidence of their existence in the period under review, except for an isolated occasion in 1937 when there was apparently an agreement on the timing of a price change. The short-run stability of prices in the industry depends partly on cost considerations (*v.* Chapter V) and partly on the existence of oligopoly. Although price cuts by any one firm are not necessarily followed by other firms, there is always the danger that they might be. A policy of price-cutting is doubly risky—it may not be profitable even if other firms do not retaliate, and it almost certainly will not be profitable if they do. In these circumstances, there is little need for price agreements to prevent short-run price cutting in the industry.

To have had any real influence price agreements would have had to apply in the long run, i.e. at the time when new models were introduced. Not only is there no proof of the existence of such agreements, but it is extremely difficult even to envisage them. For such price agreements to have any meaning, it would not be enough to agree on the prices of all new models. There would have to be a 'quality freeze' as well. This would be well nigh impossible in an industry with highly differentiated products, a rapid rate of product improvement and change, and great competitive advantages to those firms with the most rapid rate of growth. Most people acquainted with the motor industry consider that it is highly competitive, despite the small number of large producers. The lack of any feasible alternative, and the heavy penalties for those who fail to expand in step with the growth of the industry, furnish a good part of the explanation for that competition.

CHAPTER VIII

The Nature of Competition in the Industry

1. PARTS AND COMPONENTS

IT has been seen in Chapter II that, although there are a very large number of manufacturers of parts and components, there is a good deal of specialization in this section of the industry, so that the degree of competition is less than might appear at first sight. There are firms, such as Triplex Glass, which have virtual monopolies, and others, such as Burman & Sons, which share almost the entire market (in this case, the market for car steering gears) with only one other firm. Even in those sections of the components industry where several firms produce a particular product, competition between them is often cut down by the fact that different firms concentrate on different types which, to some extent, are non-competing. Another factor tending to cut down competition in the components industry is ownership of component firms by vehicle manufacturers. Even where there is nominally competition between these subsidiaries and independent firms it is usually the case that the subsidiaries' products are taken by the manufacturers:[1] a portion of the total market is thus in effect reserved for the subsidiary, leaving the independent firms to compete for the rest of the business. In this sector, competition may be very fierce, especially as the independents may have to compete with the subsidiary if it has more than enough production to satisfy the demands of its parent firm. Alternatively, it may be the case that the subsidiary may not be able to supply all the requirements of the manufacturing firm, so that outside firms are also able to supply the manufacturer concerned. This happens with carburettors, where only part of the BMC requirements are supplied by SU, and most of the remainder by Zenith. A certain number of carburettors are actually sold by SU to car firms outside BMC, but the numbers concerned are much less than those bought by BMC from outside. In the carburettor case, incidentally, competition is less than might appear,

[1] This need not, however, mean that competition from outside firms has no effect. This question is discussed more fully below.

because Solex and Zenith, the two dominant independent firms, are under common ownership: they work and compete as separate concerns, but it does not really matter to them which of them gets the business.

A further factor which tends to reduce competition in the components field is the existence of patents. In general, however, the effect of these is not important. It is not difficult in the engineering industries to design a product which is substantially similar to an existing one without infringing any patents. There are patents covering the manufacture of carburettors, for example, but it is not the existence of patents in this field which keeps the number of manufacturers low. Several firms have tried to make carburettors in the past, but have failed primarily because they were unable to produce a good enough article. In this case the 'know-how' involved in the manufacture of a complicated product was clearly far more important than the existence of patents.

The fact that a cross-licensing patent agreement has existed in the United States motor industry since 1915 gives, at first sight, weight to the notion that patents are comparatively unimportant in the motor industry generally and not only in the components sector. However, this arrangement did not retain the very liberal features which characterized the first agreement of 1915–25.[1] The comparative absence of patent litigation in the United States and United Kingdom motor industries (apart from the early litigation in both countries over general patents such as the Selden patent in the USA) is perhaps a more convincing proof that patents have not in general been an important bone of contention in the industry. The Ford-Ferguson patent battle, which did not end until the early 1950s, was an exceptional incident from this point of view, if rather a noteworthy one. In the motor industry, timing is all important for competitive success. In many cases, it does not matter much if a competitor does copy your product if he can only do so after a considerable time lag. Only where designs do not alter frequently is copying likely to be a major source of trouble. In most aspects of motor vehicle design, however, changes occur so fast that patents of two or three years back are often of no great interest to a manufacturer. When this factor is considered, along with the comparative ease with which many patents can be circumvented, it is difficult not to draw the conclusion that

[1] *v.* Federal Trade Commission, *Report on the Motor Vehicle Industry*, pp. 58–63, for the details of how agreements after 1925 progressively excluded more and more patents from the cross-licensing arrangements.

patents have not on the whole been, and are not now, an important limitation on competition in the motor industry.

To return to the components section of the industry alone: a factor limiting competition which is almost certainly of more importance than the existence of patents is that there are a large number of trade associations in this field. Many of these are non-restrictive, having been formed to exchange information and views on matters affecting the trade, to make representations to Government departments and other bodies, and so on. The most comprehensive of these non-restrictive trade associations is the Society of Motor Manufacturers and Traders, which is the chief trade association in the motor industry. It has a section for accessory and component manufacturers which contains all the major firms, but this section concerns itself only with general policy matters. It is in some of the smaller and more specialized trade associations, such as the Tyre Manufacturers' Conference and the British Starter Battery Association, that examples of agreements on prices, conditions of sale and so on, can be found. It appears to be the case, however, that comparatively few of these associations engage in price-fixing. Even where price-fixing agreements do exist, they are generally confined to sales through wholesalers and retailers. In sales of components to vehicle manufacturers for use in their vehicles as 'original equipment' there is nearly always very keen competition. It is clear from the Monopolies Commission's report on tyres, for example, that the Tyre Manufacturers' Conference has in effect controlled the prices of its members' tyres to all purchasers except the large vehicle manufacturers.[1] It is true that the Commission found that in 1952 even the large manufacturers were paying identical net prices for tyres when they bought comparable quantities,[2] but they attributed this fact to the bargaining power of the vehicle manufacturers[3] and the price leadership of Dunlop rather than to any agreement between the tyre manufacturers themselves.

It is easy to understand why competition for original equipment sales is very keen on the part of component manufacturers who sell their products to the public as well as to vehicle manufacturers. In the first place, there is the size of the original equipment market itself. In the case of tyres, for example, it represented between a quarter and

[1] Monopolies and Restrictive Practices Commission, *Report on the Supply and Export of Pneumatic Tyres*, HMSO, 1955, pp. 36 and 45.
[2] Monopolies Commission, op. cit., p. 38.
[3] This bargaining power no doubt explains why collusion among component suppliers selling to vehicle manufacturers is so rare, *v.* p. 130 below.

a third of the total sales of the industry in 1951–2.[1] In the second place, once original equipment sales of a product have been made, there is a very good chance that replacement sales will be made also. Car owners are very likely to reach the conclusion that if a manufacturer supplies a particular make of component with his car, then that make of component is the best type for it and should be bought when a replacement is needed: indeed, some vehicle manufacturers say as much, quite forcibly, in the instruction manuals they issue with their cars. The effect that original equipment sales may have on replacement sales is a particularly important consideration in those cases, such as sparking plugs, where replacement sales are much more important than original equipment sales.

It is not surprising that, in these circumstances, some component manufacturers should be prepared to take very low prices for their original equipment sales, even to the extent of selling at a loss. There is no doubt that the prices charged are often not much more than enough to cover prime costs, and it has been alleged that in some cases they do not even do this. Of course, the larger the proportion of sales represented by the original equipment market, the less profitable is it to sell at very low prices. In the case of tyres, for example, positive profits were made, on the average, on original equipment sales in each of four years investigated by the Monopolies Commission. Indeed, in one exceptional year, when replacement sales were very low, profits on original equipment sales were higher than those on replacement sales.

TABLE 1
Five Largest Tyre Manufacturers
Profits as a Percentage of Sales (Weighted Average)[2]

	Replacement Sales	Original Equipment Sales
1937	—	8.7
1948	18.4	2.5
1951	12.0	1.5
1952	4.8	6.1

The figures above are averages for the five largest firms. When the range of profits is examined, it is evident that none of the five firms made losses on replacement sales in 1948 and 1951, but that at least one of them (not necessarily the same one) made losses on original equipment sales in all four years.

The intensity of competition between component manufacturers

[1] Monopolies Commission, op. cit., p. 93.
[2] Taken from Monopolies Commission Report on tyres, op. cit., pp. 95–6.

for original equipment sales helps to explain why there should be pressure for agreements on retail prices, at least on the part of those selling for original equipment. Such agreements are found in starter batteries, for example, as well as in tyres. The leading car battery manufacturers, Lucas, Chloride Batteries, Oldham, etc., are members of the British Starter Battery Association and agree on common retail prices.[1] Not all battery firms are in the Association, however; Edison Swan (a member of the AEI Group) is the most important outsider, and charges lower retail prices for its batteries than the others. The sparking plug firms deny that they have any agreement on prices, but all the leading manufacturers—Champion (which has the greater part of the original equipment business), A-C Delco, KLG, and Lodge —charge 5s retail for their plugs and have done so since before the war. The only outsider is a small new firm, Wico-Pacy, which charges 3s 6d retail for its plugs.

Common retail prices for components do not necessarily imply that conditions of sale are identical, or that identical margins are granted to dealers. One of the ways in which members of the British Starter Battery Association compete, for example, is in the guarantee conditions that they offer to consumers, and one of the ways in which sparking plug manufacturers compete is in the margins that they offer to dealers. In the sale of some components, considerable differences in the retail margins granted by different manufacturers are found. The price of outbidding other manufacturers in original equipment sales may be that lower retail margins have to be given than by manufacturers who concentrate on the replacement market alone. The large number of parts manufacturers who do not sell to the public, on the other hand, have to rely entirely for their profits on the margins they can earn on original equipment sales.

Where such small numbers are involved as in the starter battery and sparking plug cases, there is no need to look to agreements to explain common retail prices. One would expect them, as long as conditions were comparatively stable, for the usual oligopolistic reasons. Certainly in the case of sparking plugs, where retail demand is very inelastic to price changes, nobody except someone determined to break into the trade at all costs would see much point in price cutting. This possibly explains why even those firms which do not have original equipment business make no attempt to disturb the common retail prices structure. What *is* difficult to understand, however, in the sparking plug case, is the stability of prices since before the war.

[1] Since February 1957, agreement has been confined to maximum discounts.

I

It has already been mentioned that one of the interesting facts unearthed by the Monopolies Commission in its Report on Tyres, was that vehicle manufacturers were paying identical prices for comparable quantities of tyres in 1952, and that, in the view of the Commission, a principal reason for this was the bargaining power of the vehicle manufacturers. In any consideration of competition in the components field, the strength of this bargaining power cannot be ignored. The obvious way in which it can be exerted is by playing one supplier off against another, so that, in the absence of collaboration between suppliers, the vehicle manufacturer can feel fairly certain that he is paying the lowest possible price. Even where one supplier is given most of the business, and has been given it for a number of years, the tacit threat is always present that the vehicle manufacturer will go to another supplier if the price charged becomes too high. At least one of the large British car manufacturers makes a practice of obtaining cost data from its suppliers, so that it can be sure that the supplier is not making too high a profit: ten per cent profit on turnover is a figure that is widely considered in the industry to be not unreasonable. Another object of obtaining cost data is to ensure that the supplier is producing as efficiently as possible. Very often the techniques and materials employed by the supplier are broadly the same as those employed by the vehicle manufacturer, so that the latter has a very good notion of what the product ought to cost if it were being manufactured efficiently. Manufacturers frequently help their suppliers to organize their production more efficiently, even when they do not go so far as to request cost information. Not all suppliers are willing to give cost information, although they have to feel themselves in a strong position before they deny it when it is asked for. At least one component manufacturer goes to the opposite extreme: he freely gives cost information even to vehicle manufacturers who do not ask for it, but this is a manufacturer who is very sure of himself both from the point of view of his technical efficiency and his market strength.

Where there is only one supplier, or one predominant supplier, it is not open to the vehicle manufacturer to use competition among suppliers as a means of keeping prices down. In the last resort, however, the vehicle manufacturer can always make the part for himself, and it is the threat that he will do this which acts as an ultimate sanction against inefficiency or excessive profits on the part of suppliers. Where the less specialized parts and components are concerned, vehicle manufacturers are always considering whether to buy out or make the parts for themselves: decisions of this sort have to be made in large numbers, particularly at times when new models are contemplated. Really big decisions of this sort are taken less frequently, such as at times when factory extensions are being planned. It is then that such questions are considered as whether a firm previously without a foundry should install one. Most firms are not now interested in vertical integration for vertical integration's sake, and the decision about whether to produce for oneself or not will, by and large, be taken on economic grounds.[1] A partial exception to this state of affairs occurs, however, when a firm is already integrated. In this event, the firm may automatically accept the product of its subsidiary without seriously contemplating the possibility of buying from an outside firm. Even where, as in the case of General Motors in the United States, there is nominally competition between the subsidiary firm and outside firms, the scales are heavily weighted in favour of the subsidiary. However, outside firms are often used as a check on the efficiency of the subsidiary. This usually helps to ensure that the subsidiary is at least comparable in efficiency with these firms, although there are some instances where past history and present inertia combine to keep in being a subsidiary which is uneconomic in size or other characteristics.

The fact that firms are always thinking actively about whether to buy out or make for themselves should not be taken to imply that relations between vehicle manufacturers and their suppliers are in general bad: on the whole, there is close friendship and collaboration, and the suppliers often keep members of their staff in the vehicle manufacturers' factories on a semi-permanent basis. Nor should it be taken to imply that vehicle manufacturers will abandon their long-established suppliers lightly. Of the 4,200 suppliers of the Chevrolet Division of General Motors, for example, 80 per cent have been supplying the Division for over twenty years.[2] If their regular suppliers do not give satisfaction, vehicle manufacturers will usually go to considerable lengths to suggest improvements which their suppliers should effect in order to remedy the trouble and thus retain the business. If, however, it becomes evident that whatever help the

[1] Included in this category, of course, are cases when the gain cannot be directly reckoned in pounds, shillings and pence, e.g. the mergers between vehicle manufacturers and body builders in 1953, which appear to have been motivated by the need to ensure regular supplies rather than by any consideration of the direct cost savings to be made.

[2] OEEC, *Some Aspects of the Motor Vehicle Industry in the USA* (Paris, 1952), p. 26.

manufacturer can give the supplier cannot make the required improvement, then the manufacturer will almost certainly decide to go to another supplier or to make the part for himself.

There are two main reasons why vehicle manufacturers continue to buy out on the scale that they do. The first and most important is that the suppliers of many parts and components are specialists, with a long experience of the manufacture of their particular product. They are almost invariably the survivors of a large number of firms who have tried to make this particular component and have failed. These specialist component firms sometimes have patents, but more important than this is the fact that they employ skilled research staff and thus are able to make gradual improvements in their product. Most vehicle manufacturers take the view that they have too much on their hands to do detailed research on every little component that they use. Sometimes vehicle manufacturers have attempted to make for themselves one or other of the components that are commonly bought out, and in several cases lack of 'know-how' has caused these attempts to end in failure. Suppliers do not only contribute specialized knowledge, however. They have made a very large investment in plant and machinery which, if they did not exist, would have had to be made by the vehicle manufacturers themselves. Moreover, when the vehicle manufacturers expand their output, they do not have to find the money to expand their suppliers' output also. As was seen in Chapter I, the presence of components suppliers enabled the United States motor industry to get off to a good start, while their comparative absence still hampers European vehicle producers in such countries as France and Germany.[1]

The second main reason why vehicle manufacturers continue to buy out on such a scale is that parts and component suppliers who sell to the entire motor industry can achieve economies of scale far greater than could be achieved if they were producing for one vehicle manufacturer alone. This is particularly important for the smaller vehicle manufacturers who are enabled to buy parts and components at prices comparable with those paid by the larger firms. Another advantage of this system is that it enables virtual standardization of many parts and components to take place throughout the industry, when there is no agreement on standardization between firms.

A less obvious way in which sub-contracting helps vehicle manufacturers is in the matter of deliveries and stocks. Manufacturers employing flow production methods need extremely regular deliveries

[1] OEEC, op. cit., p. 36.

of parts and do not like to hold more than a very minimum of stocks. With their great buying power, they are in a powerful position to demand very frequent deliveries (often daily or twice daily) and to place the major part of the burden of stock holding on to their suppliers. In this way also, therefore, costs are absorbed by suppliers that would otherwise have to be incurred by the vehicle manufacturers themselves.

Sub-contracting has disadvantages as well as advantages, however. Vehicle manufacturers working on very strict production schedules have to rely for vital parts on firms over which they have no direct control. Bad labour relations, for instance, may cause a strike in the supplying firm which completely holds up production of vehicles: it is said that one of the reasons prompting Ford to merge with Briggs in 1953 was concern over labour relations in the latter firm. In order to safeguard themselves against breakdowns in supply, as well as to stimulate competition between suppliers, some vehicle manufacturers insist on having two suppliers for all major parts and components. It is not always economical to do this, nor is it always possible, but in many cases it can be done. This is, of course, a form of long-term rather than short-term insurance. If one supplier, with half the business in a particular part, were suddenly to stop supplying, it would not usually be the case that the other supplier could at once step up his production to the extent required. In time, however, the adjustment could probably be made. As an added form of insurance against strikes, it is the custom in the industry for vehicle manufacturers to own the special tools used by their suppliers. The theory is that if there were a strike in the supplying firm the tools could be moved elsewhere. In practice, as in the BMC strike in mid-1956, when action was taken to prevent tools from being moved, things may not always work out in this way.

It is clear that from some points of view, vehicle manufacturers may have an interest in being integrated backwards. When demand falls off in a depression, however, there may be an advantage in not being integrated backwards. In some cases the advantage arises from the fact that outside prices are lower than internal costs. In others it arises from the fact that spare capacity in the vehicle manufacturer's plant can be utilized to make non-specialized parts so that supplies from outside firms can be cut down to a corresponding extent. In this way the suppliers may bear the brunt of the fall in demand. It should not be thought that this is done indiscriminately. Most manufacturers would hesitate to cut down purchases from a regular supplier to such an extent that the supplier's existence was placed in jeopardy. However, suppliers cannot but be aware of the fact that they may lose business either for this reason or for any of the other reasons that may induce a vehicle manufacturer to produce for himself. Many suppliers have therefore sought to diversify their production on this account, even to the extent of manufacturing products that have no more connection with vehicles than that they are made with similar materials and methods of manufacture.

Everything that has been said so far has emphasized the powerful position of vehicle manufacturers *vis-à-vis* their suppliers. However, when component suppliers have a monopoly or a virtual monopoly, either because they have access to big economies of scale or possess very specialized knowledge, it is neither easy for manufacturers to dispense with their services nor to put effective pressure on them to reveal costs or reduce prices. Among British component suppliers, Joseph Lucas, which dominates the production of electrical goods (although it by no means has a monopoly in all fields) is often mentioned as a powerful firm which is well able to stand up to the vehicle manufacturers. It has been suggested from time to time that this company, as well as others in similar circumstances, have taken advantage of their strong position to earn excessive profits. There is not enough information publicly available for this question to be settled one way or the other. As far as Joseph Lucas itself is concerned, it is known the company has reduced the prices of some of its products to vehicle manufacturers considerably over the years, relatively to prices in general.[1] It has also shown much initiative in promoting standardization, and there is good reason to believe that in the production of many components Joseph Lucas is technically very efficient. It is difficult to conclude, on the basis of the available evidence, that vehicle manufacturers would get their electrical goods significantly cheaper if the Lucas position were less dominating. In view of the economies of scale to which Joseph Lucas has access at present, it might very well be that vehicle manufacturers would have to pay more. However, the powerful position of Lucas, whether exercised or not, is a factor that cannot be ignored. Even if a vehicle manufacturer were convinced that he could produce one of the Lucas lines for less than he is paying for it, he might still hesitate to do so. This is partly because he could not be sure of how far Lucas *could* reduce the price if they wished, and partly because he would still be dependent on

---

[1] PEP, op. cit., p. 133.

Lucas for many other products and would not wish to take action which, in his view, might forfeit their good-will.

2. VEHICLE MANUFACTURE

The attention that most vehicle manufacturers pay to the price of the components they use, and to their costs generally, is a reflection of the keen competition that exists between them. There is, it is true, a great deal of contact between vehicle manufacturing firms. They are members, along with representatives of the Trade Unions and of the Government, of the National Advisory Council for the Motor Manufacturing Industry, whose purpose it is to discuss the broad problems of the industry. They are members also of the Motor Industry Research Association which carries out common research for the industry. They meet frequently under the auspices of the Society of Motor Manufacturers and Traders and other trade bodies, and they co-operate over such matters as standardization. Under a plan introduced by the Society of Motor Manufacturers and Traders in 1948, at the same time as the 'Big Six' standardization committee was set up, vehicle manufacturers went so far as to agree that they would make their premises available for inspection by one another and by component firms and would exchange a good deal of technical information. Even the Ford Motor Company, which before the war was not a member of the Society of Motor Manufacturers and Traders and used to run its own Motor Show, has co-operated fully with the rest of the industry since the war, and is taking part in all these arrangements. In spite of the fact that the larger firms see so much of each other, however, all the evidence (including that examined in Chapter VII) suggests that no agreement to limit competition has been made between them. The fact that new entry into the industry has now become virtually impossible has had little or no effect on competition between the existing firms in the British industry, all of which, whether British- or American-owned, have, for the moment at least, their full share of the competitive spirit.

'Competition' is a notoriously ambiguous word, and when it is said that the vehicle manufacturing section of the industry is very competitive this could be taken to mean anything from competition in product alone to competition in all its forms, including vigorous advertising and price competition. In fact, competition as it occurs in the British motor industry, comes somewhere between the possible extremes. No industry which consists effectively of half a dozen large firms could carry on for long without evolving some *modus vivendi*. Moments of breakdown and struggle excepted, it is inevitable that some rules of the game will emerge and will be respected. The examination of competition in the car market that was carried out in Chapter VII has made clear the rules of the game that have been accepted in the British motor industry for the last thirty years. Put briefly, these are price stability in the short period, allied with model-price competition in the long period.

It is perhaps appropriate to attempt at this point a fuller explanation than has so far been given of why these particular rules of the game have been evolved, and also to discuss certain aspects of competition between vehicle manufacturers that could not appropriately be discussed in Chapter VII. These aspects include competition in advertising and salesmanship and also in dealer representation.

It is important to realize, in the first place, that the pattern evolved in the 1930s differed a good deal from that which applied in earlier years. In particular, the period up to 1930 saw many more cases of price reductions on existing models than the period since that date. It is impossible to mention price competition in the early days of the industry without recalling the famous case of the Model T Ford. At the time of its introduction in the United States in 1908, the car was very good value for money but not outstandingly low in price. As its sales increased Henry Ford was quick to grasp the economies of scale that became possible, and he followed the policy of gradually bringing the price down as costs fell, until the Model T was the cheapest car on the market. Ford sales increased by leaps and bounds, as did the American market for cars. By 1914, Ford had captured half the entire market. He continued to make the Model T Ford until 1927, modifying it technically during the period but never fundamentally changing it. After 1925, however, Ford sales and profits began to drop at a time when General Motors sales and profits were rising rapidly. It is clear now that Ford continued too long with his policy of virtually pure price competition. By the late 1920s the United States market was becoming relatively saturated and Ford lost ground to competitors who were producing more up-to-date models. After 1927 Ford had to match them with a new model, the Model A, which was introduced at the end of 1927, and then, not much more than four years later, by another new model, the V-8. Ford had to conform to the pattern of competition that became characteristic of the United States car market in the 1930s: comparative stability of prices, and the introduction of models which were new in some major particular, every two or three years. The emphasis gradually shifted to building a bigger and better car within a conventional price range. The Ford policy of low prices continued, but in this altered context.

The same process that was at work in the United States before the war was at work in this country. The 1920s was a period of severe price competition arising from the fact that it was not until then that British producers really began to introduce mass-production techniques. By the 1930s, however, as has been seen in Chapter VII, price competition had come to play a relatively unimportant part. Not only were prices stable in the short period, but they altered little throughout the period, and it became the practice to build increasingly better cars to compete within a fairly definite price range. The price of the Austin Seven, for example, had fallen by nearly 25 per cent between 1924 and 1929, but between 1931 and 1939 its price varied relatively little, while its performance and quality improved greatly. Ford's attempt in 1935 to reduce the price of an existing model was not emulated by other firms, and Ford was forced to return to a policy of model-price competition.

The course that competition in the car market took during the 1930s and, to a considerable extent, still takes, has often been criticized on grounds that it involved vehicle manufacturers in higher costs than they need have had. The question that has often been asked is—why did model-price competition take the form of ever more luxurious models for the same price rather than lower prices for simple models, which were kept up-to-date by being improved technically as major advances were made but which were not burdened with luxuries? Perhaps the most convincing answer that has been given to this question, at least in the United States context, was that provided by Paul Hoffman of Studebaker, in his evidence before the Temporary National Economic Committee:

'From some thirty years' experience in this business I would say that the competition from used cars . . . would be so keen and fierce that any stripped car that you put on the market . . . simply could not attain a volume to justify the investment. You see, this thing has been tried time and again and it has always failed. The public has always preferred the fully equipped used car one year old to the stripped car brand new.'[1]

The danger of competition from used cars may explain why manufacturers were reluctant to produce cheap, austere models. It cannot

[1] TNEC *Hearings*. Part 21, December 6, 1939, p. 11223.

explain why models were changed so frequently. To explain this, it is necessary to recall the relatively saturated position of the market in the United States before the war. Most of the business that was to be had was replacement business, and in order to stimulate sales, vehicle manufacturers had to induce motorists to replace their old cars with new cars. To achieve this, they introduced new models every few years in order to make old models look old-fashioned. In the intermediate years, they gave their models 'face-lifts' so that each year's models should be clearly distinguishable from the next. Those motorists who felt it important to possess the latest models had, therefore, to change their cars every year, and this undoubtedly did speed up replacement. If there had been only one manufacturer in the industry, he could probably have got away with less frequent model changes than actually occurred. With several manufacturers, however, once one of them made a change, the others were forced to follow suit.

In the British market, similar forces were at work, even though the market was less saturated than the American. The majority of new car sales in the 1930s were replacement sales, in spite of the fact that the total market was still expanding. British manufacturers needed, therefore, to stimulate owners to replace their cars for the same reasons as their American counterparts, and they did so by similar methods. Models were changed every few years and 'face-lifts' were often resorted to in the intermediate years.

So far, model-price competition has been discussed in terms of the frequency of model changes and the tendency of manufacturers to build bigger and better cars to sell at a conventional price. As has been seen, however, it has further ramifications than this. Model-price competition also takes the form of each manufacturer producing a large variety of models, and, what is more, models which are similar to those produced by his rivals. It is not difficult to understand why manufacturers do this. If they were to rely on one model only, they would be putting all their eggs into one basket. Model variations need not be expensive, provided that salesmen's pleas to multiply basic parts like engines and body pressings are resisted. In these circumstances, large manufacturers would regard themselves as tempting fate if they did not offer a wide range of models—saloons, convertibles, estate cars and the rest. Another factor inducing such a wide range is unwillingness—perhaps foolish unwillingness—to let rivals keep to themselves any important part of the field. The small car market, for example, is clearly a very large one in this country, and the majority of big manufacturers (Vauxhall and Rootes being the exceptions) produce small cars. All the big manufacturers in this country produce medium-sized cars, of approximately $1\frac{1}{2}$ litres, and they all produce larger cars of approximately $2\frac{1}{2}$ litres also. Where the larger cars are concerned, the market is smaller (less than 20 per cent of all car sales on the home market in 1955) but it is not negligible, especially in certain export markets, and manufacturers apparently feel they cannot afford to let their competitors completely capture the market.

An additional factor inducing manufacturers to produce a number of models is that their dealers are always urging them to produce as wide a range of models as their competitors. Dealers naturally hate to turn away a customer because the customer wants a car of a type that the dealer cannot offer him. In the long run, the number of satisfactory dealers that a manufacturer can keep loyal to him will be affected by the range of models he produces.

An interesting development in the American industry since the war has been a narrowing of the range of cars manufactured. With the exception of cars made in negligible quantities by small specialist manufacturers, all American cars are of the mass-produced type. They are virtually all very large and very powerful. Perhaps the most striking aspect of product competition in recent years has been the 'horse-power race', in which each company has tried to exceed the others in the power generated by the engines of its cars: one of the effects of this policy, incidentally, has been to cause a multiplication of basic engine types. As part of this process, the differences between cars have narrowed greatly. The Chevrolet, for example, at one end of the General Motors price range, is very much the same sort of car, on a smaller scale (but by no means on a *small* scale) as the Cadillac, at the other end of the range. This closeness in type is reflected in the price ratio between the cars. An average-price Cadillac in 1956, for example, cost not much more than twice as much as an average-price Chevrolet. The other major American companies follow broadly the same policy as General Motors, concentrating on the same types of car, with the same close relationship between all the types they produce. There are very few cars produced by these companies which do not fit into the standard categories. The situation can be summed up by saying that, to most non-Americans, all American cars look almost exactly the same. Fortunately for United States manufacturers, most American consumers are far more aware of the differences than of the similarities.

Model competition in the British motor industry has not led to quite the same uniformity as in the American. The size difference between the smallest and largest of the mass-produced cars manufactured by the British Motor Corporation or Ford, for example, is considerably more marked than in the case of the Chevrolet and the Cadillac. The price difference is less, however, if the Ford Popular is ignored for the time being: an Austin A95 Westminster, for example, costs far less than twice as much as an Austin A35, and the same is true of the Ford Zodiac and Anglia. In Britain, the expensive cars are of the 'specialist' type, a type which virtually cannot be made in the United States because of the high labour content they require. Many of these cars, particularly those made by the 'specialist' firms, cost very much more, in relation to the cheapest cars, than is the case in America. This is true even when the most expensive cars, such as Rolls-Royce and Bentley, are left out of the reckoning. Taking the whole range, therefore, there is far more variety in the British scene than in the American. If mass-produced cars, which account for the great majority of sales, are considered alone, it is still true that the differences in type of car both within firms and, to a less extent, between firms, are greater than in the United States. The increasing similarity between the mass-produced cars of different British manufacturers, however, suggests that competitive forces are acting in the same direction in both countries.

The Continent presents a rather different picture as regards model competition. In France, Western Germany and Italy, the three main producing countries, there is comparatively little similarity between the products of the different producers. This can be attributed to some extent to the less oligopolistic structure of the motor industries of these countries. In Italy, the industry is dominated from the production point of view by one firm, Fiat, and in Germany Volkswagen is considerably larger than any other mass producer. The structure of the French industry is nearest to that of the British, with four large mass-producing firms, Renault, Simca, Citroen and Peugeot, but Renault is a good deal bigger than any of the others. The differences between the models of different companies cannot only be attributed to these considerations, however. Possibly the main reason for these differences is simply that Continental manufacturers are more ready to seek individuality than their British or American counterparts. An aspect of this is that Continental manufacturers have not hesitated to produce cars that by British or American standards are extremely unconventional. The very successful Volkswagen is, of course, just such a car, as is the Fiat 600, both of them rear-engined; in France there is the rear-engined Renault 4 c.v. and Dauphine, and the front wheel drive Citroen. Another difference from the British and American pattern is that models are changed much more slowly. This may partly be because several models, when introduced, were well ahead of their time, but this certainly cannot be the whole explanation. The less prosperous domestic markets of the three countries, and the smaller emphasis on conspicuous consumption, at least as far as motoring is concerned, may be factors tending to reduce the incentive to produce new models frequently. Almost certainly, also, the lack of fierce competition that stems from the structure of the Italian industry in particular must form part of the explanation.

When discussing the form that model-price competition takes in the industry, it is tempting to talk as though the prices of all models competing in a particular price class are very much the same. In fact, however, price differences exist which can by no means be ignored. Although the price elasticity of demand for vehicles in general is not very high, the cross elasticity of demand between vehicles of different makes is undoubtedly considerable. The technical and aesthetic differences between different makes of car help to disguise price differences to some extent, but if price differences are great, those manufacturers who charge more than their rivals for any particular type of car cannot, in general, get away for long with the excuse that their cars cost more because they are superior in quality. The consequence of this has been that those wishing (or having) to charge somewhat higher prices than their rivals for any particular type of car have had to make their vehicles seem better in some way: they have had to cultivate a reputation for more solid engineering, or for better quality trimmings, or for some other superior feature. In this way, a number of firms have, from time to time, been able to charge above average prices for essentially average vehicles. Where there are big cost differences between firms, however, it is not always possible for the high-cost firms to charge a sufficiently high price completely to overcome their cost disadvantage.

A certain amount of light on how prices are arrived at in the motor industry has been given by a vice-president of General Motors.[1]

[1] Donaldson Brown, 'Pricing Policy in relation to financial control'. Reprinted from *Management and Administration*, Vol. 7, in Homer B. Vanderblue, *Problems in Business Economics* (1924). See also Homer B. Vanderblue, *Harvard Business Review*, Summer 1939, Vol. XVII, No. 4. Donaldson Brown was writing in the early 1920s, but it is believed that the type of calculation that he described is still, broadly speaking, carried out by General Motors.

According to him, a basic price for any particular model is arrived at on the assumption that production will be at a 'standard' volume which is less than plant capacity—he suggests that this might be 80 per cent of practical capacity. To average costs calculated on the basis of the standard volume a profit margin is added sufficient to achieve the economic return on capital that is desired. In this way the 'base price' is arrived at. This price should change with persistent changes in raw material and labour prices, but not with volume fluctuations. Actual prices may deviate from base prices because of temporary competitive conditions, temporary cost changes, etc. In periods when sales are low, reduced prices are desirable to stimulate demand, but these cannot be below the base price unless the resulting loss of profits can be recouped through higher prices when sales are high. However, there is a danger in higher prices at times of high volume because they might attract others to the industry. As Donaldson Brown puts it, they might 'intensify the attraction of competitive capital in speculative or ill-advised conditions'.

There seems little doubt that other firms as well as General Motors think in this sort of way when deciding on the prices they will charge. However, not all firms can make their decisions with as much independence as General Motors. They must take very prominently into account the costs of their rivals. Donaldson Brown admits that the economic return on capital that is aimed at is affected by any advantage in costs, etc., that there may be over competing firms. Presumably this means that a greater profit margin than might usually be thought adequate will be taken if costs are sufficiently low. Where firms are not so favourably placed as General Motors as regards costs, the problem may pose itself the other way round—they may have to take a lower profit margin than their competitors rather than a higher one. They may temper the wind by charging a little more for their cars, or by producing cars of slightly inferior quality at the common price, but they do not have a great deal of room to manoeuvre in this way. In the long run, consumers seem to be able to gauge fairly accurately how the value for money offered by different firms compares. This is particularly true of purchasers of commercial vehicles, whose business interests are closely involved, but it is also true of private purchasers of mass-produced cars.

The fact that different firms have to take very different profit margins, even though their cars sell at comparable prices, is clearly brought out in the profit figures given in Chapter IX. In the years 1953–5, Ford and Vauxhall were making appreciable profits per vehicle. They were followed by BMC, with Rootes and Standard well behind. Ford and Vauxhall in particular appeared to have a good deal in hand during this period, and could have operated profitably even if vehicle prices had been reduced considerably. It could be argued that Ford and Vauxhall were setting their prices less in relation to their own costs than in relation to the costs of such firms as Rootes and Standard. Their reasons for doing this are not difficult to understand in view of their desire to finance much of their capital expansion from internal sources. There is certainly no reason to believe, however, that they would necessarily pursue such a policy in more difficult market conditions.

A word should be added about price policy in export markets. Here there is competition from foreign firms who do not hesitate to cut prices in a manner and to an extent quite unknown on their own or the British home market. Keen competition for business in these markets, and the fact that most exporting firms sell an appreciable proportion of their output in protected home markets, makes active price competition in export markets inevitable. British firms, like their foreign rivals, indulge in price discrimination of the classic type between home and export markets, and in many markets prices are certainly well below the level of full average costs at capacity, especially when the high costs of selling overseas are taken into account. In some markets at particular times, losses on the marginal costs of selling in those markets are certainly made.[1] Firms are reluctant to abandon the more important markets, however, for several reasons; among these are the possibility that such markets will become profitable in the future, the desirability of keeping a foot in markets where local manufacture is eventually contemplated, and the wish not to displease their own Governments who may threaten unpleasant sanctions if exports are not maintained at a sufficiently high level.

---

[1] It was seen in Chapter V that, for a typical car, variable costs represent 80–90 per cent of average costs at capacity working. If manufacturers are to cover variable costs and make some contributions to overheads, therefore, they must not charge a price below 85 per cent or so of average costs at capacity. The calculations carried out in Appendix C suggest that export prices in certain markets at the end of 1956 varied between 10 per cent and 20 per cent below home market prices, depending on the model of car under consideration. Since home market prices at the end of 1956 were almost certainly above average costs at capacity, it looks as though in most of the cases considered in Appendix C export prices were sufficient to cover variable costs. The position is not always so favourable, however.

Before the war the German industry received a subsidy to encourage exports of cars,[1] but it does not appear that in the post-war period any such subsidy has been paid. Nor does any other exporting country appear to be subsidizing vehicle exports in a direct manner.[2] However, subsidies have in effect been given in certain European countries since the war—to exports generally and not merely to vehicle exports—by means of foreign exchange concessions to exporters and other similar devices.[3]

Competition in advertising, etc.

When the market is starved of vehicles, as it was in the United Kingdom before 1955, it is not necessary for the vehicle manufacturer to incur heavy advertising costs. His advertisements serve mainly as an insurance for the future. Once market conditions become difficult, however, advertising becomes important. This is particularly true in the case of cars. The more saturated the market, the more competition takes the form of changes in product, real or superficial, and of advertising expenditure incurred to bring home the changes to the public. The less important the change, indeed, the more necessary is it to exaggerate its importance in the eyes of the public. Really important advances virtually announce themselves.

To see advertising competition at its most fully developed, one has to go to the United States. One observer has commented[4] that

'mass sales promotion through newspapers, magazines, radio, TV [is] as big a sales factor in the current sales picture as the cars themselves ... as I see it, it is as important [for the vehicle manufacturers] to build better advertising men as better cars in America today.'

In the British industry, different market conditions made the role of advertising a less crucial one than in the United States before

[1] PEP *Motor Vehicles*, p. 117.

[2] OEEC *Situation in the Automobile Industry in Member Countries in 1950*, p. 47.

[3] In France, complete vehicles did not enjoy the indirect subsidies (tax and social contribution repayments, etc.) allowed (until mid-1957) to other exports, although these subsidies did apply to vehicles exported unassembled. (*Financial Times*, September 15, 1955.) In Italy, 5 per cent of the export price is refunded by the Government as relief from the turnover tax, and there is also a refund of 3*d* per pound of weight as relief from duty on imported raw materials (*Financial Times*, August 23, 1955). In Germany, the tax rebate of 3.85 per cent on exports was terminated at the end of 1955 (*Financial Times*, February 28, 1956).

[4] *Autocar*, February 11, 1955, 'Detroit Notebook'.

1955–6. Now, however, British vehicle manufacturers are paying a good deal of attention to sales promotion through newspapers and other media. They are also competing in related ways. In September 1956, for example, the British Motor Corporation took the initiative in granting more generous guarantee conditions on its vehicles than was previously the practice in the industry, and it was soon followed by other firms.

Competition in dealer representation

No vehicle manufacturer who wants a high volume of sales can hope to achieve this without ensuring that stocks of spare parts for his vehicles, and skilled personnel to service them, are widely available. The wider the distribution of these facilities, the more popular will his vehicles be with intending purchasers. Purchasers will be concerned, however, not only with the total number of points at which their vehicles can be serviced, but also with the proximity of such points to their homes or places of business. Some may even buy a make of vehicle which has relatively few service points throughout the country so long as one of those service points happens to be near at hand. If one vehicle manufacturer can offer service for his vehicle in a particular place, therefore, and another cannot, the first manufacturer is more likely, other things being equal, to sell his cars to people living in or near that place than the second. For this reason, manufacturers cannot afford to let their rivals be represented in too many places where they are not represented themselves. This is especially important to manufacturers of cars.

It does not follow from the fact that manufacturers need to offer spares and service in most of the places where their rivals do so that they also need to offer new vehicles for sale at all these points. Indeed, motorists living in villages or towns often go to the nearest city to buy their cars and then get them serviced by their local dealer. However, manufacturers are aware that some purchasers prefer the convenience of buying their vehicles locally, and also that there is an element of 'impulse' buying even in the case of such expensive commodities as motor vehicles. A vehicle of a particular make is sometimes bought because it is continually seen, not because it has been decided on objective grounds that this is the best vehicle to buy. Manufacturers cannot, therefore, ignore the possibility that by distributing selling points for new vehicles widely they may make greater sales than they otherwise would. In any event, they would probably have considerable difficulty in securing adequate distribution of spare parts and service if they did not induce dealers to offer such service by giving them the opportunity of earning attractive discounts on sales of new vehicles. When vehicle sales and service are linked, moreover, manufacturers are able to exercise considerable control over the quality of service provided by their dealers. The manufacturers' power to withdraw the franchise for their vehicles enables them to insist on adequate stocks of spares being kept, on mechanics being sent to their factories for training, on standardized charges for repairs, on used car warranty schemes, and so on. For these reasons, sales and service naturally go together in the eyes of manufacturers, and in practice they appoint the same agent to provide both.

Competition between manufacturers has the effect, therefore, of inducing them to provide sales as well as service outlets wherever their rivals do so. It is not surprising, in the light of this, that during the 1930s manufacturers should have made such strong efforts to increase their dealer representation throughout the country. In the early 1930s particularly, the number of retailers appointed as dealers grew very rapidly indeed. It is not surprising either, in view of the keenness of competition between manufacturers, that they should have exerted considerable pressure on their dealers to increase their sales of vehicles. The lengths to which manufacturers in the United States went before the war to encourage greater sales have been clearly brought out in a study by the Federal Trade Commission.[1]

Commercial vehicles

Although a good deal that has been said in this chapter is applicable to commercial vehicles, the discussion has been carried on mainly in terms of cars. Several of the characteristics of the car market derive from the fact that a high proportion of cars are sold to ordinary motorists. Commercial vehicles, on the other hand, are sold only to business users, and such users are naturally more closely concerned with price, running costs, and intrinsic technical merits than the normal car owner. Models of commercial vehicles are changed less frequently than those of cars, and attempts have been made by the larger manufacturers to introduce a high degree of standardization without sacrificing flexibility in the final product. In the sale of the heavier vehicles, price competition is perhaps less important than in the sale of the lighter types, since so many heavy vehicles are designed to carry out specialized work. This field has,

[1] Federal Trade Commission: *Report on the Motor Vehicle Industry* (Washington 1939).

however, become increasingly competitive in recent years. The 'Big Five' car manufacturers, who already dominate the market for light commercial vehicles, have been moving into the heavy vehicle field. They now produce some vehicles of a weight comparable with those produced by the heavy commercial vehicle manufacturers, which are powered by diesel engines of their own manufacture. In these circumstances, the heavy commercial vehicle manufacturers are having to concentrate even more than in the past on specialized types, and they are having to scrutinize their costs and prices closely. Nevertheless, the market for these heavy vehicles is a wide one, and the largest firm, Leyland, did well in 1956 at a time when the 'Big Five' all showed reduced profits. Clearly, the competitive strength of firms such as Leyland should not be underestimated.

3. THE RETAIL TRADE

The nature of competition between the retailers of motor vehicles was much affected before the war by the efforts made by vehicle manufacturers to expand their outlets. The growth in the number of firms handling new cars in the early 1930s outpaced the growth in new car sales, and competition between dealers became much more intense. One of the ways in which they competed for business was by giving very high allowances for the used cars they took in part exchange for new cars. As a consequence, a great part of the discount on the new cars was eaten up by losses on the resale of used cars. Discontent among dealers led to co-operation between them and the vehicle manufacturers to strengthen the Motor Trade Association (now the British Motor Trade Association), which had been founded in 1910 to maintain the wholesale and retail prices of cars as laid down by the vehicle manufacturers. In 1934, vehicle manufacturers made it compulsory for their agents to belong to the Motor Trade Association. In the following year, the Association attempted to deal with the used-car problem by issuing the National Used Car Price Book in which maximum allowances were laid down for used cars taken in part exchange for new cars. Before the institution of this system, resale price maintenance had been largely a dead letter in the industry because dealers had been able effectively to cut the prices of new cars through over-allowances made on part-exchange transactions. Even after the used car price book system had been adopted, losses on used car business were made by many firms. The existence of the system did, however, serve to reduce price competition, and probably caused losses on used cars to be smaller than they would otherwise have been.

The enforcement of resale price maintenance was no problem in the years immediately following the war. There was much more likelihood that new vehicles would be sold at prices above those laid down by the manufacturers than below them. The British Motor Trade Association attempted to deal with this situation by instituting the Covenant scheme. Under this scheme sanctions were imposed on dealers who sold vehicles for more than list prices, and on motorists who broke a compulsory undertaking not to resell their vehicles within a period which varied at different times between one and two years. This scheme was abandoned early in 1953 when the supply of new cars became easier. The position after that date was that the British Motor Trade Association protected the price of new cars and of certain accessories, but that the pre-war scheme for preventing over-allowances on used cars was not reintroduced. Quite possibly it would have been reintroduced had it not been for the passing of the Restrictive Trade Practices Act in 1956, which outlawed the practice of collective resale price maintenance. Despite the absence of a used car price book scheme, however, and despite more difficult market conditions, competition in the retail trade had not returned to anything like its pre-war intensity by the time the Restrictive Trade Practices Act was passed.

The 1956 Act made collective resale price maintenance illegal, but it permitted individual resale price maintenance to survive, and indeed strengthened it by the enactment of the 'non-signer' clause. Immediately after the Act was passed, all the major vehicle manufacturers announced their intention of maintaining the resale prices of their cars. The BMTA continued in existence in an altered form after the passing of the Act, with the principal function of aiding individual manufacturers to enforce price maintenance effectively. It is already evident that resale price maintenance in the industry is being enforced as strictly since the Restrictive Trade Practices Act was passed as before, and that the Act has brought about no real change in the situation.[1]

The merits and demerits of resale price maintenance, both collective and individual, have been debated at great length in recent years in the Report of the Lloyd Jacob Committee (1947) and many other places. There is no need to repeat the general discussions here. There is no doubt that many of the objections to resale price maintenance

[1] *The Economist*, February 22, 1958, p. 684.

that have been put forward by economists and others do apply to resale price maintenance in the motor industry. However, it is questionable whether resale price maintenance has led to as great a waste of resources in the retail motor trade as it may have done in some other retail industries. This is because those firms who sell new cars are only a minority of those in the retail motor trade. The majority earn their living by the sale of fuel and by servicing and repairing vehicles. If the abolition of resale price maintenance were to lead to a reduction in the number of new car dealers, as it well might, many of those who ceased to sell new cars would fall back into the ranks of the ordinary garage trade. It is difficult to believe that many garages would close down altogether. Some resources would no doubt be saved, but not as many as might at first be thought.

Another aspect of resale price maintenance in the motor industry that needs attention is the repercussions that it has had on competition between the vehicle manufacturers themselves. One thing that it has certainly done has been to bring them together in such bodies as the BMTA, but it is doubtful whether contact in organizations such as this has made any real difference to the keenness of the competition between them over models and prices. It is doubtful also whether resale price maintenance has had any marked indirect effects in reducing competition among manufacturers. It can scarcely be argued in the motor industry, as it was by the Monopolies Commission in their report on tyres, that competition between manufacturers would only be really possible if resale price maintenance were abolished. The lack of uniformity of product in the motor industry allows competition between manufacturers to take forms that would scarcely be possible in the tyre industry, where the products of different manufacturers are inevitably very similar. Resale price maintenance in the motor industry certainly reduces slightly the *area* of competition between vehicle manufacturers, in that they all know that competition between their dealers is unlikely to take the form of direct margin-cutting on new cars, and they have not therefore had to formulate policies to deal with this eventuality: policies that might well have become competitive. However, competition between dealers does take the form of over-allowances on used cars. This is something that has been very hard to prevent in the past, and in their relations with their dealers vehicle manufacturers have had to take it into account in the margins they have allowed them. Manufacturers have also had to assist dealers in many other ways—for example, by improving the quality of their mechanics through the provision of training schools—in order to improve their ability to meet competition at all points. On balance, it is doubtful whether the existence of resale price maintenance in the retail motor trade has significantly affected the degree of competition between the vehicle manufacturers themselves.

CHAPTER IX

Profits and Sources of Funds

1. FLUCTUATIONS IN PROFITS, 1929–38

INFORMATION about industrial profits in pre-war years is extremely inadequate. This is true not only for individual industries but also for industrial profits as a whole. In the absence of comprehensive data on profits, an attempt has been made to gather together some figures for the motor industry. These are not very satisfactory, but may perhaps serve as an indication of the course of profits in the industry over the period 1929–38. Figures were not collected for the period before 1929, mainly because such rapid changes were taking place in the industry during the 1920s that the profit figures would have been very difficult to interpret. By the end of the 1920s, on the other hand, the industry had begun to approach maturity, and it is possible to gain some impression of what was happening in the industry as a whole by studying the course of events in a small number of leading firms.

The only published figures for motor industry profits covering the whole period 1929–38 are those collected by *The Economist* from the published accounts of public companies.[1] Figures for the motor industry alone are not available: *The Economist* calculations are for the motor, cycle and aviation industries. On the basis of these figures a chain index of profits during the period 1929–38 has been constructed. This shows very great fluctuations in motor, cycle and aircraft profits—far greater than those shown in *The Economist* index for industrial profits as a whole.

In absolute terms, the profits after tax of the motor, cycle and aircraft companies included in the 1929 computation amounted to about £4,750,000. The profits of the motor, cycle and aircraft companies included in the 1932 computation amounted to about £200,000 only. These are of course net figures, after deduction of losses. This is brought out by the fact that in 1932 the profits of four of the most

---

[1] Calculations for the period 1924–35 have been made by Ronald Hope, 'Profits in British Industry from 1924 to 1935', *Oxford Economic Papers*, Number 2, June 1949.

TABLE 1
The Economist *Index of Profits (After Tax)*
1930=100

Profits earned in*	All industries	Motor, Cycle and Aviation†
1929	118	130
1930	100	100
1931	73	27
1932	69	2
1933	77	42
1934	92	54
1935	103	63
1936	120	82
1937	136	89
1938	126	86

* The figures are drawn from accounts published in years ending June 30, beginning with the year ending June 30, 1930. They cover, very approximately, the profits actually earned in the preceding calendar years.

† Profits of motor firms dominate this index. Cycle and aviation profits were small in relation to those of motors, and their pattern of fluctuation was much the same.

successful car manufacturers[1] amounted to £1,360,000 after tax. *The Economist* figures greatly overstate the fall in profits of the successful firms: they show as great a fall as they do because, among the lesser lights of the industry, the slump was accompanied by very heavy losses. Even the leading firms, however, were severely affected by the slump. This is shown by a profit index that has been constructed for five of the six leading car manufacturers and the two leading heavy commercial vehicle manufacturers in the period under review. The firms concerned are Austin, Morris, Vauxhall, Standard and Humber[2] on the car side and Leyland and ACV on the heavy commercial vehicle side. The figures for Ford have been omitted because this firm moved its factory from Old Trafford to Dagenham in the early 1930s and, largely as a consequence, suffered a severe decline in profits in 1931 and 1932.

The 'Earned for dividends' column in Table 2 is on the same basis as that for 'Motor, cycle and aviation' in Table 1. The figures show a fall in profits for the seven firms of 20–30 per cent between 1930 and 1932 as compared with a fall of nearly 100 per cent for the industry

[1] Austin, Morris, Standard and Vauxhall.
[2] Humber Ltd. is responsible for all the vehicle manufacturing activities of the Rootes Group.

TABLE 2
Seven Leading Vehicle Manufacturers*—Index of Profits
1930=100

Profits earned in†	Trading Profits	Net Profits‡	Earned for dividends§
1929	89	89	97
1930	100	100	100
1931	81	71	70
1932	80	74	77
1933	89	78	90
1934	120	108	126
1935	144	140	161
1936	179	184	201
1937	178	170	169
1938	160	138	123

* Austin, Humber, Morris, Standard, Vauxhall, ACV, Leyland.

† Where necessary, figures for financial years have been adjusted to a calendar year basis. Adjustments have also been made to ensure comparability where consolidations, etc., have taken place.

‡ Trading profits less depreciation, directors' fees, debenture interest, etc. Actual figures for the leading car firms are given in Appendix D, Table 9.

§ Net Profits less accrued taxation and taxation provisions.

as a whole. By 1936 the seven firms were earning, after taxation, twice as much as in 1930, whereas for the industry as a whole 1930 was the best year of the 1930s. The importance of the Ford results in causing this marked difference between the figures for the seven firms and those for the industry can be seen from the fact that if the figures had been calculated for the seven firms plus Ford, the 'earned for dividends' index would have been 45 in 1931 and 29 in 1932. In 1932 Ford made a loss, after tax, of some £725,000, while the other seven firms earned for dividends some £1,500,000 only.

Figures of the amount earned for dividends by an industry, although of considerable interest in themselves, are unsatisfactory as an indication of the trend of profits in the industry because they are affected not only by changes in profits but also by changes in rates of taxation. It is usual, for this reason, to concentrate on movements in net profits, before tax, when studying the trend of profits, but in the case of the motor industry figures of net profits have their drawbacks as indicators of profit trends. The principal reason for this is the sharp changes from year to year that motor firms make in their provision for depreciation. It is the custom to write off jigs and tools for new models in a very short space of time—between one and three years usually—even though the life of the tools is often much greater than this. The result is a big divergence between net profits and trading profits in some years but not in others. As an indication of the relationship between profits and sales—a relationship which will shortly be investigated—an index of trading profits is more satisfactory than an index of net profits, and for this reason attention will for the moment be concentrated on trading profits.[1]

The figures for trading profits in Table 2 for the seven leading vehicle manufacturers have been divided in the table that follows into the figures for the five car manufacturers included in the index and for the two heavy commercial vehicle manufacturers. A column is also included showing the effect on the car figures of the inclusion of Ford.

TABLE 3
Index of Trading Profits
1930=100

Profits earned in	Leyland and ACV	Five car firms*	'Big-Six' car firms†
1929	105	84	85
1930	100	100	100
1931	81	82	71
1932	53	87	64
1933	39	102	99
1934	69	134	134
1935	83	160	154
1936	114	196	184
1937	137	189	179
1938	132	167	159

* Austin, Humber, Morris, Standard, Vauxhall.
† Five firms plus Ford.

[1] Table 2 shows clearly the divergences that can occur between the trend of trading profits, net profits and the amount earned for dividends. Trading profits were affected less than net profits by the slump, but rose by more in the early stages of the recovery and by rather less in the later stages. The 'earned for dividends' figures fell by slightly more than net profits in the slump but rose more rapidly than either trading profits or net profits in the recovery. The differences between trading profits and net profits were due to the fact that provisions for depreciation, etc., fell relatively little in the early stages of the slump, then rose by nearly 60 per cent between 1932 and 1934, but only rose again by some 13 per cent between 1934 and 1936. The differences between net profits and the amount earned for dividends were due primarily to the fact that taxation, after falling by much the same proportion as net profits between 1930 and 1932, was practically the same in 1934 as in 1932, although net profits were some 45 per cent higher in 1934 than in 1932. Taxation more than doubled between 1934 and 1936 while net profits rose by some 70 per cent, but over the period 1930 to 1936 taxation rose by only about 50 per cent as compared with the rise in net profits of 84 per cent.

Profits and Sources of Funds

The experience of Leyland and ACV was markedly less satisfactory than that of the leading car firms, and was subject to a much greater degree of fluctuation.[1] The index for the five car firms alone shows a slightly smaller fall in profits in the slump and a markedly greater expansion in the boom than the seven-firm index in Table 2. The inclusion of the Ford figures has a depressing effect on the car index, but less so in the boom (by which time Dagenham was producing vehicles in considerable volume) than in the slump.[2] However, the depressing effect of Ford's figures is exaggerated by the fact that in 1930 the profits of the Continental Ford companies were included in the company's accounts, but soon afterwards were excluded.

An interesting difference between the trend of profits of the larger car firms, such as those considered here, and the 'specialist' car firms, is brought out by a computation made by *The Economist* in 1937. An index of profits was calculated for three firms producing 'popular' cars, Morris, Austin and Standard, and for four firms producing 'more expensive' cars, Rover, Riley, Humber[3] and Alvis. The index for the popular cars was much the more stable of the two. *The Economist* suggested that the reason for this was that the normal effect of depression was to divert replacement demand from more expensive to less expensive models.[4]

---

[1] Hope, op. cit., p. 163, shows that in 1924–35 the degree of fluctuation of the profits of six commercial motor firms was markedly greater than that of eight car firms. Commercial motor profits were much more severely hit by the slump.

[2] It will be noticed that the inclusion of Ford's trading profits makes far less difference to the index than did the inclusion of Ford's profits after tax to the 'earned for dividends' index (see p. 153 above). In the case of Ford, the behaviour of both the depreciation and the taxation figures makes the trading profits much the most satisfactory index of profits to use in an investigation of the relationship between profitability and sales.

[3] There was some overlap here: the profit figures for Humber cover Hillman as well as Humber cars.

[4] *The Economist* figures were as follows:

Profits* 1930=100

	'Popular'	'More expensive'
1929	98	79
1930	100	100
1931	68	†
1932	75	†
1933	58	123
1934	79	273
1935	115	263
1936	142	n.a.

* Presumably profits after tax.   † Combined losses recorded for these years.
Source: *The Economist*, August 21, 1937, p. 392.

2. PROFITS AND OUTPUT, 1929–38

In this section a comparison is made between changes in trading profits and changes in the output of vehicles by the industry and in the value of the industry's sales. For this comparison it has been thought best to use the index of trading profits for the 'Big Six' car firms given in Table 3. These six firms were responsible in 1938 for some 90 per cent of total car production, 80 per cent of total commercial vehicle production, and 88 per cent of the combined production of cars and commercial vehicles. It should be possible, in these circumstances, to draw some meaningful conclusions from a comparison of these firms' trading profits with vehicle output and the value of sales for the industry as a whole.[1]

TABLE 4
Profits, Output, Prices and Turnover
1930=100

	Trading Profits*	Number of Vehicles Produced†	Vehicle Prices‡	Value of Vehicle Sales§
1929	85	100	105	105
1930	100	100	100	100
1931	71	95	92	87
1932	64	98	82	80
1933	99	121	81	98
1934	134	145	82	119
1935	154	171	69	118
1936	184	195	68	133
1937	179	212	67	142
1938	159	188	69	130

* 'Big Six' car firms—Austin, Ford, Humber, Morris, Standard and Vauxhall.
† Calculated from SMMT figures of UK car and commercial vehicle production.
‡ Estimate based on SMMT indices for car prices and commercial vehicle prices, lagged by one year.
§ Calculated from the output and price series. The resulting index has been checked against sales of motor vehicles, parts and accessories as shown in the Census of Production for 1930 and 1935 and the 'Import Duties' data for 1934. The figure shown in the table for 1934 is higher than the corresponding 'Import Duties' figure (102), but the calculated figure for 1935 is very close to that deduced from the Census (117).

[1] Sufficient information is not available for it to be possible to compare the trading profits of the 'Big Six' firms with their own output of vehicles and the value of their own sales.

Conclusions drawn from this table rest on shaky foundations, for the indices of both vehicle prices and vehicle sales are based on incomplete data, particularly the index of vehicle sales. Another point that should be borne in mind is that the profits under discussion result from sales of parts and accessories as well as from sales of vehicles, but it is not possible to calculate figures of the overall sales of vehicle firms except in one or two years. When all the reservations have been made, however, the indices given in the table probably do indicate the overall trend reasonably well, although figures for individual years may be suspect. Before conclusions are drawn from the table, it will be helpful to calculate two further indices from it—profits in relation to output (i.e. the number of vehicles produced) and profits in relation to turnover (i.e. the value of sales).

TABLE 5
Profits in Relation to Output and Turnover
1930=100

	Profits/Output	Profits/Turnover
1929	85	81
1930	100	100
1931	75	82
1932	65	80
1933	82	101
1934	92	113
1935	90	130
1936	94	138
1937	84	126
1938	84	122

The fall in vehicle prices between 1929 and 1932, and again between 1934 and 1935, caused the value of sales to fall by more than the output of vehicles in the slump and to rise by very much less in the recovery. Trading profits fell in the slump by even more than the value of sales, but in the recovery rose much more rapidly; not as rapidly, however, as the output of vehicles. The result was a considerable rise over the period in profits on turnover, but a fall in profits per unit of output. It is clear that costs of production, as well as prices, must have fallen—part of the fall no doubt being attributable to the much greater emphasis on small car production after 1930—and that in the years following 1932 the fall in costs must have been greater than the fall in prices. If it is assumed that trading profits as a proportion of turnover were 10 per cent in 1930, then, assuming the information in Tables 4 and 5 to be broadly correct, costs per unit of output in 1937 must have been approximately 35 per cent lower than in 1930.[1] The fall in prices (33 per cent), although not as great, was such that an absolute decline took place in profits per unit of output in spite of the fall in costs. If profits per vehicle had been £20[2] in 1930, the figure would have fallen to £17 in 1937.

It is possible, by combining the available data with a certain amount of guesswork, to make approximate calculations of profits per unit of output for individual manufacturers.[3] The most striking fact that appears to emerge from these calculations is that for Ford the fall in profits per unit over the period seems to have been greater than for any other of the 'Big Six' firms. If such a fall took place, it may have been partly due to the marked change in emphasis towards small car production after 1931, but the Ford figures for the early 1930s are suspect—because of the different basis on which profits were calculated before and after the move to Dagenham—and it may be that they exaggerate the extent of any fall in profits per unit of output that actually occurred. The figures for the years after 1933 are not subject to this qualification, however, and it is interesting to note that between 1935 and 1936, following the introduction of the £100 car, Ford profits per unit of output fell by over 15 per cent at a time when, as Table 5 shows, profits per unit of output were rising for the 'Big Six' as a whole.

The results for Morris over the period, which are more reliable than those for Ford, also show a big fall in profits per unit of output, particularly after 1932. Austin did better, profits per unit of output not falling by as much as the 'Big Six' average until 1935. The remarkable thing about the Austin figures is their strength in 1931 and 1932, as compared with the overall weakness shown in Table 5. Standard also did very well in 1931 and 1932 and, what is more, did appreciably better than the average in the later 1930s: profits per unit of output were actually higher after 1935 than in 1930. Humber did well

---

[1] There are some indications from Census of Production and other data that a figure of 10–15 per cent for profits on turnover may have been about right on the average for the larger firms. If in the example in the text 15 per cent instead of 10 per cent had been taken as representing profits on turnover, the estimated fall in costs per unit of output between 1930 and 1937 would have worked out at 36 per cent.

[2] A figure of this order is broadly consistent with the assumption of 10 per cent profits on turnover and has some independent support.

[3] It is not possible to calculate profits on turnover also, since a general index of vehicle prices is the only index available, and it would clearly be inappropriate to use this for individual firms.

also, but it started from such a weak position that, having achieved fair success after 1933, the profit figures naturally improved very greatly in relative terms. Similar considerations applied to Vauxhall, which had the most successful record of all: profits per unit of output were more than 50 per cent above the 1930 level throughout most of the period. In absolute terms, trading profits per vehicle produced in 1937 appear to have been highest for Vauxhall; Austin was next highest, followed by Morris, Ford, Standard and Humber, in that order. It has to be borne in mind, in interpreting these figures, that Vauxhall was not selling an 8 or 10 horse-power car in 1936, whereas the other firms were selling one or both of these types. Vauxhall was selling a higher proportion of commercial vehicles also. Other things being equal, therefore, one would expect Vauxhall's absolute profit per vehicle to be somewhat higher than the average.

To return to a consideration of the figures for the 'Big Six' as a whole: it was calculated earlier that costs per vehicle produced may have fallen by something like 35 per cent between 1930 and 1937. Over this period, the output of the industry more than doubled. It is tempting to deduce from the figures, suitably adjusted for price changes,[1] a relationship between costs and volume of output, but unfortunately the result would not have a great deal of significance. One of the main reasons for this is the trend towards the production of smaller cars during the period: in 1930, new registrations on the home market of cars of 12 horse-power and under represented only 53 per cent of the total, whereas by 1938 they represented 78 per cent.[2] The fall in costs was undoubtedly associated with the increase in the scale of the industry that took place during the 1930s, but there is not sufficient data available to trace the exact connection. To understand the effect on costs of a growth in output, a more direct approach, such as is employed in Chapter VI, is required.

3. RETURN ON CAPITAL, 1929–38

It is usually considered that the most satisfactory way to judge the

[1] The general level of prices did not alter greatly over the period 1929 to 1938. The index used by Dr Prest (*Economic Journal*, March 1948, pp. 58–9) shows a fall of some 15 per cent between 1929 and 1933 and a rise of 11 per cent between 1933 and 1938. In 1937 prices were approximately 2 per cent below the 1930 level. The Board of Trade wholesale price index for intermediate products was slightly more variable, but whichever index is taken it still seems to be true that the effect of general price changes on the level of costs must have been relatively small during this period.

[2] PEP, op. cit., p. 65.

profitability of a firm is to work out the relationship between its profits and the assets it employs. In practice, considerable difficulties arise when such calculations are attempted,[1] so that figures purporting to show rates of return on capital have to be taken with a large grain of salt. This is true for firms in the motor industry as much as for firms in general. The figures in Table 6, which show the relationship between net profits[2] and assets[3], should not therefore be taken too seriously.

TABLE 6
Rates of Return on Capital,* 1929–38

	1929 %	1930 %	1931 %	1932 %	1933 %	1934 %	1935 %	1936 %	1937 %	1938 %
Austin	21	25	19	14	15	18	16	15	16	11
Ford	12	11	3	†	†	7	4	6	5	3
Humber	†	4	†	†	7	22	14	14	14	8
Morris	16	17	11	12	6	8	15	19	16	12
Standard	†	19	24	48	27	19	25	23	26	9
Vauxhall	n.a.	n.a.	12	18	41	54	58	47	38	24

* Net profits in financial year in relation to net tangible assets at the end of financial year. Austin financial year ends July 31; Humber and Standard, August 31; Ford, Morris and Vauxhall, December 31.

† Loss.

The very high figures shown for some companies in Table 6 are related in several cases to an undervaluation of net assets, due to high depreciation provisions. This is clear in the case of Vauxhall, for example, which allowed £2,250,000 for depreciation in the period 1934–38, while its net assets at the end of the period were only £3,055,000. It is true that Vauxhall was making good profits, even after depreciation, between 1934 and 1938, so that the undervaluation of assets is not by any means the whole of the story, but the figure of 58 per cent for earnings on capital in 1935 must certainly be treated with reserve.

In spite of the difficulties caused by such problems as the undervaluation of capital, Table 6 does throw up some interesting points. It reflects the steady profit performance of Austin over the period, for example, and the fluctuations in Morris profits after 1930, especially the steep fall after 1932. The Ford losses in 1932 and 1933 were clearly

[1] *v.* Silberston and Solomons, 'Monopoly Investigation and the rate of return on capital employed', *Economic Journal*, December 1952.

[2] It seems more appropriate to consider net profits than trading profits in this particular context.

[3] i.e., net tangible assets as calculated by Moody's Services Ltd.—fixed assets, net of depreciation, plus current assets, less current liabilities and provisions.

linked with the move to Dagenham. The low returns on capital earned by Ford in the later 1930s can be explained partly by the fact that Ford, with its completely new plant, had the highest net assets in the industry—although Ford sales were not the highest—and partly by the relative stability of Ford trading profits between 1934 and 1938, in spite of the fact that car output more than doubled over the period 1934 to 1937. High depreciation provisions were also a factor: depreciation, etc. reduced Ford net profits to less than 50 per cent of trading profits in all but one of the years between 1934 and 1938.

4. DIVIDENDS, RETAINED EARNINGS AND RECOURSE TO THE CAPITAL MARKET, 1929–38

In common with industry in general, the motor industry distributed a high proportion of its net earnings as dividends before the war. Mr Kaldor has calculated that in 1938 some 75 per cent of the total post-tax income of companies, after deduction of depreciation allowances, was distributed as dividends.[1] For the 'Big Six' car firms the proportion over the whole period 1929–38 was rather lower than this; it was 66 per cent, leaving 34 per cent of net earnings retained.[2] The proportion of earnings retained was somewhat higher in the earlier years than in the later, as the following table shows:

TABLE 7
Proportion of Net Earnings Retained.* 'Big Six' Car Firms

	1929–33 %	1934–38 %	1929–38 %
Austin	33	31	32
Ford	20	23	22
Humber	†	53	17
Morris	50	25	35
Standard	80	40	53
Vauxhall	72	42	45
	38	32	34

* Net undistributed profits as a proportion of total amount earned for dividends (i.e. net profits less all taxes, including income tax paid on dividends on behalf of shareholders).

† Net earnings were negative (c. —£300,000) over this period while dividends of c. £80,000 were paid.

[1] N. Kaldor, *An Expenditure Tax*, p. 161.

[2] Hope, op. cit., p. 177, found that in 1924–35 the proportion of earnings retained by vehicle manufacturing firms was appreciably higher than the average for all industry. He gives a figure of 10.5 per cent for the proportion of net earnings

The high proportions retained by Standard and Vauxhall in 1929–33 can no doubt be explained by their small net earnings over this period. In 1934–38, with the exception of Humber, which was building itself up after the slump, their proportions retained were still the highest. Austin and Ford pursued a policy of high dividends throughout. The big change in the figures for Morris in the two periods is linked with the fact that ordinary shares of Morris Motors were issued to the public for the first time in 1936.[1]

Retained earnings were, for the six firms as a whole, slightly more important as a source of funds than the capital market.

TABLE 8
1929–38. Funds Available, Internal and External (Long-term)[2]
£'000

	Retained Earnings	Depre-ciation	Total	Long-term Capital Raised*	Date
Austin	1,625	1,362	2,987	nil	
Ford	819	4,635	5,454	4,620	(1931)
Humber	103	501	604	725	(1935, 1937, 1938)
Morris	2,997	1,689	4,686	650	(1935, 1936)
Standard	565	604	1,169	970	(1935, 1937)
Vauxhall	1,589	2,893	4,482	550†	(1936)
Total	7,698	11,684	19,382	7,515	

* Only issues which actually raised capital have been included.
† From General Motors.

If retained earnings and depreciation allowances are taken together,[3] they were considerably more important as sources of funds than long-term capital raised externally. For three firms, Austin, retained by all industry, as compared with 45.4 per cent for commercial motors and 61.6 per cent for non-commercial motors. His figures are expressed as a percentage of net earnings for *ordinary* shares (i.e., after payment of preference dividends) and are therefore higher than they would be if total net earnings were taken as a base, as they are in Table 7.

[1] The change was even greater than appears at first sight. The figures given in the table, which were calculated from the accounts of Morris Motors, underestimate the proportion of profits retained inside the whole Morris group of companies before 1936. Ordinary share dividends were paid by Morris Motors to the Morris holding companies during the period 1930–36. *v.* Andrews and Brunner, *The Life of Lord Nuffield*, pp. 209 *et seq.* and pp. 340–1.

[2] The figures given in this table are approximate only, since they have had to be culled from the limited data that is available.

[3] They represented, between them, 51.5 per cent of gross earnings (net earnings plus depreciation) over the period.

Morris and Vauxhall, internal funds were of predominant importance; Austin indeed raised no capital at all externally until 1948. The other three firms, Humber, Standard and Ford, all leant heavily on the capital market: Humber and Standard did not go to the market before 1935, by which time their profits were much higher than during the depression years. Ford went to the market for a very large sum as early as 1931, when Dagenham was being built, and in the later 1930s financed itself internally, primarily by making very heavy provision for depreciation, as Vauxhall did also during these years.

The changes in the net assets of the six firms between 1929 and 1938 are shown in Table 9. It will be seen that the two firms whose net assets increased most in absolute terms during the period were Ford and Morris, the Ford expansion taking place mainly in the early period and the Morris expansion mainly in the later period. In relative terms, the biggest increases in net assets were shown by Standard and Vauxhall, both firms which had small net assets at the beginning of the period and which expanded their production greatly during it.

TABLE 9
*Net Assets** £'000

	Increase in Net Assets			Value of Net Assets
	1929–33	1934–38	1929–38	1938
Austin	530	525	1,055	5,138
Ford	4,452	467	4,919	12,555
Humber	−204	908	704	2,033
Morris	457	3,617	4,074	11,464
Standard	305	1,218	1,523	1,771
Vauxhall	495†	1,506	2,001	3,055
Total	6,035	8,241	14,276	36,016

* Net tangible assets as calculated by Moody's Services Ltd.
† 1931–3 only.

Since retained earnings plus long-term capital raised externally amounted to £15.2 million during 1929–38 (Table 8), these two sources of funds were alone more than sufficient to finance the net expansion in assets. This was true for each firm individually, with the exception of Morris, as well as for the six firms taken together.

5. THE TREND OF PROFITS 1947–56

Profit information for the years since the end of the war is a good deal better than for the 1930s. *The Economist* now prepares quarterly figures in some detail, and the National Institute of Economics and Social Research has carried out a large-scale analysis of the sources and uses of funds in public companies for the years 1949–53. *The Economist* figures for the motor, cycle and aircraft industry and for all industries are given below.

TABLE 10
*Gross Trading Profits**
(1947=100)

Profits earned in	Motors, Cycles and Aircraft	All Industries
1947	100	100
1948	130	120
1949	154	124
1950	214	148
1951	254	178
1952	275	168
1953	321	174
1954	388	201
1955	436	224
1956	382	232

* Gross trading profits, before provisions and before tax. The indices have been constructed from the figures given in *The Economist* quarterly profits analyses.

These post-war figures, in contrast to those for 1929–38 in Table 1, show a much more vigorous upward trend in the profits of motors, cycles and aircraft firms during the period 1947–55 than in the profits of all firms taken together. Even when profits fell on the average between 1951 and 1952, the rise in motor, cycle and aircraft profits continued, although at a reduced rate. The rapid increase in profits over this period was not surprising in view of the relatively easy market for vehicles that prevailed up to 1955 and the much greater rise in vehicle output than in output in general.[1] In 1956, however, the experience of the motor industry was a good deal worse than that of industry in general, and the profit figures reflect this.

If figures for the motor industry alone are studied, the rise in profits and output in the years before 1956 is seen to be even greater than is indicated by the figures for all types of vehicles taken together. Between 1949 and 1953, the period covered by the NIESR survey, the total profits of car and commercial vehicle firms rose by 134 per

[1] The official index of industrial production shows a rise of 48 per cent for all industries between 1947 and 1955, as compared with a rise of 89 per cent for the 'vehicles' component of the index. For cars, commercial vehicles and tractors only, the increase in output between 1947 and 1955 amounted to 174 per cent.

cent as compared with the rise of 108 per cent shown by *The Economist* index.

TABLE 11
Index of Trading Profits[1]
(1949=100)

Profits earned in*	Car Manu- facturers†	Heavy Commer- cial Vehicle Manufacturers‡	Total	Components§
1949	100	100	100	100
1950	177	108	161	124
1951	204	99	180	136
1952	218	137	200	146
1953	250	130	234	139

* Profits relate approximately to calendar years: the method used by the NIESR is to sum the profits of companies with accounting dates falling in the year April–March (April 1949–March 1950, etc.).

† Twenty-one firms. Motor cycle manufacturers are included, but their influence on the figures is small.

‡ Thirteen firms.

§ Thirty-eight firms.

Table 11 brings out the fact that heavy commercial vehicle manufacturers did considerably less well than the car manufacturers. The component manufacturers also had a less successful profit record than the car manufacturers, but a more successful one than the heavy commercial vehicle manufacturers. One probable reason for the relatively poor showing of the heavy commercial vehicle manufacturers was that they expanded their output a good deal less than did the car manufacturers during the period 1949–53. Between these years, heavy commercial vehicle output[2] rose by only 3 per cent as compared with 32 per cent for cars, light commercial vehicles and tractors.[3]

6. PROFITS AND OUTPUT, 1947–56

Since the profit figures calculated by the NIESR cover the period 1949–53 only, it has been decided to use *The Economist* profit index

[1] The figures in this table have been derived from computations specially prepared for the authors by the National Institute of Economic and Social Research. We wish to express our gratitude to the Institute for having undertaken the considerable amount of work involved in preparing these computations.

[2] i.e. the output of all commercial vehicles over six-ton weight and all public service vehicles. (The majority of vehicles of these types is made by the heavy commercial vehicle manufacturers.)

[3] Between 1953 and 1955, however, the rise in heavy commercial output (55 per cent) was greater than that in the output of cars, etc. (45 per cent).

when dealing with the whole period 1947–56. It is clear from the NIESR figures that *The Economist* index understates the rise in motor vehicle manufacturers' profits during 1949–53, but since the two indices move in a similar way, it probably does not give too inaccurate a picture if *The Economist* index is used. This index is shown again in Table 12, together with indices of vehicle output, prices and the value of sales.

TABLE 12
Profits, Output, Prices and Turnover
(1947=100)

	Trading Profits	Number of Vehicles Produced*	Vehicle Prices†	Value of Vehicle Sales‡
1947	100	100	100	100
1948	130	125	101	126
1949	154	143	105	150
1950	214	180	110	198
1951	254	174	122	212
1952	275	162	132	214
1953	321	188	129	242
1954	388	234	127	298
1955	436	274	128	351
1956	382	222	135	300

* Cars, commercial vehicles and agricultural tractors. Tractors have been included in the index because of the greatly increased importance of tractor output in relation to car and commercial vehicle output since the war.

† Estimate based on movements in the wholesale home market prices of a number of types of cars and commercial vehicles, and on movements in the average export value of cars and commercial vehicles.

‡ Calculated from columns * and †. There is quite good agreement between this index and changes in the gross output of the industry as shown in the Census of Production figures for the years 1948–53.

With the use of these indices it is possible to calculate figures for profits in relation to output and turnover in the way that was done for the pre-war decade.

The post-war story is clearly a very different one from that of the pre-war years. Taking the period 1947–55, to begin with, profits per unit of output rose a good deal, and their rise outstripped that in profits on turnover.[1] What happened during the period up to 1953

[1] The general picture given by the table would not have been significantly changed if the profit figures calculated by the National Institute of Economic and Social Research, and the gross output figures given in the Census of Production had been used. The biggest difference, using NIESR and Census of Production

TABLE 13
Profits in Relation to Output and Turnover
(1947=100)

	Profits/Output	Profits/Turnover
1947	100	100
1948	104	103
1949	108	103
1950	119	108
1951	146	120
1952	170	128
1953	171	133
1954	166	130
1955	159	124
1956	172	127

was that, although in absolute terms gross profits per vehicle rose by 70 per cent, the rise in costs of production was such that it prevented profits on turnover from rising to anything like the same extent. Nevertheless, profits on turnover went on rising until 1953 and did not fall until 1954 when absolute profits per vehicle fell. The period during which the discrepancy between the indices of profits/output and profits/turnover really became marked was 1950 to 1952. It was during this period that costs rose particularly steeply. Assuming gross profits on turnover in 1953 of approximately 10 per cent,[1] the implication of the figures is that costs per unit of output rose by about 30 per cent between 1947 and 1952, nearly 20 per cent of the rise taking place between 1950 and 1952. Between 1952 and 1953, costs appear to have fallen by 4–5 per cent and then to have risen again by about 1 per cent between 1953 and 1955. Over the whole period 1947–55 costs per unit of output appear to have risen by about 25 per cent.

In considering these movements in costs it should be borne in mind that the composition of the industry's output was not stable throughout the period 1947–55. In the earlier years the proportion of small cars produced fell considerably, only to rise again in the early 1950s. By 1955, it was back to the 1947 level. The rise in costs per unit since

figures, is that the rise in both profits/output and profits/turnover that took place between 1949 and 1951 occurred to a greater extent than is suggested by the table between 1949 and 1950. Figures of trading profits as a percentage of turnover derived from the annual reports of the Commissioners of Inland Revenue also support this conclusion.

[1] A figure of this magnitude seems plausible in the light of Inland Revenue figures and has some support from other data.

1950 would no doubt have been greater had it not been for the swing towards smaller cars.

The increase in costs, profits and prices in the motor industry must of course be placed against the background of rising prices in the economy as a whole. Between 1947 and 1955, when vehicle prices appear to have risen by something like 30 per cent and costs per unit of output by 25 per cent, retail prices as a whole rose by about 50 per cent and wholesale prices[1] by about 70 per cent. It is evident that, in real terms, both costs and prices in the motor industry fell during the period. It is particularly interesting to compare the years 1950 and 1955 from the point of view of the real change in costs, since in both of these years the industry was utilizing a high proportion of its capacity. The calculations suggest that between 1950 and 1955 vehicle prices rose by 15–20 per cent and costs per unit of output by about 15 per cent. Over this period, the Board of Trade index of the wholesale prices of materials used in mechanical engineering rose by nearly 50 per cent, and the average weekly earnings of employees in the metals, engineering and shipbuilding industries by about the same percentage. In real terms, therefore, costs per unit of output may have fallen by 20–25 per cent[2] between 1950 and 1955, a period during which the industry's output rose by nearly 50 per cent, from 903,000 to 1,371,000 vehicles. A good deal of this fall in costs must have been due to the economies afforded by larger-scale production, but very probably the spreading of overheads played some part, since in 1950 the industry's output was almost certainly held at a lower proportion of capacity than in 1955 by shortage of raw materials.

So far, figures derived from *The Economist* profits figures for motor, cycle, and aircraft firms during the period 1947–55 have been discussed. In 1956, *The Economist* figures, used in conjunction with those of vehicle output and the value of vehicle sales, suggest that, although total profits fell, profits per vehicle rose in absolute terms and also in relation to turnover. However, when the 1956 accounts of the 'Big Five' car producers are examined these conclusions are not borne out. They show that, for the five firms, trading profits fell by 34 per cent, as compared with 12.5 per cent in *The Economist* index, and that profits per vehicle fell steeply both in absolute terms and in relation to the value of vehicle sales. In 1956 the profits of

[1] Of manufactured products.

[2] Possibly rather less than this for a vehicle of given specifications, in view of the trend towards smaller cars during this period.

leading commercial vehicle and aircraft firms rose, and this prevented *The Economist* index from falling as much as it would have done if it had reflected the results of the car firms alone.

Figures for a number of individual firms are given in Table 14. Since the war vehicle firms have been far less reticent than formerly in publishing information about their production, but the only large car producers to publish details of turnover regularly are Ford and Vauxhall.

TABLE 14
*Ford, Vauxhall, BMC and Standard Profit/Output
Ford and Vauxhall Profit/Turnover*

	Ford Trading Profit per Vehicle £	Ford Trading Profit/ Turnover %	Vauxhall Trading Profit per Vehicle £	Vauxhall Trading Profit/ Turnover %	BMC* Trading Profit per Vehicle £	Standard† Trading Profit per Vehicle £
1947	42	13.5	43	11.6	–	n.a.
1948	41	12.8	36	10.3	–	n.a.
1949	40	11.3	44	12.3	–	n.a.
1950	63	17.3	47	13.1	–	31
1951	66	16.1	59	12.9	–	29
1952	72	14.0	95	16.9	–	24
1953	77	17.0	110	20.6	53	n.a.
1954	78	17.7	107	21.0	60	30
1955	61	14.1	93	17.4	57	35
1956[1]	43	9.5	77	13.2	36	23

* Years ended July 31
† Years ended August 31.

The figures of absolute profits per vehicle are not directly comparable between the four companies, both because their range of activities differ and because of the different average values of the vehicles they sell: in particular, the vehicles produced by Vauxhall, which comprise a higher proportion of commercial vehicles than is the case with Ford, BMC, or Standard, are on the average a good deal higher in price than those of the other firms. For these reasons, the comparative changes in the profit per vehicle figures over time are more revealing. Over the period 1947–53, the rise in Vauxhall's profits per vehicle was very considerable. The same was true of the rise in Vauxhall's profits on turnover, although Vauxhall suffered a

[1] Net profit (i.e. trading profits less depreciation, etc.) per vehicle was £32 for Ford in 1956 and £52 for Vauxhall. Net profit as a percentage of turnover was 7.0 for Ford in 1956 and 8.9 for Vauxhall.

temporary check in their rate of profit after 1950 in the face of the post-Korean rise in costs. The Ford results follow a similar pattern to those for Vauxhall, but are a good deal less buoyant in the years 1951–54. In accordance with the general trend in the industry, profits per vehicle and profits on turnover fell after 1954 for both Ford and Vauxhall. Vauxhall's profit per vehicle actually began to fall after 1953, and BMC's profit per vehicle began to fall after 1953–4. For Standard, however, the fall did not begin until after 1954–5.

Turnover figures are not available for BMC, so that it is not possible to chart the movements in BMC's profits/turnover ratio from year to year. Over the period, the indications are that BMC profits on turnover were lower than those earned by either Ford or Vauxhall, but BMC had the excuse during the years following 1952 that it was still reorganizing after the Austin-Nuffield merger. In any event, BMC profits on turnover in 1952–6 were almost certainly better than those of either Standard[1] or Rootes. In judging Standard's profits, however, it must be remembered that some 40 per cent of Standard's output is of tractors which it produces for Massey-Harris-Ferguson. On these the profit margin earned by Standard is presumably smaller than it would be if the Ferguson tractor were entirely a Standard product.

It is interesting to compare what can be deduced from the Ford and Vauxhall figures regarding changes in profits and costs with what has been deduced earlier from the figures for the industry as a whole. Taking the years 1950 and 1955 again,[2] the proportionate rise in profits per vehicle for Vauxhall well exceeded the average for the industry, but Ford profits per vehicle actually declined slightly. The implication of the Ford figures is that costs per unit of output rose by almost 24 per cent, while the average value of Ford vehicles rose by only 19 per cent: hence the decline not only in profits on turnover but also in absolute profits per vehicle. Vauxhall, on the other hand, appears to have had a rise in costs per unit of output of 43 per cent during the period, but a rise of 50 per cent in the average value of its output: hence the increase in both profits per vehicle and profits on turnover. In comparing these figures with those previously given for

[1] Standard has published turnover figures in 1950–51 and 1951–2 only. In those years its trading profit/turnover ratio was 7.8 per cent and 6.2 per cent respectively.

[2] For both firms, as for the industry as a whole, output fell off after 1950, and was below the 1950 level until 1953. For both firms also, as for the industry, 1955 was a peak year for production.

the industry as a whole (a rise of 15 per cent in costs and of 15–20 per cent in prices), it has to be borne in mind that the industry figures are based on very shaky foundations, being the outcome of a long series of estimates. Even in looking at the figures for Ford and Vauxhall, however, several provisos have to be made, especially about the figures of profits per vehicle. In the first place, only the sales of vehicles by these firms is known: nothing is known about the proportion of sales represented by spare parts in different years. A change in this proportion could bring about an apparent change in profits 'per vehicle' when no change has in fact taken place. In the second place, the proviso about the changing composition of vehicle output that was made when the industry figures were under discussion applies even more strongly to figures for individual firms. The rise in costs per vehicle and in the average value per vehicle in Vauxhall's case, for example, can almost certainly be associated with the production by Vauxhall of larger cars and more diesel-engined commercial vehicles. These considerations do not, however, explain away the high profits on turnover that both Ford and Vauxhall were making before 1955–6, since profits on turnover depend on the relationship between prices and costs and not on their absolute level.[1]

7. SHORT-RUN MOVEMENTS IN PROFITS, 1955–7

It is appropriate at this stage to add a word about the relationship between movements in profits and the short-run structure of costs in the industry. Nothing has been said about this at an earlier stage in this chapter because movements in profits over periods of several years have been considered, and during these periods the productive capacity of the industry increased very considerably, thus making analysis of short-run changes very difficult. If, however, attention is concentrated on what happened in the period 1955–7, when output fell considerably and then rose again, something can be said about the way in which profits were affected by changes in the proportion of capacity worked. Even during this period the capacity of the industry was growing, but it seems probable that the effect of short-run changes in the proportion of capacity worked had a more important effect on costs and profits than the overall growth in the capacity of the industry. In studying this period, the experience of the Ford Motor Com-

---

[1] It is true that a rise in the proportion of spares in total sales is likely to increase profits on turnover, because profit margins on spares are usually higher than those on vehicles. Whether such a rise occurred between 1950 and 1955 is not known.

pany will be discussed in an attempt to focus attention on the problems involved in analysing short-run profit changes. A good deal of guesswork is involved in what follows, but it is hoped that the general impression given is a more or less correct one.

The experience of the Ford Motor Company during the period 1955 to mid-1957 was as follows:

TABLE 15
Ford Motor Company. Profits and Sales 1955–57

	Year 1955	1st half 1956	2nd half 1956	1st half 1957
		(Annual Rate)		
Number of vehicles produced '000	351	357	285	332
Value of sales* £m.	152	155	136	160
Net profits £m.	18.1	11.3	8.7	18.3
Percentage net profit on turnover	11.9	7.3	6.4	11.5
Average selling price per vehicle £	432	436	477	480
Average profit per vehicle £	52	32	31	55
Average costs per vehicle £	380	404	446	425

* The financial results shown here derive from the sales of spare parts as well as of vehicles. Nothing is known about spare part sales, but unless the proportion of spare part sales to total sales changed greatly over the period under review, the broad conclusions drawn from the figures should not be greatly affected.

Several commentators, in remarking on the considerable fluctuations in profits during this period, have attributed them to the heavy burden of fixed costs in the industry. As has been seen in Chapter V, however, the burden of fixed costs is not particularly high in the industry. The fixed costs of firm 'A' were only 16 per cent of total costs at standard volume. For the purpose of this analysis, fixed costs for Ford, as a highly integrated concern, will be put at 20 per cent of total costs at standard volume. If it is assumed that Ford had a capacity of 450,000 vehicles per annum during the period under review, then standard volume (80 per cent of capacity) would have been approximately 350,000 vehicles. If these figures are accepted for the sake of argument, how can Ford's profit record during 1955–7 be explained?

Year 1955–1st half 1956

Between these periods the volume of output scarcely altered, but costs per unit of output rose by 6 per cent. Since output did not alter, the rise in costs cannot have been due to a rise in fixed costs per unit of output.[1] The rise in costs must have been due to a rise in variable costs. Since selling prices scarcely altered between the two periods, the rise in variable costs was entirely responsible for the fall in profits. Trading profits fell by the same proportion as profits per vehicle.

1st half 1956–2nd half 1956

The volume of output fell by 20 per cent between these periods. On this account, average fixed costs per unit of output would have risen by approximately £20. But costs per unit of output rose by £42[2]. Variable costs must therefore have risen by approximately £22, or 7 per cent. However, the fall in costs per unit was virtually offset by a rise in the selling price per unit. Profits per unit of output therefore fell only slightly, and trading profits fell by much the same proportion as the volume of sales.

2nd half 1956–1st half 1957

Between these periods the volume of output rose by one-sixth. On this account alone, average fixed costs per unit of output would have fallen by approximately £16. They actually fell by £21. There was probably, therefore, a small fall in variable costs per unit of output.[3] Since selling prices rose only slightly between the two periods, the rise in profits per unit of output was due almost entirely to the fall in costs. Trading profits more than doubled. They would, of course, have risen by only one-sixth if the increase in the volume of sales had not been associated with a fall in costs per unit of output.

If this analysis is even broadly correct, then what happened in the first two periods under review cannot be explained—except to a very small extent—by changes in average fixed costs brought about by changes in capacity working. What happened between the second half of 1956 and the first half of 1957, however, can very largely be explained by the fall in average fixed costs that must have taken place as output rose. As far as Ford was concerned, therefore, those who attributed most of the changes in profits during 1955–7 to the heavy

[1] Even if an allowance is made for some rise in fixed costs on account of an increase in productive capacity this conclusion is scarcely altered.

[2] New and more expensive models were introduced during the first half of 1956. To some extent, the rise in costs per unit must have been associated with the introduction of these models.

[3] Possibly this arose from more efficient working as the new models got into full production.

burden of fixed costs in the motor industry were wrong during the period 1955–6. They were right to point to fixed costs during the period 1956–7, but not to *heavy* fixed costs.

Ford's experience in the period 1956–7 illustrates the fact that although fixed costs are not a high proportion of total costs at capacity (or even at standard volume), profits in the motor industry may nevertheless be highly sensitive to movements in output. This is because the changes in average fixed costs that come about as output alters, although they do not affect costs per unit of output very greatly, do affect profits per unit of output greatly. And since profits per unit of output and the volume of output rise or fall together, total profits are very highly geared to changes in the level of output. This conclusion is an important one, but it would apply to many other industries besides the motor industry. In so far as motor industry profits were singularly volatile in 1955–7 this was due not to any peculiarity in the structure of motor industry costs, but to the impact on a normal structure of costs of sharp rises in variable costs in 1955–6 and of a peculiarly volatile demand—a demand that was affected not only by normal economic forces but also by Government measures affecting the industry.

8. RETURN ON CAPITAL, 1947–56

Profits in relation to capital employed were very healthy in the industry between 1947 and 1955. This conclusion remains true even when account is taken of the undervaluation of fixed assets caused by the post-war inflation.[1]

It is interesting to compare the years when each company's rate of return on capital achieved a peak. In the case of Rootes and Standard this was as long ago as 1950–1, although after that year there was a contrast in the experience of the two companies: Rootes' profits on capital fell away steadily, while Standard's recovered in 1953–4 after a fall in 1951–2.[2] The year of peak profits on capital for Vauxhall was 1953, for BMC 1953–4, and for Ford 1954. The fall in Vauxhall's rate of return that took place in 1954 was not marked, but there was a big fall in 1955 and again in 1956. For BMC and Ford, a steep fall did not

[1] It is relevant, in this connection, that the increase in net assets between 1947 and 1956 amounted to two-thirds of the value of net assets in 1956. The bulk of net assets in 1956 had been acquired, therefore, at post-war prices.

[2] The recovery was associated with the introduction of 8 and 10 h.p. models at the end of 1953. Small cars (other than the Triumph Mayflower) had not been produced by Standard since 1948.

TABLE 16
Rates of Return on Capital,* 1947–56

	1947 %	1948 %	1949 %	1950 %	1951 %	1952 %	1953 %	1954 %	1955 %	1956 %
Austin	28	16	17	44	51	—	—	—	—	—
Morris	21	12	21	48	—	—	—	—	—	—
BMC	—	—	—	—	—	(14)†	31	38	34	19
Ford	22	23	19	34	28	26	35	36	30	15
Rootes‡	—	—	18	37	40	35	31	30	20	10
Standard	7	14	18	18	31	22	22	28	27	5
Vauxhall	29	25	23	21	20	35	59	56	32	14

* Net profits in financial year in relation to net tangible assets at the end of the financial year. Austin and BMC financial year ending July 31; Humber and Standard, August 31; Ford, Morris and Vauxhall, December 31.

† Based on figures for four months only.

‡ Rootes figures are available from 1949, when Rootes became a public company. They include the results of Humber Ltd., although Humber figures are published separately also.

occur until 1955–6 and 1956 respectively. Too much weight should not be put on the apparent difference between the experience of Vauxhall on the one hand and Ford and BMC on the other, however, because the comparison is distorted by exceptional changes in Vauxhall's assets during this period. Table 14 above, which gives profits on turnover, is a much more reliable guide to the trend of profits, and shows that, as far as profits on turnover are concerned, Vauxhall suffered less severely than Ford between 1954 and 1956. It also shows, in the case of Ford and Vauxhall at least, that the high profits on capital indicated in Table 16 cannot be explained away by arguments about the undervaluation of assets, either on account of inflation or of rapid amortization. In the years before 1956, Ford and Vauxhall certainly earned very high profits on turnover as well as on capital employed.

The variations in the rates of return earned by different companies between 1950 and 1955 reflect, to some extent at least, their relative success in expanding their sales and maintaining their profit margins during a period when competition in the industry was gradually becoming more intense. The experience of 1955–6, however, was one that was shared by all the companies under review: they all experienced stable or falling output,[1] combined with rising costs. The

[1] Ford output fell by 8.5 per cent in 1956 and Vauxhall output by 13 per cent. Standard output fell by over 20 per cent in the year ended August 31, 1956. BMC output was 5 per cent higher in the year ended July 31, 1956, than in the

market situation was such that they were unable to raise the selling prices of their vehicles sufficiently to prevent a squeezing of their margins of profit.

9. DIVIDENDS, RETAINED EARNINGS AND RECOURSE TO THE CAPITAL MARKET, 1947–56

It was shown earlier that, in the pre-war decade, the six largest car firms retained only 34 per cent of their net earnings after tax. Since the war the proportion retained has been far higher.

TABLE 17
Proportion of Net Earnings Retained. 'Big Five' Car Firms 1947–56

	%
Austin (1947–51)	72
Morris (1947–50)	39
BMC (1952–)	68
Ford	79
Rootes (1949–)	79
Standard	52
Vauxhall*	74
	73

* A substantial proportion of the very large dividends paid to General Motors in 1953 and 1954 was reinvested in Vauxhall almost immediately. These reinvested sums have been treated as net earnings retained. If they had been treated as distributions, the proportion of net earnings retained would have worked out at 33 per cent only.

In the two cases, namely Morris and Standard, where the proportion of profits retained was well below the average, this appears to have been caused by a policy of maintaining dividends in the face of falling profits rather than by a deliberate policy of distributing a high proportion of net earnings.

For all the firms taken together, retained earnings were a larger source of funds than depreciation allowances and a far larger source than funds raised on the capital market.

Ford's record is the most striking: no capital raised externally and a bigger total of funds ploughed back internally than that for any previous year. There are no published figures for Rootes' output, but in his review issued with the 1955–6 accounts, the Chairman stated that turnover had been maintained while cost increases had not been passed on to the public in the form of higher prices: this implies little or no change in the output of vehicles.

Table 18
1947–56. Funds Available, Internal and External (Long-term)
£'000

	Retained Earnings	Depreciation	Total	Long-term Capital raised*	Date
Austin (1947–51)	5,553	2,794	8,347	2,589	(1948)
Morris (1947–50)	2,006	2,213	4,219	—	—
BMC (1952–)	19,594	11,498	31,092	4,117	(1954)
Ford	39,257	20,462	59,719	—	—
Rootes (1949–)	7,024	4,102	11,126	5,485	(1949, 1954)
Standard	3,126	13,849	16,975	7,385†	(1948, 1954, 1955)
Vauxhall‡	19,796	14,950	34,746	17,680§	(1954, 1955, 1956)
Total	96,356	69,868	166,224	37,256	

* Only issues which actually raised capital have been included.

† In addition, £1,560,000 had been raised in 1945 by the issue of ordinary shares.

‡ See footnote * to Table 17.

§ In June 1957, Vauxhall made arrangements to raise additional sums of £6 million by the sale of preference shares to General Motors and approximately £5 million by a private placing of loan stock.

other firm. Standard ploughed back much less over the whole period than any of the other 'Big Five' firms and raised a good deal of capital on the market, but to balance its small retentions it did make very heavy provision for depreciation. Vauxhall, in spite of high retentions, raised far more funds externally than any of the other firms. This was a reflection of the rapid rate at which the company's productive capacity was expanded in the mid-1950s. A £36 million expansion programme, begun in September 1954, was substantially completed in 1957. Between 1953 and mid-1957, General Motors helped to finance this expansion programme by taking up shares in Vauxhall and extending loans which amounted in total to approximately £3 million more than the dividends paid during this period by Vauxhall to General Motors. In addition, Vauxhall raised loans amounting to some £20 million from British sources.

Table 18 provides an interesting contrast with Table 8 regarding the relationship between depreciation allowances and retained earnings before and after the war. Table 8 shows that during the period 1929–38 depreciation allowances for the six firms taken together amounted to 50 per cent more than retained earnings. Table 18 shows that during the period 1947–56, on the other hand, retained earnings were nearly 40 per cent greater than depreciation allowances. Possibly the division between these two categories was not very meaningful between 1947 and 1956, owing to the post-war rise in prices and the difficulties caused thereby in calculating the sums that ought to be set aside for depreciation.[1] For this reason, it is of interest to consider retained earnings and depreciation allowances together. If this is done, the two together are seen to have amounted to 82 per cent of gross earnings (net earnings plus depreciation) during the period 1947–56 as compared with 51.5 per cent during the period 1929–38. Even on this basis, the proportion of earnings retained since the war is seen to be very much greater than before the war, but the difference is less than when the pre-war and post-war relationship between retained earnings and net earnings alone is considered.

Turning to the changes in the net assets of the five firms, the figures for Ford are again noteworthy.

TABLE 19
*Net Assets** £'000

	Increase in Net Assets 1947–56	Value of Net Assets 1956
Austin (1947–51)	7,854	—
Morris (1947–50)	2,338	—
BMC (1952–)	24,727	62,609
Ford	40,983†	65,349
Rootes (1949–)	10,628	16,891
Standard	10,485	14,254
Vauxhall	36,562	44,646
Total	133,577	203,749

* Net tangible assets as calculated by Moody's Services Ltd.
† Increase 1948–56 only. Consolidation of accounts in 1948 make 1947 asset figures not comparable with those for later years. The 1947 accounts show net assets at £17.4 m. as compared with £24.4 m. in the consolidated 1948 accounts.

The increase in Ford net assets over the post-war period has been greater in absolute terms than that for any other firm, and by the end

[1] The sums shown for depreciation in Table 18 are those in the companies' own accounts and not those allowed by the Inland Revenue. It is very probable that the companies wrote off new assets in their own accounts during this period at a rate faster than that allowed by the Inland Revenue authorities for taxation purposes. The depreciation allowances shown here, therefore, may not amount to much less than they would have done if they had been calculated on a replacement cost basis. Of course, taxation relief was not calculated on this basis, and this had repercussions on the sums available to the companies for retention and for distribution as dividends. The offsetting effects of investment allowances, etc., should not be forgotten, however.

of 1956 the value of Ford's total net assets had surpassed that of the British Motor Corporation in mid-1956. The increase in Vauxhall's net assets has also been very substantial, especially when Vauxhall's relatively small size in 1947 is considered. The Vauxhall figures are even more striking when it is borne in mind that the mergers with Briggs and with Fisher and Ludlow have inflated the figures of net asset growth for Ford and BMC respectively. At the time of the merger with BMC, Fisher and Ludlow's net assets were valued at about £4.5 million, and Briggs' net assets were probably rather higher than this at the time of the merger with Ford. In relative terms, Vauxhall showed the greatest increase in net assets during the period, followed by Standard, Ford, Rootes and BMC,[1] in that order.

Over the period 1947–56, for all the firms taken together, retained earnings plus long-term capital raised were just about sufficient between them to finance the net expansion in assets. This was substantially true also for every firm but Ford,[2] and in Ford's case the gap would probably be eliminated if the expansion of assets caused by the merger with Briggs were excluded.

For the years 1949–53 a much more detailed account of sources and uses of funds in the motor industry is available as a result of the work on company accounts done by the National Institute of Economic and Social Research. For car manufacturers, the Institutes' figures are given in Table 20 overleaf.

One of the points that these figures make clear is the relative unimportance of capital issues or bank advances in providing funds during the period 1949–53.[3] Additions to reserves, together with increases in the credit received from trade creditors and the tax authorities, were by far the most important sources of funds. The figures also make clear that a high proportion of the increase in assets during the period was in liquid assets, i.e. cash and securities. Only one-third of the funds available was expended on fixed assets. The increase in stocks over the period was about one-half of that in fixed assets.

Looking at the changes in sources of funds from year to year during the period 1949–53, it appears that the rate of addition to reserves

[1] Including the increase in net assets of Austin and Morris before 1952.
[2] Assuming that net assets really did increase between 1947 and 1948, i.e. that the increase was not entirely a consequence of the consolidation of the accounts in 1948.
[3] As Table 18 shows, however, large sums were raised externally after 1953, notably by Vauxhall.

TABLE 20
Car Manufacturers—Sources and Uses of Funds, 1949–53
£'000

Sources of funds			Uses of funds	
Additions to reserves, etc.			Increase in fixed assets	61,753
(a) retained profits	51,240			
(b) depreciation	39,647		Increase in value of stocks	31,124
(c) tax reserves	15,701	106,588		
Increase in credit received:			Expenditure in acquiring subsidiaries	9,978
(a) from banks	1,215			
(b) from trade creditors	35,439		Increase in debtors	19,231
(c) tax due	20,056		Increase in liquid assets	49,610
(d) dividends and interest due	3,069	59,779	Other	7,327
Issue of capital:				
(a) debentures	106			
(b) preference shares	—67			
(c) ordinary shares	7,667	7,706		
Other		4,950		
Total		179,023	Total	179,023

was a fairly steady one, with a peak in 1951, but that the increase in credit received fluctuated a good deal, being particularly high in 1951 and particularly low in 1952. The most important periods for capital issues, on the other hand, were 1949 and 1952–3. Turning to the uses of funds, the figures show a fairly steady rate of addition to fixed assets throughout the period, but a good deal of fluctuation in addition to stocks. Stocks rose by £2½ million in 1949, and £4–£5 million in 1950, and then rose by £20 million in 1951, at a time when production and sales were falling off. In 1952, the rise in stocks was only £10 million, and in 1953, when home sales were expanding vigorously, stocks actually fell by £6 million. Changes in liquid assets were also very marked: increases of £6 million in 1949 and £13–£14 million in 1950 were followed by a fall of some £4 million in 1951. Then came an increase of £7 million in 1952 and finally a very steep increase of £28 million in 1953. Clearly, the fall in liquid assets in 1951 and the rise in 1953 were connected, to some extent at least, with the opposite movement in stocks that took place in those years.

It is clear from the accounts for years since 1953 that although the liquid assets of certain companies, notably BMC, Ford and Vauxhall, continued to rise for a time, liquid assets as a whole fell very considerably between 1955 and 1956.[1] Comparing 1955 and 1956 balance sheets, Ford showed a fall in liquid assets of over £15 million, BMC of over £13 million, Vauxhall of nearly £11 million, Standard of over £6½ million, and Rootes of nearly £3 million. In all, the fall amounted to nearly £50 million. Over the same period, all five companies showed substantial increases in the value of stocks and of buildings, plant, etc. Much of the rise in stocks and work in progress (nearly £25 million for the five companies) was no doubt an involuntary one, stemming from the fall in vehicle sales. Since this fall in sales caused a fall in profits as well as a rise in stocks, and since the motor firms continued to push ahead with their expansion programmes, it is not surprising that liquid assets fell heavily, even for those firms which had recourse to the capital market.

---

[1] i.e. between the financial years ending during 1955 and 1956 respectively.

CHAPTER X

Future Prospects

DURING 1954 nearly all the large vehicle manufacturers announced ambitious plans for future capital expenditure. Ford, for example, said that they intended to spend £65 million during the period 1955–60 and Vauxhall that they intended to spend £36 million. Part of these sums was destined for plant renewal and modernization, but considerable amounts were to be spent on an expansion of output. Vauxhall, for example, intended to double their output over the period 1955–60 and the British Motor Corporation to increase output by 25 per cent in eighteen months. The Nuffield-Austin merger made it possible for the British Motor Corporation to achieve substantial additions to output, with comparatively little new capital expenditure, by reorganizing and rationalizing production. In the face of this, manufacturers like Ford and Vauxhall needed to make heavy expenditure if they wished to keep their share of the market, let alone if they wished to expand it.

When all the expansion plans announced in 1954 have been completed, as they should have been by 1960, the industry is expected to have capacity for producing one and a half million[1] cars and commercial vehicles per annum. This compares with the 1955 peak output of one and a quarter million cars and commercial vehicles, divided between home market sales of approximately 675,000 vehicles and export sales of approximately 535,000 vehicles.

When the industry's expansion plans were first mooted, it was said that the industry expected to sell half its output abroad in 1960, as it had done in 1954. The implied export sales of 750,000 vehicles were nearly 40 per cent higher than exports in 1950, the best post-war year. Whether sales of this magnitude will in fact be possible will depend on a number of factors, among which the trend of world incomes, increased competition from other producing countries, and increased vehicle production in overseas markets are clearly very important. Even assuming that world incomes continue to rise, it is by no means

[1] Some estimates put the figure as high as 1¾ million cars and commercial vehicles.

certain that British vehicle exports will increase to 750,000 vehicles by 1960. Foreign competition, particularly from Germany, is being increasingly felt. West Germany had less than 10 per cent of the export market for cars in 1950; by 1955 she had 31 per cent and by 1956 nearly 35 per cent. It is true that British exports were hit particularly hard in 1956 by import restrictions in such staple markets as Australia and New Zealand, but the tendency for Britain's share to fall was unmistakable before 1956. Between 1954 and 1955, for example, British car exports scarcely rose, while French car exports rose by 30 per cent, Italian by 70 per cent and West German by 55 per cent. On the commercial vehicle side, Britain is in a stronger position. Exports were higher in 1955 than in any previous year, and in 1956 fell by only 8 per cent. Between 1954 and 1955, British exports rose by 25 per cent, while French, Italian and West German exports all remained stable. Britain's commercial vehicle exports were well under half her car exports in number in the period 1954–6, although in value they were two-thirds as great in 1954–5 and an even higher proportion in 1956.

Increased production in overseas markets is particularly serious from the point of view of British vehicle exports because Australia is one of the main countries affected. Australia has been by far the most important market for British vehicle exports in the post-war period. In 1955, for example, it took 27 per cent of total exports of cars and 23 per cent of exports of commercial vehicles. Since the war, however, Australia has begun to produce her own car, the General Motors Holden, in increasing quantities, and other manufacturers, both British and Continental, have been making a higher and higher proportion of their vehicles in Australia.[1] In February 1956, for example, the British Motor Corporation stated that within eighteen months Austin and Morris motor-cars built in Australia would incorporate 90 per cent of local components. At the same time, BMC announced plans for a £A5 million expansion scheme, which would enable the total output of Austin and Morris vehicles to rise to 50,000 per annum, and stated that the Corporation was aiming to capture 45 per cent of the local car market. It was envisaged that 'in the not too far distant future' Australia would take its place as an exporter of

[1] In 1954–55 General Motors Holden produced about 60,000 of the 230,000 new vehicles registered in Australia. About 70,000 of the total was accounted for by vehicles of other makes assembled (and partially manufactured) in Australia. Holden plan to produce 100,000 cars in 1958 and total Australian production may be 170,000 vehicles. (*Financial Times*, December 23, 1955.)

motor vehicles with a particular interest in the markets of South East Asia. If the British Motor Corporation and other British firms are successful in their efforts to capture a large share of the Australian market, the United Kingdom will clearly benefit in the shape of higher profits earned overseas but exports of vehicles to Australia will certainly fall. This is the more likely to be the case since the guaranteed margins of preference for British goods in Australia were reduced appreciably in February 1957, so that foreign manufacturers were put in a stronger position to compete for what was left of the Australian import market.

Taking into account both increased competition from other countries and the prospect of declining imports into traditional markets, particularly Australia, there must clearly be doubts about the ability of the British motor industry to increase its exports appreciably during the period ending in 1960. These doubts remain even after taking account of the high level of exports to the United States in 1957. The conclusion of a survey of export markets for cars carried out in 1955 was that world car exports might actually fall during the period 1955–60,[1] and that the United Kingdom's share of the market was more likely to fall than to rise in the period immediately ahead.[2] In the view of the authors of the survey, it would be unrealistic to expect a significant increase in British car exports before 1960. If this view is accepted, then the prospects for British exports of 750,000 vehicles by 1960 must appear very uncertain, even when account has been taken of the possibility that commercial vehicle exports will be more successful than car exports.

If export markets cannot be relied on to take up their share of the increasing output capacity of the industry during the period ending in 1960, then either the home market must do so or surplus capacity will emerge in the industry. To forecast the future demand for vehicles on the British home market would be a difficult exercise at any time, but is perhaps peculiarly difficult in the conditions of the late-1950s, since the industry has recently passed through a number of abnormal years. The position was abnormal even in 1955, since a high proportion of the cars on the roads were still pre-war models. Events prior to 1955 clearly cannot be relied on to give a firm indication of the factors affecting the demand for vehicles in the post-war world, and the

[1] Consumption was expected to rise by 12 per cent, but exports were expected to fall because of increased production of cars in overseas markets.

[2] Quoted in *The Times Review of Industry*, February 1955, p. 78, from 'Motor Business' (Economist Intelligence Unit).

events of 1956 were, in their different way, so abnormal that they too cannot be taken as a guide. In 1957 also, much of the year was taken up with the repercussions of the Suez crisis at the end of 1956. Another major difficulty in the way of forecasting future demand is uncertainty about future levels of vehicle and fuel taxation and about hire purchase regulations.

In spite of these difficulties, a number of estimates of the future home market for vehicles have been attemped, mainly by the staff of *The Economist*. The most detailed of these estimates[1] suggest that car sales on the home market in 1960 may amount to between 584,000 and 654,000 vehicles. The lower estimate assumes that the ratio of car prices to the general level of prices will be the same in 1960 as in 1956. The higher estimate assumes that the ratio will fall by about 10 per cent. If a previous estimate made by *The Economist* of commercial vehicle sales in 1960 is added to these figures, then total vehicle sales on the home market would be between 735,000 and 810,000 by 1960. This compares with home market sales of 675,000 vehicles in the peak year 1955.

Looking at the prospects for sales in export markets and on the home market together, it is impossible to avoid the conclusion that the industry is very likely to have surplus capacity by 1960. This is true even if the higher of the estimates for home market sales is taken and if exports are put at, say, 600,000 vehicles as compared with the 535,000 actually exported in 1955. It is to be anticipated, in these circumstances, that competition between manufacturers will be extremely keen during the next few years. This is certainly what manufacturers themselves expect, and some of them have admitted that they are relying not only on an expansion of the total market but also on increasing their own share of the market at the expense of other British manufacturers.

These guesses about the future apply to the medium-term prospect only. Wars and catastrophes apart, the world market for vehicles will clearly go on expanding for a very long time to come.[2] If the British motor industry maintains its present share of world vehicle production it will have no difficulty at all in disposing of far more than

[1] *Motor Business*, 'The long-term growth in domestic passenger car demand', September 1956.
[2] *The Economist* estimates of total UK sales of cars and commercial vehicles in 1970 vary between 1,755,000 and 2,080,000 vehicles, depending on whether Britain joins a European Free Trade Area or not. Economist Intelligence Unit, 'Britain and Europe' (1957), p. 147.

one and a half million vehicles in 1965–70. Even an appreciable drop in Britain's share would be compatible with sales well in excess of the capacity which is planned at present.

In assessing Britain's share of world vehicle output in the long run, the crucial question to ask is, 'What is the competitive strength of the British motor industry?' Even though it is certain that many countries will build up domestic motor industries behind tariff walls, it is equally certain that there will still remain many other countries wishing to import vehicles. Imperial preference, where it still exists, is likely to become of less and less importance. Britain's share of the import markets that remain open will therefore depend primarily on her competitive strength, unaided by preferences. In the British home market, the existence of a tariff of 30 per cent *ad valorem* on imported vehicles is at present a great protection against foreign competition. If, however, the plans for a European free trade area are implemented, the protective duty, as it applies to Britain's chief competitors, the European vehicle manufacturers, will be gradually lowered over a period of years and will vanish altogether by 1970 or so. Although transport costs from the Continent will give the British industry some protection, the crucial factor on the British home market, as well as in export markets, will be the competitive strength of the British industry, particularly its strength *vis-à-vis* its Continental rivals.

It is dangerous to discuss long-term competitive strength in the light of such factors as present comparative wage-rates in the motor industries of different countries. The relationship between the level of wages in different countries—at present unfavourable to Britain in comparison with the main Continental producers—can change greatly over a period of time, although it would be realistic to assume that this relationship will remain unfavourable for some time to come. It is dangerous also to base comparisons of future competitive strength on the present relationship of raw material prices, which is on the whole favourable to the United Kingdom, particularly as raw material prices in Britain may rise if a European free-trade area is formed.[1] The long-run competitive strength of the British motor industry must primarily be assessed by reference to its scale of produc-

---

[1] Iron and steel are the crucial raw materials to consider here. However, it has been argued that the rise in steel prices that would occur if coal and scrap prices were to rise to the European level has been much exaggerated. Sara, E. T., *Free Trade in Steel?*, p. 11 (paper read to the Manchester Statistical Society, November 13, 1957).

tion and its comparative efficiency in producing, designing and selling vehicles.[1] As far as scale is concerned, the British industry is certainly large enough at present in relation to the motor industries of Continental countries for it to be possible for it to reap economies of scale on as great, if not a greater, scale than they. It has the advantage also of a components industry which is more developed and better organized for large scale standardized production than that of any other European country and which should itself greatly increase its exports in a free-trade area. At present, British cars, and even more British commercial vehicles, are very competitively priced. As far as productive efficiency is concerned, there is no reason to believe that the British industry is inferior to its competitors, and if at present design and sales efficiency seem to be at a comparative disadvantage, these are matters which can be remedied within a short span of years.

It would appear, therefore, that the British motor industry is well placed fundamentally in comparison with its closest rivals for the competitive struggle that lies ahead. This does not mean, however, that the industry will necessarily be able to compete effectively as it is at present organized. In particular, individual models of cars are produced on a larger scale in some European countries than they are in Britain. The chief example is the Volkswagen, with an output of about 400,000 a year in 1957, while no British model is produced at a scale of much more than 100,000. The Renault Dauphine is also in very large scale production—at a rate of about 200,000 vehicles a year in 1957. Well before the time that the protection of the import duty has been removed, the British industry will have to concentrate production in such a way that the scale on which individual models are produced is not markedly below that of European models. It may also find it necessary to produce 'economy' cars on a large scale if European imports are not to flood the British market.[2] This sort of adjustment is likely to come about a good deal more easily if motor vehicle taxation in the British home market is reduced and the market thus allowed to expand with fewer restraints than at present, but even

[1] Changes in the comparative efficiency of *other* British industries might, of course, affect the rate of exchange between sterling and other currencies, and hence affect the competitive strength of the motor industry. Such general changes are very difficult to forecast, and they cannot be taken into account here.

[2] It may be that in post-war circumstances the Hoffman thesis (p. 137 above) is no longer applicable. 'Economy' cars make an appeal not only because of low initial costs but also because of low running costs. Bigger second-hand cars may be as cheap to buy but they are a lot dearer to run.

so it is not likely to come about without shocks and dislocations. It is likely to come to a limited extent only from a reduction by individual manufacturers in their range of models, unless one or more of them succeeds in producing a really outstanding model which will oust his other models from the production lines. Very probably, the concentration that will be necessary to meet European competition will have to be brought about by mergers, not only mergers between small companies, or mergers between small companies and large ones, but mergers between the 'Big Five' manufacturers themselves.

The prospects for the motor industry in the event of a European free-trade area being formed have been discussed at some length in recent years by various commentators. The most detailed analysis has been carried out by *The Economist* Intelligence Unit,[1] and the conclusions of their study are broadly similar to those reached above. One of the factors that *The Economist* Intelligence Unit stresses most is the importance of suitable designs for the European market, and another is the particularly good prospects for commercial vehicles. It is foreseen that if the European Free Trade Area is formed, total British exports of cars will, by 1970, rise by 80 per cent over the 1955 level and exports of commercial vehicles will double. If, however, the Common Market is formed but no European Free Trade Area, Britain will find it very difficult to penetrate European markets. In this event, it is foreseen that British exports of cars to Europe will actually be below the 1955 level in 1970 and exports of commercial vehicles only slightly higher. Total car exports might be 9 per cent higher and commercial vehicle exports 30 per cent higher.

Estimates of future sales such as those made by *The Economist* Intelligence Unit cannot purport to be more than an intelligent appraisal of future possibilities. Whether their details turn out to be correct or not, however, the broad orders of magnitude seem reasonable. Mr H. H. Liesner[2] has pointed out that at present the motor industry is not as successful an exporter to the Continent as many other British industries, but it could plausibly be argued that up to now the designs of many British vehicles, and the facilities for servicing them, have not been outstandingly good. With improvements in these directions, the performance of the industry in Europe might take an appreciable turn for the better. It is an interesting fact that, when questioned about their willingness to enter a European Free Trade Area, several British motor manufacturers have expressed

[1] *Britain and Europe* (1957), pp. 133–148.
[2] *The Economist*, September 14, 1957, pp. 869–70.

themselves in favour of the proposal. One spokesman has said that free imports of Continental cars would not worry the industry much, and another has expressed his belief that the industry stood to gain by the wiping out of tariffs and quotas all round.[1]

This favourable reaction on the part of the industry has probably been motivated partly by fears of what would happen if the Common Market were to be set up but not the Free Trade Area. Nevertheless, there seems no reason to doubt that the industry is genuinely confident of its ability to compete in any Free Trade Area that may be formed.

---

[1] *Manchester Guardian* 'Survey of Industry, Trade and Finance, 1957', p. 40.

CHAPTER XI

Conclusions

IN the course of this study, two important facts relating to costs of production in the motor industry have been brought out. The first is that in the short run the vehicle manufacturer's fixed costs are a relatively small proportion of his total costs—certainly less than 20 per cent—unless his plant is working at very low levels of output. The evidence for this conclusion is set out in Chapter V. The second is that in the long run the cost of manufacturing vehicles falls steeply as the scale on which they are produced grows larger. In other words, there are very great economies of large-scale production in the industry. It is suggested in Chapter VI that, in the present state of technique, firms can continue to reap significant economies up to a scale of production of one million vehicles per annum. As the whole motor industry expands, the gains are greater than for the individual firms because economies are gained by component and material suppliers. It is argued in Chapter VI that if the scale of car production in the United Kingdom were to double, from one million per annum—a level which is now being approached—to two million per annum, it seems possible that costs per vehicle might fall by approximately 15 per cent.

While it is widely accepted that there are considerable economies of large-scale production in the motor industry, the fact that fixed costs are a relatively small proportion of total costs is much less widely known. It is, indeed, often assumed by commentators on the motor industry that fixed costs are a heavier burden in the motor industry than in most other industries, and the motor industry itself has often put forward arguments that are based, implicitly at least, on the assumption that the burden of fixed costs in the industry is an exceptionally heavy one. It is often said, for example, that the home market needs to be a large one so that overheads can be spread over a large volume of production, or that short-run rises in purchase tax, or the tightening of hire-purchase regulations, throttle the industry because they cut down sales in the home market and thus raise costs of production so much that the industry cannot compete abroad. Another way of putting the same point is to argue that the last little bit of production is vitally important to the industry because it makes all the difference between profits and losses. What becomes of these arguments if they are looked at in the light of the fact that fixed costs in the industry are not exceptionally high? It seems clear, to begin with, that the effect on costs per unit of output of small changes in output are not very significant. A temporary tightening in the home market is not likely to lead to such a ruinous rise in costs that the competitive ability of the industry in export markets will be seriously impaired. However, a really serious fall in home market sales would bring output down to the regions where fixed costs per unit of output do become very high. Costs would rise significantly, and profits would fall very greatly. Indeed, as has been seen in Chapter IX, profits are very highly geared to changes in output, because even small changes in costs per unit of output lead to big changes in profits per unit of output. One can draw the conclusion, therefore, that the motor industry is not so exceptionally tender a flower that the Government should at all costs hesitate to reduce its sales temporarily by such devices as raising purchase tax or the minimum hire purchase deposit. However, the Government has to be careful with this industry, as with other industries, because too drastic a fall in sales makes it very difficult for the industry to cover its fixed costs, and reduces its profits very considerably. Low profits, in their turn, might reduce the industry's willingness to expand at the same time as they reduce its ability to do so.

In the longer run, high purchase tax, high taxes on fuel, or stringent restrictions on hire purchase, may have a more serious effect on costs of production in the industry, and hence on its ability to compete, than restrictions which cause the industry to work below its full capacity for short periods of time. If the home market is kept a good deal smaller over a period of years than it could otherwise be, this will lead to a smaller expansion in the motor industry than would otherwise be the case. The industry's ability to grasp economies of scale will be reduced and its costs will be higher than they would be if the home market were larger. In emphasizing this point, the spokesmen for the motor industry are on solid ground. In emphasizing the weight of taxation in the United Kingdom, however, and the effect that this has on the size of the market, there is a tendency to overlook one point: although the British purchase tax is higher than that in the main Continental motor manufacturing countries, the fuel tax is lower than that in some of them, notably Italy and France. It is clear that the total weight of taxation on motoring in the United Kingdom is a good deal higher than in the United States, but it is by no means as obvious that it is higher than in such countries as France or Italy, or indeed, West Germany (*v.* Chapter III). However, since vehicle sales are probably inhibited more by a high initial price than by high running costs, the high level of British purchase tax in comparison with purchase taxes in Continental countries is probably a factor making for lower sales and hence for a comparatively smaller home market.

Even if the burden of taxation in the United Kingdom were a good deal lower than it is, it would still be true that individual firms in the motor industry would be working at well below the optimum size. It was said earlier that firms can continue to reap significant economies up to a scale of production of one million vehicles per annum. The gains taper off as this level is approached, and most of the economies that are possible can be attained with a production of 500,000 vehicles per annum (*v.* Chapter VI). But even this level of production is far beyond the reach of any British manufacturer at present. When it is said that the optimum level of production is approached at a level of output of 500,000 vehicles per annum, this should be taken to mean 500,000 identical, or nearly identical vehicles. The British Motor Corporation is the biggest British vehicle manufacturer, producing 440,000 vehicles in the year ended July 31, 1956, but it is doubtful whether any one model was produced at a scale of much over 100,000 per annum during this period. The economies of scale actually achieved by BMC are greater than can be inferred from the number of any particular model they produce because many parts are used which are common to a number of their models. Even when this factor is taken into account, however, it is obvious that the British Motor Corporation has not achieved anything like all the economies of large scale production that can be realized, and neither has any other British firm. In the United States, on the other hand, the three largest firms, General Motors, Ford and Chrysler, produce on such a scale that it is open to them to grasp virtually all worthwhile economies of scale. On the Continent, only one firm, Volkswagen, is anywhere near the optimum scale of production from a technical point of view.

In discussions of the optimum scale of production it is often said that the technical optimum may be greater than the managerial optimum. Putting it another way: very large scales of production, although desirable from a technical point of view, may not be desirable from a managerial point of view because they lead to inefficiency. There is no doubt that considerable managerial problems do arise in the motor industry, as in other industries composed of large firms, and there are cases to be quoted in the industry of inertia, complacency, bad labour relations and other signs of poor management. It would be difficult, however, to argue that bad management is rife in the motor industry. The industry provides many examples of managements which work well because they have delegated responsibility and have in other ways recognized and attempted to solve their managerial difficulties: indeed, the largest vehicle producing firm in the world, General Motors, is a text-book example of such a firm. The motor industry is one which produces a great challenge to management, then, but it is a challenge which it has proved by no means impossible to meet.

Another factor that needs to be considered in this context is the marketing optimum. It is usually said that as far as this optimum is concerned large firms have an advantage over small firms: they can buy on better terms and their selling expenditure per unit of output is less because selling expenditure does not increase proportionately with sales. There is no reason to doubt that these considerations apply to the motor industry. Although on the side of buying, the small vehicle manufacturer is helped very considerably by vertical disintegration, there is no doubt that large firms can achieve greater economies than small. On the side of selling, everything is in favour of the large firm. Large firms often give lower retail margins than small firms, but their sales are so large that they have no difficulty in recruiting numerous retail dealers, scattered all over the country, and this in itself is a potent factor influencing consumers to buy their vehicles. Large firms can also advertise more extensively than small firms, and this helps to give their vehicles the reputation with consumers that is so important for sales. In addition, large firms can set up world wide selling organizations, together with assembly plants in import markets, and can thus facilitate export sales very greatly. Clearly, in the motor industry, the marketing optimum is very large.

When the technical, the managerial and the marketing optima are considered together, there is no reason to conclude that it is desirable for vehicle producing firms in the industry (other than producers of very specialized types of vehicle) to be smaller than is indicated by technical considerations. Whatever might be said about the possible managerial inefficiency of large firms, technical economies of scale in this industry, together with marketing economies, are of such importance that they overwhelm the other factors which have to be taken into account when considering the optimum scale of individual firms.

If the minimum possible costs of production are to be achieved in the motor industry, it follows from what has just been said that it would be desirable for the major firms in the industry to be large enough to achieve all the possible economies of large-scale production. However, as has been seen, no British firm is within sight of such a goal. What conclusions follow from this? In the first place, it is clear that at present the total market for British vehicles is too small. In 1955, the year of peak production, only 900,000 cars and 340,000 commercial vehicles were produced by the entire industry. For optimum technical efficiency to be approached, production on this scale would have to be divided between two basic types of car and one basic type of commercial vehicle only. It would clearly be very foolish to aim at such a goal. On the production side, it would entail extreme concentration of the industry. On the sales side, it would make for great difficulties in view of the variety of markets in which British vehicles are sold, and the failure of one model would lead to disaster for the whole industry. There is no doubt that the market for British vehicles needs to be very considerably larger than it is at present before the optimum scale of production for individual models of vehicle can be approached. However, the fact must be faced that over the next few years the market for British vehicles is unlikely to exceed one and a half to two million cars and commercial vehicles per annum, even if purchase tax in the home market is greatly reduced. In these circumstances it cannot be hoped that optimum scales of production will be achieved in the foreseeable future. They could, however, be approached more closely than they are at present if there were some reduction in the number of models produced by the large manufacturers.[1]

It is clear from the discussion in earlier chapters that there is a good deal less variety in the number of models produced by individual firms than was the case before the war, and that there is a much greater use of common parts among different models. There has also been great progress in the standardization of components since before the war, and the production of some of these, being for the

[1] The very large number of models produced by the small manufacturers is scarcely relevant to this issue, since costs in the industry as a whole are affected primarily by what is done by the large manufacturers who account for the great bulk of production.

Conclusions

whole motor industry, has approached the technical optimum. However, in spite of the progress that has been made, very much more standardization would be needed before the production of individual models could even begin to approach optimum levels of production. This could be achieved in two ways: either existing firms could produce a smaller range of models than at present, or the number of firms could be reduced. In the latter event, each of the remaining firms could produce a fairly wide range of models, but individual models could be produced on a greater scale than at present.

What has been said so far flows purely from a consideration of the optimum scale of production in the industry. Nothing has been said about how greater concentration in the industry, if it is desirable, is to be achieved, and what the repercussions on the efficiency of the industry might be of different methods of achieving greater concentration. Nor has anything been said about how far the efficiency of the industry depends on factors other than those connected with costs of production: for example, the design of vehicles and the efficiency of sales and service. Before any conclusions can be drawn regarding changes in the industry that might be desirable from the point of view of the public interest, factors such as these must be examined as well as those concerned with the technical optimum. In order to do this, the structure and behaviour of the industry has to be considered, and, in particular, the relationship between the extent of competition in the industry and the industry's present and future efficiency.

It is clear from what has been said in Chapters VII and VIII, that the motor industry is a highly competitive one. This has not been true in the past of the retail motor trade, so far as the sale of new cars is concerned, because collective resale price maintenance was firmly enforced before the Restrictive Trade Practices Act was passed at the end of 1956, and individual resale price maintenance has been firmly enforced since the Act was passed. Nor has it been true of certain sectors of the components industry, e.g. tyres, although restraints on competition in these sectors of the industry have been confined primarily to wholesale and retail sales and not to sales to vehicle manufacturers. Collective restrictive practices have, however, covered only a small part of the whole field of activity of the industry. In particular, they have been noticeably absent on the vehicle manufacturing side.

In so far as there are limitations on competition in the manufacture of components and vehicles, therefore, they arise for the most part out of the structure of the industry rather than out of deliberate attempts to suppress competition in it. As far as structure is concerned, it has been seen in Chapter VIII that in the components section of the industry there are a number of cases of single firm monopoly, or near monopoly. In most of these cases, however, the fear that vehicle manufacturers might manufacture components for themselves acts as a restraint on any tendencies towards monopolistic behaviour that there might be. On the vehicle manufacturing side, there are only five major producers left in the industry, but there is a high degree of competition between them. At first sight this may seem surprising, but it should not be forgotten that these firms manufacture products which differ a great deal from one another, and that these products are constantly changing. If in these circumstances the major vehicle manufacturers wanted to make an agreement to restrain competition, they would find it very difficult to do so. It would not be sufficient to make an agreement on prices. Agreement would have to be reached on types of model to be produced, on types of model changes to be made, on the frequency of model changes, and on a host of other matters. It could no doubt be done, if there were the will, but it would not be easy to do. As it is, there is not the will, and the fact that two of the largest and fastest-growing firms in the British industry, Ford and Vauxhall, are owned by American firms—firms moreover which are keen rivals in the United States—is a guarantee that in the foreseeable future no combined action on prices or products is likely to take place in the industry. It would be unfair to the remaining large British producers not to add that they, for their part, show no sign of a lack of the competitive spirit.

When all this has been said, it remains true that competition among vehicle producers takes place according to certain fairly clear rules, even though these are never explicitly formulated and are not the subject of any agreement among firms. These rules stem partly from the structure of costs in the industry (see Chapter V) and partly from the small number of large producers. They dictate a policy of 'model-price' competition, as it has earlier been called. Straight price competition is very rare in the industry. Normally, prices remain fixed for long periods of time, being changed by manufacturers when costs change for the industry as a whole, or when new or 'face-lifted' models are introduced. Competition between manufacturers takes the form, by and large, of an attempt to build models which are better than those produced by competing firms but which sell within the same price range. Efficiency in manufacture, deriving from large-scale production or from technical excellence, is reflected either in models which give better value for money or in bigger profit margins, or possibly in both, rather than in lower prices. When manufacturing efficiency is allied with models whose qualities appeal to the public —the two do not necessarily go together—profits can be very high. As was seen in Chapter IX, the profits earned by different firms, selling cars in approximately the same price range as each other, often differ widely.

With this pattern of behaviour, the motor industry cannot be said to be other than very imperfectly competitive in the text-book sense of the word, but it will probably be generally agreed that in the layman's sense it is very competitive. Competition takes place in quality rather than in price. Firms which achieve low costs or offer good products for sale succeed in growing while those which do not, decline. There is a constant pressure on firms in the industry to keep on their toes technically and otherwise if they are to continue to be successful. New firms are free to enter the industry without any other handicap than that automatically created by the fact that others are already well established there.[1] It is true that this makes entry very difficult in practice, but entry is not artificially restricted and efficient small firms are able to expand, as Jaguar has done since the war. One can conclude that the British motor industry, if by no means perfectly competitive, is what American economists would call 'workably competitive', and is likely to remain so in the foreseeable future.

It is natural to inquire how far the type of competition that exists in the motor industry has led to efficiency in the past and is likely to do so in the future. Before an answer to this question can be attempted two difficulties must be faced. The first is that 'efficiency' is an ambiguous term and there is no one definition of it on which everybody would agree. The second—and this is by far the greater of the two difficulties—is that, even when agreement has been reached on the meaning of 'efficiency', it is very hard to decide how far any particular industry or any particular group of firms can be said to be efficient. The task becomes a little more manageable perhaps when it is realized that the interesting question is not 'is this industry efficient?' but 'how efficient is this industry?'—as compared, for example, with motor industries in other countries or with other industries in the same country. Even so, value judgments become of predominant importance in questions of this sort, and it is very likely that different answers would be given to them by different commentators. The

[1] Corwin D. Edwards, *Maintaining Competition*, McGraw Hill, 1949, pp. 9–10.

paragraphs which follow must be read in the light of these considerations, and what is said in them must be regarded as the opinion of two commentators only—an opinion which others may not share.

There would perhaps be fairly wide agreement for the view that the efficiency of an industry can be assessed by reference to what has happened to real costs of production in the industry over time, to the amount of technical progress that has taken place in the industry, and to the industry's ability to survive and grow in a competitive environment. Other criteria could be suggested, but it would probably be agreed that those mentioned are among the most important of those which need consideration. It would probably be agreed also that of the three criteria, the last is by far the most important. Few would deny that real costs of production have been greatly reduced over the years in the British motor industry, or that considerable technical progress has been made. But the motor industry is not alone in these achievements. Other British industries have made considerable progress also, as have industries in other countries, including the motor industries of other countries. There is little doubt that the motor industry is among the most progressive of British industries, but then it is generally true that the motor industry of any major manufacturing country is among the most efficient of its industries. This is, in a sense, a tribute to motor industries in general, but to say that most motor industries are progressive does not help to throw light on the competitive efficiency of the British industry. Undoubtedly the most searching test of the industry is to examine how far it has been able to survive and grow in competitive conditions. Perhaps the most acceptable way of making such an examination in the case of the motor industry is to point to comparative prices and comparative sales performance in export markets. By this criterion, the British motor industry was not very efficient before the war, especially in comparison with the United States industry. Since the war, the industry has, it is true, done very much better, its performance being particularly impressive in the years immediately following the war. The American industry has been prevented from being an effective competitor by restrictions on dollar imports, but in any event the type of car now being produced in the United States does not appear to be very suitable for most other markets (*v.* Appendix B). It was not until the mid-1950s that a really serious competitor to the United Kingdom, in the shape of Germany, emerged in the car market and, to a lesser extent, in the commercial vehicle market. It is true that circumstances were generally favourable to the British industry during the post-war decade, but it is also true that, by and large, the industry took advantage of its post-war opportunities with both hands. The setback to exports in 1956 led to a reassessment of the industry's competitive strength in export markets. It showed up weaknesses in sales and service which had been partly obscured by the boom conditions of previous years, and it gave pause to those who held that the British type of car—four wheels, four doors, four-cylinder engine, water-cooled and placed at the front—was the ideal design. However, the export successes of 1957 revived the faith of those who had always asserted that British cars were just as good as Continental cars and that 1956 had been a bad year for British exports for exceptional reasons. It seems fairly clear that on the score of prices in export markets (v. Appendix C) British cars are on the whole fully competitive with those from other Continental countries with the exception of the German Volkswagen. It is suggested in Appendix C, after a study of prices in home as well as in export markets, that the indications are that British costs of production at the end of 1956 were by no means out of line with costs in other European countries.

As compared with the motor industries of other countries, then, the British industry shows up fairly well on its performance since the war. It seems to have been fully competitive on the score of costs of production, but has perhaps been somewhat less impressive—although not to the extent that many of its critics would argue—as regards vehicle design, salesmanship and service. These last remarks apply particularly to cars. Where commercial vehicles are concerned, and particularly heavy commercial vehicles, the British industry has been in the forefront from a design point of view.

What of the future? The pattern that competition has taken in the British motor industry in the past shows no signs of any fundamental alteration. It is likely that firms will continue to rely on a combination of quality and price competition, and that they will continue to compete by introducing new models, or substantially new models, every few years. It is also likely that each of the large firms will continue to produce a fairly wide range of models with a high proportion of common parts. It does not seem probable, for reasons explained in Chapter VIII, that the Volkswagen pattern of concentration on a single model will deliberately be adopted by the large firms in this country, although if any firm produces a model that turns out to be outstandingly successful it will no doubt concentrate a very substantial part of its production on it. As far as types of car are concerned, it seems probable, for the present at any rate, that the cars produced by the large British firms will continue to be of the traditional type. If, however, the very small cars now being sold in such large numbers on the Continent continue to be successful, the large firms will eventually be forced to produce them.

In these circumstances, there will undoubtedly continue to be a good deal of duplication between firms, and individual firms will continue to expend a good deal of energy in adding, for competitive reasons, new features to their models. Many of the features will be of little real value to the motorist, but if the past can be taken as a guide, some will certainly embody real progress in design. The out and out advocate of rationalization will not be happy at this state of affairs, because it will leave the scale of production in the industry a long way from the technical optimum. There will still be far too many models for the lowest possible costs of production to be achieved. Unfortunately, the critics do not always face up to the implications of the position they have adopted. As long as there are five major producers, there are bound to be ten or more different models of car produced. In decrying what they consider to be an excessive number of models, the critics are really asking for a major change in the structure of the industry, i.e. a 'Big Two' or 'Three' instead of a 'Big Five'.

Once this is realized, the proponents of model reduction must ask themselves such practical and awkward questions as: who is to be eliminated and how is this to be accomplished? A policy of fewer models means fewer firms—and this can only be brought about by competitive elimination of firms, by mergers, by nationalization, or by cartelization. The first method has certainly been effective in the past, but its great weakness is that it takes time: it can only be a long-run solution to the problem. The second method—mergers—is not such a simple and easy means of concentrating productive resources as might be supposed. Mergers cannot be arranged at short notice, for they are the outcome of particular circumstances and personalities, and are associated with competitive elimination. The entire history of the British motor industry reveals very few mergers between *successful* firms: almost invariably one of the parties to a merger has been bankrupt or on the verge of liquidation. The British Motor Corporation is the exception rather than the rule. Nationalization or cartelization (i.e. some form of industry-wide agreement on rationalization of production and allocation of markets) might perhaps supply a speedier solution to the problem. However, they raise a number of other issues and both, of course, mean the abandonment of competitive enterprise, with or without changes in ownership and control.

In short, a policy of fewer models means fewer companies; and this structural change can only be brought about by one of the methods outlined above. Nothing can be gained by agitating for fewer models in the manner of the preacher denouncing sin. The number of models depends on the pattern of demand and the number of major firms, and not, by and large, on the wickedness or stupidity of the car manufacturers. The demand pattern and the number of large firms surviving have both been historically determined by the interplay of consumer tastes and competition, and neither are likely to change in the near future unless very positive and far-reaching steps are taken to alter them. In considering whether such steps should be taken it should not be forgotten that competition has in the past been a potent source of technical progress. It is doubtful whether technical progress would have taken place on the scale it has, in the British industry and in the motor industries of other countries, if competition in the industry had been less keen. An imposed scheme of rationalization might well lead in the short run to greater economies of large-scale production and lower costs, but in the long run it might lead to a diminution in the competitive strength of the industry because it would remove, wholly or partially, the impetus given by the uncertainties of active competition.

If one concludes that the case for some form of control over the motor industry, in order to bring about greater rationalization, is a weak one, one is faced with something of a dilemma. As at present constituted, the industry is producing vehicles on a scale which is far from the technical optimum. This has not so far prevented it from producing vehicles at costs as low as those of most of its rivals on the Continent, but then they too are for the most part producing at scales below the optimum. The one firm—Volkswagen, whose production is on a scale approaching the optimum, appears to have lower costs than any other, although it is true that its low costs are also attributable to the fact that it has been producing the same model for many years. With the prospect of a European Free Trade Area, the market possibilities facing firms in the motor industry are bound to widen. It was suggested in Chapter X that the British industry is well placed fundamentally for the struggle that lies ahead but that it may not be very successful unless the scale of production of individual mass-produced models is appreciably increased. An approach towards the technical optimum is particularly desirable, therefore, in view of the prospects of a Free Trade Area in Europe, but the case for some form of control over the industry to bring this about is not a strong one.

There are, fortunately, grounds for hoping that this dilemma may be resolved, at least in part, as a consequence of the natural workings of competition in the industry. As was seen in Chapter X, competition in the industry is likely to intensify a good deal in the immediate future, and it will intensify even more if a European Free Trade Area is set up. The industry deserves credit for the extent to which it has expanded its output in response to post-war demand at home and abroad, but potential output is now so high that overcapacity in the industry may well arise during the course of the next few years unless demand at home and abroad proves to be extremely buoyant. Manufacturers are aware of the prospect and have been preparing themselves for it, but it is not to be expected that all will be equally successful when the time comes. Given the history and the circumstances of the motor industry, it seems very likely that the outcome of this situation will be a further round of horizontal mergers. Some of these are likely to be between 'Big Five' firms and specialists, but further mergers among the members of the 'Big Five' cannot be ruled out as a possibility. Perhaps the BMC merger will prove more typical of the future than of the past. It is these latter mergers particularly that are likely to make it possible for really substantial economies of large-scale production to be reaped. As for the smaller firms, the tendency may well be for more and more of the smaller car manufacturers to give up the unequal struggle, although such firms as Jaguar, with their outstanding competition record, will no doubt survive and grow. The disappearance of many makes of car will be regretted by the enthusiast for motor cars, but will make relatively little difference either to the pattern of competition in the industry or to its efficiency at home and its success abroad. On the commercial vehicle side, there may well be a further reduction in the number of independent specialist firms, although the bigger firms, such as Leyland, will almost certainly continue to play an important role in the industry. The speed with which all these developments are likely to occur, if indeed they do occur, is likely to be in direct proportion to the strength of competitive pressure at home and abroad.

So far, attention has been concentrated on the possibility of changes in the structure of the industry in the direction of greater horizontal integration. It should not be forgotten that during the last few years the structure of the industry has been modified considerably by greater vertical integration, and there is every possibility that further integration in this direction will take place during the next few years. Some observers have welcomed this trend. They have pointed out that in the United States and on the Continent firms are more highly integrated than in Britain, and they have therefore concluded that further vertical integration in this country is bound to be a step in the right direction. However, these observers have ignored the fact that the United States and the Continent are in completely different categories. There is so much vertical integration in Continental countries because their components industries are much less highly developed than in the United Kingdom, where components firms are able to secure great economies by producing for the industry as a whole. Certainly, if a European Free Trade Area is formed, the British components industry is well placed to increase its exports to the Continent very considerably. In the United States industry, on the other hand, the situation is a fundamentally different one. There, the largest firms, like Ford and General Motors, are so large that they can produce for themselves many (but by no means all) of the components they need on a scale sufficient to reap all worthwhile economies of large-scale production. General Motors, after all, is far bigger than the entire British motor industry.

Some British firms, influenced by the American example, clearly have ambitions to become more vertically integrated themselves. Their claim that this is because they want to lower costs of production is not, however, an entirely convincing one. Further vertical integration would almost certainly involve the sacrifice of important economies of scale in the case of processes in which the optimum scale of production is high, and which are now being performed by one or two suppliers for the whole industry. For processes in which the optimum lies within the scale of the integrating firm, there does not appear to be much scope for reducing costs, unless the car manufacturer can be assumed to be more efficient than the supplier.[1] While there may be individual cases where such an assumption is warranted, there is no evidence to suggest that a general move in the direction of vertical integration is justified on the grounds of inefficiency of the parts and components section of the industry.

It is sometimes argued that vertical integration reduces costs to the

[1] Some savings might be obtained in transport, and in greater control over quality and the timing of deliveries, but these are not likely to be of great significance.

car manufacturer by eliminating the supplier's profit, the implication being that car prices can be reduced accordingly. But all that usually happens in this connection, when the services of an efficient supplier are dispensed with, is that the profit derived from the process is transferred from the pockets of the supplier to those of the car manufacturer.[1] The latter will not normally invest in the additional plant and equipment required for the new process, and hire the extra labour necessary to operate it, unless a reasonable profit can be made by doing so. There is no reason to suppose that the acquisition of car body firms in recent years by some of the major car manufacturers has lowered the total cost of producing cars any more than it has resulted in lower prices.

From the standpoint of the individual firm, vertical integration possesses certain advantages which, at times, outweigh the disadvantages. But this stems primarily from strategic calculations rather than from cost considerations. In a rapidly expanding market, the integrated firm can increase its output with less fear of shortages, or of high prices, of essential parts and components. Its wider control over its activities gives it greater scope in a depressed market for meeting intensified competition.[2] It is notable that since the war vertical integration in the British industry has taken place for strategic rather than cost reasons, and it seems very likely that much of the vertical integration that is contemplated at present is based mainly on strategic reasons also.

From the point of view of the public interest, however, it is doubtful whether there are strong arguments for very much more vertical integration in the British industry while it remains at about its present size. Vehicle manufacturers have the opportunity to buy, on equal terms, standardized products manufactured on an industry-wide scale. There is a danger that further vertical integration might reduce competition in the industry by denying supplies on equal terms to firms other than those which have become integrated. In so far as it leads to smaller scales of production, as it well might, it will also raise costs in the industry. Changes are certainly desirable in the components field, particularly in the direction of further standardization, but it seems likely that such changes will be brought about much

---

[1] If the supplier has been making monopoly profits, then, of course, these can be eliminated. But for the reasons given in Chapter VIII, monopoly profits on the part of suppliers are not likely to be great.

[2] Although, if it relied on suppliers, it might well benefit by obtaining parts and components at below their full cost of production.

more readily by standardization committees than by further vertical integration.

In the circumstances of the industry, it seems then that further horizontal mergers should, in general, be welcomed. They are unlikely to lead to monopoly, and should enable the technical optimum to be approached. Where further vertical integration is concerned, however, the balance of gains and losses is far less clear.

APPENDIX A

The Capital-Output Ratio in the Motor Industry

THE fact that the motor industry employs a great deal of machinery and equipment sometimes leads observers of the industry to the conclusion that the motor industry is highly capitalized in relation to other manufacturing industries. For example, the following comment appeared in *The Economist* early in 1957.[1]

'The gulf between a large profit and a small one is narrow in an industry that uses capital as heavily as motor manufacture does. A small fall in production can have a shattering effect on earnings.'

The truth of this statement is challenged in Chapter V, where it is shown that, at outputs near normal capacity, the proportion of fixed costs in total costs is quite small. A more direct refutation can be given by reference to the ratio of capital to output in the motor industry as compared with other manufacturing industries.[2] The most detailed calculation of the capital-output ratio in manufacturing industry in the United Kingdom is that carried out by Barna. Barna calculated, from fire insurance values, the replacement cost of the assets (excluding vehicles) used in British manufacturing industry in 1954. These figures make no allowance for the depreciation of assets, and therefore show the value of assets gross, at replacement values. Barna also calculated the value of fixed assets per person employed for different manufacturing industries and the ratio of fixed assets to value added (i.e. to net output) in these industries. His conclusions were as follows:[3]

---

[1] *The Economist*, March 16, 1957, p. 943.
[2] The relationship between a low proportion of fixed costs and a low capital/output ratio is not entirely a straightforward one. If capital is very short-lived, a low capital/output ratio is compatible with a high proportion of fixed costs in an industry. However, in the motor industry the life of most capital assets is not exceptionally short, so that a low capital/output ratio and a low proportion of fixed costs go together. The relationship is also complicated by the distinction between gross output and net output (i.e. gross output less the cost of raw materials). *v.* footnote 1, p. 208 below.
[3] T. Barna, 'The replacement cost of fixed assets in British manufacturing in 1955', *Journal of the Royal Statistical Society*, Volume 120, Part I, 1957, p. 24.

	1954 Fixed assets per person employed[1] £	Ratio of fixed assets to value added
Motor, cycle and aircraft	1,740	2.1
All manufacturing industries	1,740	2.2

It would appear, therefore, that both the amount of fixed assets per person employed in the motor industry and the ratio of assets to net output are very much the same as in manufacturing industry in general.[2] The capital-output ratio in motor manufacturing is very much lower than in those industries which really are highly capitalized, e.g. oil refining with a ratio of 7.9, and coke ovens with a ratio of 7.7. Even textiles have a much higher ratio (3.9) than the motor industry.

Confirmation of these conclusions is given in calculations that have been made for the United States by Creamer.[3] Creamer's calculations are on a different basis from those of Barna, and are therefore not directly comparable with his. His measure of capital is of fixed plus working capital at balance sheet values, i.e. *after* the deduction of depreciation. His measure of output is less satisfactory than Barna's, being taken gross,[4] i.e. the total value of sales adjusted for stock changes, with no deduction made for purchased raw materials, etc. Creamer's capital figures are lower in most cases than if they had been calculated on the Barna basis and his output figures are always higher. One would normally expect his capital-output ratios to be a good deal lower than if they had been calculated in the Barna manner.

Creamer found that in 1948 the ratio of capital to output in the industry producing motor vehicles, complete or parts, was .439. This was with capital at book values and output at current prices. At 1929 prices for both capital and output the ratio was .519. For all manufacturing industries the

[1] In the motor, cycle and aircraft industries, two-thirds of the value of fixed assets was accounted for by plant. In manufacturing industry as a whole the ratio of plant to buildings was slightly lower. (Barna, op. cit., pp. 16–17.)

[2] This statement refers, strictly speaking, to the motor, cycle and aircraft industries taken together. According to Barna (op. cit., p. 19), assets per head appear to be relatively low in the manufacture of some components and relatively high in the making of engines and the assembly of motor vehicles. The range is from about one-half the group average to one-half above it. In aircraft manufacture the level of assets is not high. It is clear from what Barna says that, even though the capital-output ratio is higher than 2:1 in engine manufacture and vehicle assembly (possibly as high as 3), it cannot, even here, be said to be exceptionally high in relation to the capital-output ratio in other industries.

[3] David Creamer, 'Capital and Output Trends in Manufacturing Industries, 1880–1948', *National Bureau of Economic Research, Occasional Paper 41* (New York, 1954).

[4] Less satisfactory because no account is taken of the big differences in the proportion of purchased materials in different industries.

capital-output ratio was .532 at reported values and .648 at 1929 values. These estimates confirm the Barna estimates, therefore, in that they show that the motor industry is not a highly capitalized industry in relation to other manufacturing industries. Indeed, whereas Barna's figures suggest that the motor industry ratio is almost the same as the average for all manufacturing industries, Creamer's figures, admittedly on a different basis, suggest that it is significantly below the average.[1]

Creamer attempted estimates of the capital-output ratio over a long period of years. His estimates for all manufacturing industries and for the motor industry are as follows.[2]

Ratio of total capital to output (1929 prices)

	Motors	All manufacturing industries
1880	–	.547
1890	2.000	.730
1900	3.529	.803
1900	3.650	.794
1904	2.714	.891
1909	2.203	.972
1914	1.215	1.008
1919	.876	1.022
1929	.575	.885
1937	.531	.741
1948	.519	.648

Manufacturing industry as a whole had an increasing capital-output ratio until 1919 and has had a declining ratio since. The motor industry ratio rose until 1900 only and has declined very significantly since that date. The capital-output ratio for motor cars was relatively much higher than the average for all manufacturing industries up to 1914, which suggests that it *used to be* true that the motor industry was relatively very highly capitalized, but that this has not been the case for the last forty years. It is significant that the first decade of this century, when very great falls in the capital-output ratio in the motor industry took place, saw the introduction of flow production methods in vehicle manufacture in the United States.

Certain other calculations of Creamer's are of considerable interest in throwing light on conditions of production in the motor industry. Creamer worked out the relation between numbers employed, capital and output in

---

[1] High bought-out costs in the motor industry no doubt help to explain why Creamer's figures give a different result from Barna's. In the motor industry gross output is very high in relation to net output because of the importance of bought-out costs. Barna's figures show that, even when bought-out costs are ignored, the relationship between capital and (net) output in motor manufacturing is not especially high.

[2] Creamer, op. cit., pp. 86–91.

several manufacturing industries. For the motor industry his figures are as follows.[1]

Motor Industry
Indices of ratios (calculated at 1929 prices)
(1929=100)

	1900	1909	1919	1929	1937	1948
Labour/output	964.9	598.2	162.3	100.0	96.5	82.5
Capital/labour	65.5	58.5	93.6	100.0	95.0	108.9
Capital/output	634.8	351.8	152.3	100.0	92.3	90.3

The capital/output figures are the same as those in the table given previously, expressed in index form. They show dramatically the fall in the capital/output ratio that has taken place, particularly between 1909 and 1919. The capital/labour figures follow the trend that one would expect—an increase in capital per worker; the rate of increase after 1919 has, however, been surprisingly small. The labour/output ratio shows the most dramatic movement of all—the twelvefold increase in productivity per man that took place between 1900 and 1948 (1909–19 again being the most significant period)[2] at a time when capital per man rose by only 67 per cent. In manufacturing industry as a whole the rise in productivity was only three-fold between 1900 and 1948, while capital per man rose by 113 per cent. The productivity of a dollar's worth of capital in the motor industry not only increased enormously over the period but it increased by far more than in manufacturing industry generally.

---

[1] Creamer, op. cit., p. 73.
[2] It is notable that the fall between 1929 and 1948 was not very great. This may partly be a question of the years chosen for the comparison. A comparison between 1935 and 1955 gives a better result. (*v.* p. 211 below.)

APPENDIX B

Comparative Productivity and Prices in the British and American Motor Industries

1. Mechanization and Comparative Productivity

The degree of mechanization in the motor industries of different countries differs a good deal. It is particularly interesting to compare the situation in the United Kingdom with that in the United States, where the scale of production is so much larger. The scale factor is probably the principal factor accounting for the greater mechanization to be found in the United States industry, but other factors include the greater degree of standardization (at least before the war) and the high level of labour costs in relation to machinery costs. This last factor gives American manufacturers a strong incentive to substitute capital for labour in circumstances where this would not be justified on cost grounds in this country.

Estimates of the comparative degree of mechanization in two different countries, even when they relate to the same industry, are notoriously difficult to make. Horse-power per operative is usually employed as the most readily available method of comparison, although it has many drawbacks as an indicator of capital intensity.[1] Taking horse-power in the British and American industries, Dr Rostas found that before the war the ratio of horse-power per operative in the two industries was between four to one and five to one. Since then the gap has narrowed appreciably in relative terms, but the ratio is still as much as three to one.[2]

Horse-power per 100 operatives in the UK and US motor industries[3]

	UK 1930	UK 1951
Motors and cycles	121	280

	USA 1939	USA 1954
Motor vehicles, etc.	565	875

[1] v. L. Rostas, *Comparative Productivity in British and American Industry*, Cambridge University Press, 1948, pp. 15–16.

[2] Nineteen fifty-four was a year of low employment in the US motor industry. Using the 1954 horse-power figures (the only ones available) and the much higher 1953 employment figures, horse-power per 100 operatives works out at only 695. On this basis, there has been in the USA a smaller absolute increase in horse-power per head than in the UK and not only a smaller relative increase.

[3] Pre-war figures from Rostas, op. cit., p. 177. Post-war figures for the UK from *Census of Production, 1951*, Summary Tables, Part II, p. 41. Post-war figures for the USA from 1954 *Census of Manufactures*, Bulletin MC-37A. Motor Vehicles and Equipment.

Appendix B

The higher degree of mechanization in the American motor industry is allied with much higher productivity per worker than in this country. Dr Rostas found that in 1935 the output of vehicles per head was three times as high in the United States motor industry as in the British motor industry.[1] Allowing for the shorter hours worked in the American industry, the ratio of productivity per man hour was four to one. In Germany, it appears, output per head in the motor industry was virtually the same as in Britain[2], at a time when German vehicle production was at two-thirds the British level.

Dr Rostas estimated that between 1924 and 1935 output per man year doubled in the British motor industry, but he made no similar estimate for the movement in American productivity over these years. Since 1935, productivity has undoubtedly increased in both Britain and the United States. Very approximate estimates suggest that the gap between the two countries may have narrowed somewhat in recent years.

Number of vehicles produced per man per year[3]

	1935	1950	1955	Ratio 1955:1935
United Kingdom	2.8	3.6	4.5	1.6
United States	8.8	10.4	11.2	1.3
Ratio USA:UK	3.1	2.9	2.5	

In looking at the figures for 1950 and 1955 it should be borne in mind that these were years of high output and employment in both the United Kingdom and the United States, but that vehicle output rose very much more in Britain than in America between 1950 and 1955—well over 50 per cent as compared with less than 15 per cent. In Britain during this period employment in firms making parts and accessories for the motor industry rose by 50 per cent, but by 11 per cent only in firms engaged directly on vehicle manufacture. Looking at the vehicle manufacturing firms alone, output per man year appears to have risen by between 35 and 40 per cent between 1950 and 1955.

Comparisons of this sort between industries in different countries are open to criticism on the grounds that like is not being compared with like. Where vehicles are concerned, it is obvious that the types of vehicle produced in the United Kingdom and the United States were not the same

---

[1] Rostas, op. cit., Appendix 17, p. 171. In motor vehicle manufacture alone (i.e. excluding those employed in making parts and accessories), the ratio was as high as five to one.

[2] L. Rostas, 'Industrial Production, Productivity and Distribution in Britain, Germany, and the United States', *Economic Journal*, April 1943, p. 46.

[3] i.e. total number of cars and commercial vehicles produced in each year divided by the total number of operatives employed in the motor industry (including those making parts and accessories). Differences in the degree of integration between US and UK vehicle manufacturers do not therefore distort the comparison.

before the war and are not the same now.[1] Nevertheless, when all the qualifications have been made, there can be no doubt that productivity per head in the American motor industry is considerably higher than in the British. It is probably true also that the gap is now less wide than it was before the war.

It would be interesting to know to what extent different factors account for the considerable difference in productivity per head that is still to be found between the British and American motor industries. Obviously, a very important factor is the difference in scale of production, leading to greater mechanization and hence to high output per head. Table 1 of Chapter VI (p. 88) indicates that, with a rise in output from 100,000 to 400,000 units, direct labour costs per unit of output might fall by 24 per cent. This implies a rise in the productivity of direct labour of approximately one-third. If, as a result of an increase in the scale of production, such an increase of productivity were to occur in the UK,[2] it would reduce the ratio of US/UK productivity from 2.5 to 1.9. If output in the UK could rise to scales above 400,000 for a single model, the gap would obviously be narrowed still more. However, it is difficult to believe on the evidence that the gap would completely disappear, even if American scales of production could be reached in this country. Other factors are certainly at work. An important one, mentioned previously, is the high level of labour costs in relation to machinery costs in the USA. This gives rise to a substitution of capital for labour (and hence to higher output per head) in circumstances where it would not be justified on cost grounds in this country. Among other factors that might be mentioned is the possibility that general managerial efficiency is greater in the USA or that operatives work harder. It is impossible to know what weight, if any, to assign to these factors. If some observers are to be believed, however, the possibility of greater managerial efficiency in the US motor industry cannot be ignored.

2. Comparative Costs and Prices

Higher productivity per head does not necessarily imply lower overall costs of production, but it is certainly the case that, in the motor industry, American costs were a good deal lower than British before the war in spite of much higher labour costs in America. Exact comparisons cannot be

---

[1] Rostas points out, however (*Comparative Productivity in British and American Industry*, op. cit., p. 167), that in 1935 the ratio of commercial vehicle to car production was much the same in the two countries and that while American cars were on the average bigger than British cars, British lorries were bigger than American lorries.

[2] The figures in Chapter VI imply that the rise would be less than this. Indirect labour costs do not fall at all, so that in relation to all labour employed productivity would not rise by as much as one-third. However, since the table probably underestimates the fall in costs that would actually take place if output increased from 100,000 to 400,000 units, it may not be unreasonable to assume an overall rise in output per head of one-third.

made because of differences in type of product. A measure that is often used for broad comparisons, although a very crude one, is average cost per pound of vehicle weight. On this basis, it has been suggested that in 1938 costs of production were 1s 3d per pound in Britain, and about 40 per cent less in the United States. By 1947, costs are said to have doubled in both countries, leaving the relationship between them the same.[1]

The British industry was given a cost advantage *vis-à-vis* the American by the devaluation of 1949. This can be seen by examining comparative wages in the two countries. In April 1949, average hourly earnings in the British motor industry were 43d compared with 100d in the American industry—a ratio of 1:2.3. In April 1950, average British earnings were 45d per hour, while American earnings, at the new exchange rate, were 150d per hour—a ratio of 1:3.3. In the years following 1950, British earnings rose faster than American. By April 1955, the ratio of British to American earnings had fallen to 1:3 and by April 1956 to 1:2.8. As far as earnings were concerned, therefore, the advantage given by the 1949 devaluation had been reduced by 1956, but it had by no means been entirely wiped out.

Movements in relative earnings can, of course, give only an indication of movements in relative costs as a whole. Another guide to movements in relative costs in Britain and America during the years under consideration is the relation between the home market prices for cars in the two countries. When this relationship is examined it is clear that car prices, calculated on a pence per lb. basis, have not been very far apart in recent years and indeed have been moving closer together. At the end of 1952, for example, the price per lb. in the United States of the Chevrolet four-door sedan (one of the cheapest American cars and in 1952 one of the most popular) was 46d per lb., and the price of the Ford 6 was 45.5 per lb. At that time, the Ford Anglia was the cheapest British car, at 45.5d per lb.[2] The average price of the five British mass-produced cars in the 1 to 1½ litre class[3] was 52.5d per lb. At the end of 1956, the most popular of the low-priced American cars were V-8s, with automatic transmission. The price per lb. of the Chevrolet V-8 was 62.5d and of the Ford V-8 59.5d. The price per lb. of the Chevrolet 6 without automatic transmission was 53.5d and of the Ford 6 54d. At that time the cheapest British car by far was the Ford Popular at 40.5d per lb. The average price of the five mass-produced

---

[1] PEP, op. cit., p. 126.

[2] In calculating American prices, prices delivered at the factory, including Federal excise tax but not local taxes, have been taken. In calculating British prices, prices excluding purchase tax have been taken. Without Federal tax, the American prices would be approximately 9 per cent lower than shown here.

[3] Austin A40, Morris Oxford, Ford Consul, Hillman Minx, Vauxhall Wyvern. This group has been taken as the group of British models with the lowest average price. The average price of the smaller Morris Minor and Austin A30 was 56d per lb.

cars in the 1–1½ litre class had risen to 54.5d per lb., but it was now much closer to the American level.

It is obvious that comparisons of this sort, based on the price per pound weight of cars, provide only the roughest of guides to comparative prices, and hence to comparative costs of production. They ignore quality of finish and bodywork, comfort, fuel economy, engine performance, ease of driving, and a host of other factors of great importance to the motorist. They may even bias results in the wrong direction: when, for example, aluminium doors are substituted for steel, the car is made lighter in weight and its performance improved, but the price per pound weight (assuming the price of the car to be unchanged) has risen, so that it would appear that the value for money offered by the car had decreased when in fact it had increased. Objections of this sort are particularly powerful when the prices per pound of two cars at any one moment of time are compared. When comparisons of the movement of relative prices per pound over time are made, however, it seems more reasonable to argue that the comparisons have some significance, even when one is comparing movements in the prices of cars so dissimilar as an American Ford 6 and a British Ford Consul.

It has sometimes been suggested that an alternative basis of comparison, one based on price in relation to (brake) horse-power, would be superior to one based on price per pound weight, since it would give a measure of price in relation to performance. Such a basis of comparison has its attractions, especially when it has been modified to take into account engine power in relation to vehicle weight—the performance of a vehicle is better judged by its power/weight ratio than by its engine power alone. If a comparison of this type is made for Britain and America, what does it show? In America, the Ford V-8 cost £5.7 per horse-power in 1952 and only £4.5 per horse-power in 1956. If the figures are adjusted to take account of the increased weight of the car, the equivalent 1956 figure becomes £5.1. In Britain, the Ford Consul cost £10 per horse-power in 1952 and £8.7 per horse-power in 1956. When the figures are adjusted for weight, the equivalent 1956 figure is £9.5. Comparing the price per horse-power adjusted for weight in the two years, the price of the American car was 57 per cent of the British car in 1952 and 54 per cent in 1956.[1] On this basis, therefore, assuming that the two cars selected are reasonably representative, the results arrived at are quite different from those arrived at previously on the basis of price per pound weight. Prices fell, not rose, in both Britain and America between 1952 and 1956. American cars were cheaper than British cars in 1952 and had become relatively cheaper still by 1956.

In assessing the value of the comparison that has just been made, it should be remembered that in the early 1950s American manufacturers

[1] American manufacturers are more generous in their assessment of the brake horse-power of their cars than British manufacturers. The numerical comparison, therefore, exaggerates the absolute difference in price.

were engaged in a 'horse-power race'. One of their main concerns, it is not unfair to say, was to get the maximum horse-power out of their engines. In Britain, on the other hand, increased horse-power was certainly a consideration but to nothing like the extent it was in the United States. Other desirable ends, for example, increased fuel efficiency, were pursued much more actively in Britain. In the circumstances, it would seem dangerous to place too much weight on price comparisons based on price per horse-power during the period 1950–56. Comparisons based on price per pound weight, although far from perfect, are probably a good deal more trustworthy as a guide to changes in the relative value for money offered by British and American cars during the period and hence to changes in relative costs of production. It will be remembered that the conclusion that is suggested by the figures of price per pound—that British and American costs have moved closer together during the last few years—is consistent with what is known of the movement in relative productivity per worker.

Whatever dispute there may be about changes in British and American car prices in relation to the quality of the vehicles, there is no doubt that in absolute terms the gap between the prices of cars in the two countries has widened very appreciably in recent years. In 1952, the price of a Chevrolet 6 in the United States was £600,[1] and the price of a Ford V-8 was £625. At that time the Ford Consul cost £470 in Britain, excluding tax, and the Austin A40 £467. At the end of 1956, the Chevrolet V-8 (with automatic transmission) cost £870, and the Ford V-8 £860. The Ford Consul had risen in price to £520 and the price of the Austin A50 was £514. The increase in the size of American cars, together with the incorporation of features, now practically standard, such as automatic transmission, had raised their prices by far more than those of British cars, whose specifications had altered much less drastically. In export markets, such as Switzerland, where motorists were able to choose between buying cars from all the major producing countries, American mass-produced cars had to be considered, in 1956, as in a completely different price class from typical mass-produced British or Continental cars. In Switzerland, in October 1956, the British Morris Minor cost £487, the Ford Consul £729, the Ford Zephyr £855, the Standard Vanguard £888, and the Chevrolet Bel Air £1,254.[2] At the same time, and in the same market, however, British and Continental cars were very competitive in price.[3] They had to be, since as vehicles they were very similar—except that there were virtually no British counterparts for the smallest Continental cars—and in direct competition with one another. Practically none of them, however, could be said to be directly competitive with American cars.

[1] With automatic transmission, the price was £695.
[2] *The Economist*, 'Motors with the Brake on', p. 3, October 20, 1956.
[3] *v.* Appendix C for a discussion of the relative prices of British and Continental cars in home and export markets.

APPENDIX C

The Relative Prices of British and Continental Cars

A COMPARISON of the current prices of British and Continental cars is obviously of interest from a short-term point of view for the light it throws on the present competitive strength of the motor industries concerned. It is of interest from a longer term point of view for any light it may throw on the possible competitive strength of the British and Continental motor industries when the European Free Trade Area becomes a reality.

To deal with export markets first: when the situation in export markets towards the end of 1956 is examined it is clear that British and Continental cars were on the whole comparable in price. Prices are given in Table 5 at the end of this Appendix of some representative mass-produced cars from the United Kingdom, France, Italy and Germany in three markets: Australia, and two European countries which do not produce cars, the Netherlands and Switzerland. In Australia, where Imperial preference helped British cars, Continental cars were appreciably dearer than British cars, size for size, with the exception of the Volkswagen which was priced very competitively. In the Netherlands and Switzerland, the prices of comparable British and Continental cars were much closer together, although in terms of pence per pound weight, British cars were, if anything, cheaper than those from other countries.

TABLE 1
Car prices in export markets. October 1956
d per lb.

British	Netherlands	Switzerland	Australia
Morris Minor 2-door	64.0	66.5	92.5
Hillman Minx de luxe	68.5	75.5	99.5
Ford Consul	64.0	71.0	96.5
French			
Renault 4 c.v.	77.0	85.5	134.5
Peugeot 203	77.0	76.5	113.0
Renault Frégate	61.0	69.0	103.0
Italian			
Fiat 600	80.5	75.5	125.0
Fiat 1100	70.5	70.5	n.a.
Fiat 1400	77.0	77.5	109.0
German			
Volkswagen	65.6	69.5	n.a.
Volkswagen de luxe	73.5	78.5	117.0
Opel Olympia Rekord	73.0	76.0	n.a.

Appendix C 217

In the Netherlands, only the Renault Frégate was cheaper, on a pence per pound basis, than all three British cars quoted, and the Volkswagen was the only other car of a comparable price. In Switzerland, where British cars were at a disadvantage on account of the longer freight, the Morris Minor was the cheapest car on a pence per pound basis of all those quoted. The only Continental cars which were cheaper than the British cars of comparable size were the Fiat 1100, the Volkswagen, and the Renault Frégate, with the Opel and the Peugeot 203 not very far away.

Comparisons on the basis of price per pound, which are not very satisfactory at the best of times (see page 214 above), are even less satisfactory when cars of such different types as the Morris Minor and the Volkswagen are compared. The Volkswagen suffers somewhat in these pence per pound comparisons from the fact that it is an exceptionally light car for its size and power, just as the Renault Frégate benefits in the comparisons from the fact that it is rather a heavy car for its size. Looking at the price of the Volkswagen in Switzerland, for example, there is little doubt that at £454 it was, quality for quality, cheaper than the Morris Minor at £487, even though it was dearer on a pence per pound basis. Apart from the Volkswagen and the Volkswagen de luxe, however, it is difficult to find any other Continental car with which British cars were not fully competitive in price in export markets at the end of 1956.[1]

The conclusion that has just been reached is scarcely a surprising one. When cars resemble each other as much as the mass-produced cars of Britain and the Continent, their manufacturers are forced to price them competitively in export markets, even though this may mean that export prices have to be lower than home market prices. It is of interest, therefore, to look at the home market prices of some of the cars whose prices in export markets have been quoted, to see whether there are any obvious cases of price discrimination between home and export markets.

In nearly all cases, the home market prices of these cars, excluding sales taxes, were well below the prices of the same cars in the three export markets quoted—the Netherlands, Switzerland and Australia (see Table 5 at the end of this Appendix). The Fiat 1100 and, to a lesser extent, the Fiat 1400 are exceptions. These cars could not have been sold in the Netherlands and Switzerland at little more than their prices in Italy unless their export price from Italy had been well below their home market price. One other exception is the Renault Frégate, which was sold in the Netherlands for less than the home market price in France.

The fact that for all cars quoted other than the Fiat 1100, the Fiat 1400 and the Renault Frégate there was a big gap between home market prices (excluding taxes) and prices (including taxes) in export markets does not of course prove that it was only these cars that were sold for export at prices

[1] Possibly the Opel Rekord was cheaper, quality for quality, than comparable British cars, but the larger Opel model (the Kapitan of 2,500 c.c.) was a good deal dearer comparatively.

TABLE 2
Home market prices. October 1956
(Prices are in £ sterling equivalent and exclude sales taxes)

	£	*d* per lb.
United Kingdom		
Morris Minor 2-door	401	54.5
Hillman Minx de luxe	515	56.5
Ford Consul	520	50.5
France[1]		
Renault 4 c.v.	330	64.0
Renault Frégate	720	62.0
Italy[2]		
Fiat 600	340	63.5
Fiat 1100	555	69.0
Fiat 1400	770	73.5
Germany		
Volkswagen	328	50.0
Volkswagen de luxe	392	58.4
Opel Olympia Rekord	545	68.5

below their home market prices. One has to take into account customs and excise duties in export markets, the cost of freight to these markets, and differences in dealers' margins between home and export markets. If this is done, it can be seen that for nearly all the cars quoted export prices must have been below home market prices. This is true for Continental exports to the UK as well as for exports to other markets by Continental and British producers. For example, the Volkswagen was sold in this country at the end of 1956 at a retail price of £422 10*s* 0*d*, excluding purchase tax. As purchase tax (£212 12*s* 0*d*) was at the rate of 60 per cent of the wholesale price, the latter must have been about £354, and the distributors' margin must have been about £68 10*s* 0*d*, i.e. just over 16 per cent of the retail price. Since the wholesale price of £354 included an import duty of 30 per cent, the landed price of the Volkswagen must have been about £270. Probably it was less than this, as no allowance has been made for administrative costs in the UK. Ignoring administrative costs, however, £270 can be taken as the approximate landed price of the Volkswagen, excluding import duty. In Germany, the retail price of the same car was £328 excluding tax. The wholesale price must have been of the order of £275. When allowance is made for freight charges between Germany and the UK, it is clear that the Volkswagen was exported to Britain at well below the home market price.

[1] French prices exclude purchase tax of 24 per cent, but include taxes levied at various stages of manufacture. These are said to amount to 15–20 per cent of the list price of a car (excluding the purchase tax).

[2] Italian prices exclude sales tax of 3 per cent, but include the turnover tax which is levied at those stages of manufacture at which raw materials, bought-out parts, etc., change hands. In all, the tax content of the list-price of a car (excluding the sales tax) may amount to something like 15–20 per cent.

A similar calculation for the Fiat 600 suggests an even greater gap between home and export prices. The Fiat 600 sold in the UK at the end of 1956 for £412 10s 0d, excluding purchase tax. The landed price of the Fiat, calculated in the same way as for the Volkswagen, must have been about £260. In Italy, on the other hand, the wholesale price of the Fiat 600, excluding tax, was about £285. A comparable calculation cannot be made for the Renault 4 c.v., which sold in the UK at the same price as the Volkswagen, since there is an assembly plant in this country, and Renault cars are imported in unassembled form. For this reason, the import duty paid on these cars, with their lower landed value, must have been less than that paid on cars imported complete such as the Volkswagen. If reasonable assumptions are made about the cost of assembly in this country, it seems possible that at the end of 1956 the Renault 4 c.v. was being landed in the UK at a price of about £290 (including cost of assembly in the UK), while the French wholesale price was about £280.

Analogous calculations can be made for cars sold in the Netherlands and Switzerland. These countries have different rates of import duty depending on whether cars are imported in assembled or unassembled form. Allowance has to be made for the appropriate import duties[1] and also for an additional import tax of 15 per cent of the duty paid value in the Netherlands and a sales tax of 5.4 per cent of the wholesale price in Switzerland. The table shows the conclusions that can be reached; it includes also the figures for the UK that were given in the previous paragraphs.

TABLE 3
End 1956

	Estimated wholesale price in home market excluding sales tax:	Estimated landed price, excluding import duties and sales taxes in:		
		Netherlands	Switzerland	UK
	£	£	£	£
Morris Minor 2-door	335	320*	300	(335)
Renault 4 c.v.	280	230	285	290*
Fiat 600	285	240	255	260
Volkswagen	275	245	285	270

* Including estimated cost of assembly in the importing market.

The table shows that in three cases only were landed prices higher than home market prices. Even in these cases—the Renault 4 c.v. in the UK and Switzerland and the Volkswagen in Switzerland—the difference between home market and landed prices were almost certainly too small to cover the cost of freight between the countries concerned. If this is so, export

---

[1] The three European cars to be considered—the Volkswagen, the Fiat 600 and the Renault 4 c.v.—are imported complete into the Netherlands and Switzerland. The British car to be considered—the Morris Minor—is imported unassembled into the Netherlands and complete into Switzerland.

prices were less than home market prices in all the cases quoted: in many of them a great deal less. Making allowance—very roughly—for freight rates, the situation may have been something like this:

TABLE 4
End 1956

	Estimated wholesale price in home market excluding sales taxes: £ (d per lb.)	Estimated export price as percentage of home market price To Netherlands and Switzerland %	To Netherlands Switzerland and UK %
Morris Minor 2-door	335 (45.5)	85	—
Renault 4 c.v.	280 (54.0)	85	90
Fiat 600	285 (55.0)	80	80
Volkswagen	275 (42.0)	90	90

In the markets under review, the Fiat 600 export price appears to have been something like 20 per cent less than the home market price as compared with 10 per cent less in the case of the Volkswagen, 10–15 per cent for the Renault and 15 per cent for the Morris. The discrepancy between home and export prices for Fiat would have been more striking if the calculations had been made for the Fiat 1100 or the Fiat 1400. As has been noted earlier, the retail prices of these models in the Netherlands and Switzerland, including tax, were not much higher than the home market prices in Italy, excluding tax. In spite of the heavy price reductions for export, Fiat cars were not outstandingly cheap in export markets. These price reductions were necessary to make these cars, which were expensive in their home market, competitive abroad. Taking both home and export prices into account, it seems reasonable to conclude that the average price of Fiat cars was higher than that of the other three cars examined in Table 4.[1]

If Table 4 is broadly accurate, there is not much to choose in the matter of price discrimination in export markets between the British, French and German cars that have been considered. However, the Volkswagen was the cheapest in its own home market, followed (on a pence per pound basis) by the Morris and the Renault, in that order. Taking home and export prices together, there is not much doubt that the average price at which the Volkswagen was sold was the lowest of the three, quality for quality. As between the Morris and the Renault 4 c.v., there is room for dispute. Con-

[1] One would expect the costs of producing such small cars as the Fiat 600 to be higher, per pound of weight, than that of producing larger cars such as the Volkswagen (v. statement of Managing Director of Vauxhall, 1957, when he said that for cars smaller than the Vauxhall Victor value was squeezed out quicker than costs). This factor has to be taken into account when appraising the relative prices of cars of different size. In the calculations above, however, the fact that the Fiat 1100 and 1400 have been taken into account helps to ensure that this factor has not distorted the comparisons as far as Fiat is concerned.

sidering the larger size of the Morris, it may not be too partisan to conclude that the Morris was the cheaper, quality for quality. If another British car such as the Ford Anglia (wholesale price c. £300=43d per lb.) had been chosen,[1] there would have been less room for doubt. The British cars would have appeared even cheaper comparatively if the Renault Dauphine (wholesale price c. £370=63.5d per lb.) had been chosen as the basis of comparison, although a comparison with the Citroen 2 c.v. (wholesale price c. £260=51d per lb.) would not have been so unfavourable to France. In examining these prices it must be remembered that the French exchange rate at the end of 1956 was almost certainly overvalued. On balance, it may be fair to conclude that at the end of 1956 the prices of the Morris Minor and other comparable British cars were, on average, less in home and export markets than that of the Renault, but that when allowance is made for the unrealistic French exchange rate, there was less to choose between the Renault and the British cars.

The calculations that have just been made refer to the average selling prices of cars in home and export markets. They cannot be taken as an indication of costs of production because they make no allowance for the taxes levied at various stages of manufacture in France and Italy. Because of the way in which these taxes are levied, it is not possible to calculate precisely how much they amount to. It is understood that a figure of 15–20 per cent may be approximately correct for both countries. If this amount is deducted from the French and Italian car prices that have been quoted, these prices are brought much more closely into line with German and British prices. Volkswagen prices would still appear to be the lowest, but it is extremely difficult to say how far there is a difference between British, French and Italian prices. Taking all the Fiat models into account, Italian prices are still perhaps the highest of the three,[2] but as between French and British prices it is impossible to choose.

Having carried out all these calculations, what one would like to do would be to draw general conclusions about the comparative costs of producing cars in Germany, France, Italy and Britain. If it is assumed—and this is probably not too wide of the mark—that comparative prices may be taken as a guide, it is, as has just been seen, extremely hard to be sure how prices, excluding taxes, really do compare.[3] What is more, the comparisons that have been made are very limited in scope. They have been

[1] The Ford Popular (wholesale price £230=34d per lb.) would have been the most favourable case to take, but it has not been considered because it is essentially a pre-war type of car, not comparable with the other British and foreign cars quoted.

[2] This conclusion is reinforced when the indirect subsidies on exports given in France and Italy (v. Chapter VIII, p. 144) are taken into account. These subsidies give scope for Italian costs, in particular, to be higher than is indicated by the prices charged.

[3] The problem is made even more difficult when it is remembered that no account has been taken in all the calculations of social security taxes on employers,

made for selected cars in three export markets only. In defence, it can be said that the cars chosen for the comparisons have been among the leading models of their respective countries and that if other important models had been chosen, or if other markets had been considered, the results would not have been very different. If these arguments are accepted, one might perhaps put forward the following conclusions very tentatively. At the end of 1956, among European mass-produced cars,[1] costs were probably lowest in the case of the German Volkswagen. Costs may have been highest for the mass-produced Italian cars, while French and British mass-produced cars possibly occupied an intermediate position. As between the costs of Italian and of French and British cars there does not, however, seem to have been a great deal to choose.

TABLE 5
Car prices in export markets. October 1956*
(Prices are in £ sterling equivalent and include local taxes)

	Netherlands	Switzerland	Australia
British			
Morris Minor 2-door (803 c.c.)	468	487	678
Hillman Minx de luxe (1,390 c.c.)	622	688	907
Ford Consul (1,702 c.c.)	658	729	990
French			
Renault 4 c.v. (747 c.c.)	395	440	691
Peugeot 203 (1,290 c.c.)	658	650	962
Renault Frégate (2,141 c.c.)	708	806	1,198
Italian			
Fiat 600 (633 c.c.)	420	403	670
Fiat 1100 (1,089 c.c.)	565	566	n.a.
Fiat 1400 (1,395 c.c.)	807	812	1,142
German			
Volkswagen (1,192 c.c.)	427	454	n.a.
Volkswagen de luxe (1,192 c.c.)	493	525	786
Opel Olympia Rekord (1,490 c.c.)	580	604	n.a.

* Source: *The Economist*, 'Motors with the Brake on', October 20, 1956, p. 3.

which are different in all the countries under consideration. However, taxes of this sort must be ignored for the present purpose. To consider the role that they play in affecting comparisons of prices would raise very broad issues about the financial structure of different countries which cannot be pursued in the present context.

[1] Ignoring the Ford Popular.

APPENDIX D

STATISTICAL TABLES

Table 1
UK Production of Motor Vehicles

Year	Cars* 000's	Commercial Vehicles 000's	Agricultural Tractors 000's
1913		34	
1922		73	2
1923	71	24	n.a.
1925	132	35	n.a.
1929	182	56	10
1930	170	67	15
1931	159	67	4
1932	171	61	3
1933	221	66	3
1934	257	86	4
1935	312	92	9
1936	354	108	13
1937	390	118	18
1938	341	104	10
1939	305	97	15
1945	17	122	18
1946	219	148	28
1947	287	158	56
1948	335	177	114
1949	412	218	88
1950	523	263	117
1951	476	259	137
1952	448	242	123
1953	595	240	109
1954	769	270	133
1955	898	341	133
1956	708	299	109
1957	861	290	144

* Includes taxis.

TABLE 2
New Registrations of Motor Vehicles in the UK

Year	Cars* 000's	Commercial Vehicles Goods Vehicles 000's	Hackneys 000's
1927	162	36	9
1929	169	54	11
1930	159	53	10
1931	142	52	8
1932	156	46	5
1933	187	55	4
1934	231	69	5
1935	281	69	7
1936	310	83	8
1937	318	78	9
1938	280	69	9
1939	236	63	7
1945	8	30	2
1946	122	103	4
1947	148	124	8
1948	113	108	10
1949	155	110	13
1950	134	94	11
1951	140	94	8
1952	191	85	5
1953	301	100	5
1954	394	112	6
1955	511	157	6
1956	407	151	5
1957	433	144	5

* Excludes taxis which are included under hackneys.

TABLE 3
*Vehicles in Use in the UK**

Year (as at August 31)	Cars† 000's	Commercial Vehicles Goods Vehicles 000's	Hackneys 000's
1913	88	53	35
1920	187	101	75
1929	998	336	100
1930	1,075	355	103
1931	1,104	367	89
1932	1,149	377	87
1933	1,227	395	87
1934	1,334	421	87
1935	1,505	442	87
1936	1,675	468	88
1937	1,834	488	87
1938	1,984	504	89
1939	2,073	497	92
1945	1,522	484	101
1946	1,807	572	107
1947	1,984	684	117
1948	2,002	785	131
1949	2,178	862	137
1950	2,307	916	140
1951	2,409	921	142
1952	2,521	949	138
1953	2,784	979	121
1954	3,135	1,014	112
1955	3,561	1,082	107
1956	3,925	1,143	102
1957	4,217	1,191	100

* Excluding vehicles exempt from registration, e.g. army vehicles. All figures are those of vehicles with current licences at the time of the annual census.
† Excludes taxis which are included under hackneys.

TABLE 4
UK Exports of New Motor Vehicles

Year	Cars Complete	Chassis	Commercial Vehicles Complete†	Chassis
	000's		000's	
1920	4	3	—	1
1921	2	1	—	1
1923	3	2	—	1
1925	18	10	—	2
1927	16	18	—	2
1929	24	10	3	6
1930	19	4	4	3
1931	17	2	2	3
1932	27	5	2	6
1933	34	7	2	8
1934	35	9	3	11
1935	44	10	3	11
1936	51	14	4	14
1937	54	24	4	17
1938	44	24	5	11
1946	70	17	23	23
1947	126	17	24	26
1948	195	32	37	38
1949	219	39	45	48
1950	344	55	75	71
1951	309	60	68	69
1952	276	34	62	66
1953	264	38	52	60
1954	316	50	58	69
1955	322	51	79	78
1956	290	28	70	75
1957	378*	25	82	64

* In 1957, one-third of the cars exported complete were unassembled.
† Includes station wagons (23,560 in 1957).

TABLE 5
Production of Cars—Chief Overseas Producers

Year	USA	Canada	France	Italy	Germany*
			000's		
1929	4,587	203	211	54†	117
1932	1,135	51	136	26	44
1937	3,916	153	177	61	264
1938	2,001	124	200	59	277
1945	70	2	2	2	n.a.
1947	3,558	167	66	25	10
1949	5,119	192	188	65	104
1950	6,666	285	257	101	216
1951	5,337	283	320	119	267
1952	4,337	285	370	114	301
1953	6,117	365	371	143	369
1954	5,559	282	444	181	518
1955	7,920	375	560	231	706
1956	5,816	374	663	280	848
1957	6,113	356	738	318	1,040

* Western Germany only from 1946
† Includes commercial vehicles

TABLE 6
Production of Commercial Vehicles—Chief Overseas Producers

Year	USA	Canada	France	Italy	Germany*
			000's		
1929	771	59	42	—†	39
1932	235	10	27	4	8
1937	893	54	24	10	64
1938	488	42	27	8	66
1945	656	131	33	8	n.a.
1947	1,240	91	71	18	14
1949	1,134	99	98	21	58
1950	1,337	106	100	27	90
1951	1,428	133	126	26	107
1952	1,218	149	129	25	127
1953	1,206	119	126	31	121
1954	1,042	68	156	36	162
1955	1,249	79	164	38	203
1956	1,104	99	164	36	228
1957	1,101	71	190	33	172

*Western Germany only from 1946.
† Included under cars, see Table 5.

TABLE 7
Exports of New Cars and Car Chassis from UK and Chief Overseas Producing Countries

Year	UK	USA	Canada	France	Italy	Germany*
			000's			
1929	39	340	65	39	24†	5
1932	32	41	10	14	6	9
1937	78	229	44	20	26	52
1938	68	162	40	19	18	65
1946	87	117	23	20	n.a.	n.a.
1947	143	267	42	58	10	n.a.
1949	258	140	17	76	15	14
1950	399	120	24	89	20	69
1951	369	217	37	93	29	91
1952	310	141	42	83	25	100
1953	302	154	28	81	30	138
1954	366	173	7	101	41	231
1955	373	212	12	133	69	357
1956	318	175	14	151	78	421
1957	403	141	16	219	111	502

*Western Germany from 1946.
† Includes commercial vehicles.

TABLE 8
Exports of New C.V.s and C.V. Chassis from UK and Chief Overseas Producing Countries

Year	UK	USA	Canada	France	Italy	Germany*
			000's			
1929	9	197	37	10	—†	3
1932	8	25	3	2	neg.	2
1937	21	166	22	5	8	13
1938	16	116	17	4	2	13
1946	46	168	45	13	n.a.	n.a.
1947	50	267	42	26	1	n.a.
1949	93	134	12	26	3	1
1950	146	131	10	29	2	15
1951	137	216	23	32	3	29
1952	128	155	38	24	1	37
1953	111	134	17	23	1	40
1954	127	185	4	31	3	67
1955	158	177	6	30	5	68
1956	146	198	5	25	9	79
1957	146	194	4	33	8	82

*Western Germany from 1946
† Included under cars, see Table 7.

Sources, Tables 1–8: SMMT *Motor Industry of Great Britain*
SMMT *Monthly Statistical Review.*

Appendix D

TABLE 9
Profits[a] of 'Big Six' Car Producers
1929–1957

Years to:	Austin July 31	Morris Dec. 31	BMC July 31	Ford Dec. 31 £'000's	Rootes[h] July 31	Standard Aug. 31	Vauxhall Dec. 31
1929	778[b]	1,285		909	−67[i]	−18	−260
1930	563	1,313		958	43	40	−65
1931	790	805		323	−96	71	78
1932	601	912		−51	−245	201	145
1933	631	463		−131	72	132	483
1934	821	644		831	245	107	838
1935	783	1,316		531	232	156	946
1936	736	2,037		773	242	240	1,137
1937	824	1,820		604	264	291	1,094
1938	556	1,356		406	279	165	731
1939	664	1,927		1,789	330	318	1,054
1940	654	1,521		1,740	709	180	478[j]
1941	737	1,635		2,430	751	308	480[j]
1942	1,024	1,799		1,223	1,782	230[j]	581[j]
1943	829[c]	1,980		1,254	1,438	223[j]	507[d]
1944	880[c]	2,384		1,340	1,708	244[j]	549[d]
1945	907[c]	1,943		1,444	1,510	267[j]	2,076
1946	1,025[c]	2,956		3,159	−41	281	1,475
1947	⎰ 1,307[d] ⎱ 1,808	⎰ 2,542 ⎱ 2,623		3,888	617	262	2,038
1948	1,110	1,514		5,544	1,229	899	1,958
1949	1,632	2,631		5,088	1,144	1,155	2,724
1950	5,200	7,136		9,741	2,772	1,258	2,742
1951	7,238	(8,749)[e]		9,751	3,404	2,258	2,725
1952			5,222[f]	9,595	3,368	1,601	5,291
1953			12,304	15,719[g]	3,267	1,615	9,884
1954			17,928	19,011	3,501	2,160	12,433
1955			20,251	18,094	3,312	3,305	10,833
1956			11,683	10,014	1,731	747	6,421
1957			7,811	20,574	−567	836	−2,255

Note: Horizontal lines indicate that accounts are consolidated after this date.

[a] Net profits before tax, i.e. trading profits, plus other income, less depreciation, directors' salaries, minority interests, debenture interest, etc., before deduction of preference and ordinary dividends and before deduction of tax.

[b] Calendar year.

[c] Profits *after* EPT.

[d] After taxation.

Footnotes continued on following page

e From Andrews and Brunner, *The Life of Lord Nuffield*, p. 341. For all Morris enterprises.
f Four months only.
g Briggs acquired during 1953.
h 1929–1937 figures are for Humber Ltd. only (year to August 31). In 1937–8 Humber net profits were £153,000. 1938–1949 figures are combined net profit of Rootes and its subsidiaries.
i Eleven months to July 31.
j After depreciation *and* taxation.
Source: Based on figures from Moody's Services Ltd.

LIST OF CHARTS
FIGURES AND TABLES

CHARTS AND FIGURES

Chapter V—
Figure 1. Short period unit cost curve 1954—large scale vehicle manufacturer .. .. *page* 66

Chapter VI—
Figure 2. The firm's technical economies of scale 94

Chapter VII—
Chart I. Prices of 'Big Six' 7–8 h.p. models 1929–39 101
Chart II. Prices of 'Big Six' 9–10 h.p. models 1929–39 104
Chart III. Prices of Class I (£360–£401 basic) models, 'Big Five' 1946–55 113
Chart IV. Prices of Class II (£498–£535 basic) models, 'Big Five' 1946–55 114

TABLES

Chapter I—
Table 1. Car and C.V. Production—UK and Main Producing Countries, 1947–55 (1937=100) 16

Chapter II—
Table 1. Estimated Unit Car Sales and Market Shares, 1954 .. 22
Table 2. Estimated Unit Commercial Vehicle Sales and Market Shares, 1954 25
Table 3. Major Bought-out Components as Percentage of Total Expenditure on bought-out Material in typical Small Car—Company Y, 1954 27
Table 4. Material Expenditure and Total Car Cost (per cent) .. 31

Chapter III—
Table 1. UK—Vehicles Subject to Hire Purchase Agreements, 1953–56 44
Table 2. Percentage of Total Car Registrations in the UK, 1938–55 51

Chapter V—
Table 1. Analysis of Total Cost of a Typical Car, 1954 62
Table 2. Unit Factory Cost of a Mass Produced Car, 1954 .. 63
Table 3. Costs and Volume, Firm A, 1954 65
Table 4. Firm A—Unit Cost Analysis, 1954 67

Chapter VI—
Table 1. Cost/Volume Relationship—Company X, 1954 .. 88
Appendix. Economies of Scale 98

232   *The Motor Industry*

Chapter VII—
Table 1. Domestic Car Sales, 8 h.p. and under, 1934–38 .. 102
Table 2. Share of Total 'Big Six' Car Production 1929–39 (by firms) 107
Table 3. Estimated Share of Total Production of Private Cars, 1946–55 (by firms) 117
Table 4. Saloon Models Selling at under £665 Basic—October 1956 120

Chapter VIII—
Table 1. Five Largest Tyre Manufacturers: Profits as a Percentage of Sales (1937–52) 128

Chapter IX—
Table 1. *The Economist* Index of Profits (After Tax) (1929–38) .. 152
Table 2. Seven Leading Vehicle Manufacturers—Index of Profits, 1929–38 153
Table 3. Seven Leading Vehicle Manufacturers' Index of Trading Profits, 1929–38 154
Table 4. Profits, Output, Prices and Turnover, 1929–38 (1930=100) 156
Table 5. Profits in Relation to Output and Turnover, 1929–38 (1930=100) 157
Table 6. Rates of Return on Capital, 1929–38 ('Big Six' Car Firms) 160
Table 7. Proportion of Net Earnings Retained. 'Big Six' Car Firms, 1929–38 161
Table 8. 1929–38. Funds Available, Internal and External (Long-term). ('Big Six' car firms) 162
Table 9. Net Assets, 1929–38 ('Big Six' car firms) 163
Table 10. Gross Trading Profits, 1947–56 (1947=100) 164
Table 11. Index of Trading Profits, 1949–53 165
Table 12. Profits, Output, Prices and Turnover, 1947–56 (1947= 100) 166
Table 13. Profits in Relation to Output and Turnover, 1947–56 (1947=100) 167
Table 14. Ford, Vauxhall, BMC and Standard Profit/Output. Ford and Vauxhall Profit/Turnover, 1947–56 169
Table 15. Ford Motor Company. Profits and Sales, 1955–57 .. 172
Table 16. Rates of Return on Capital, 1947–56 ('Big Five' car firms) 175
Table 17. Proportion of Net Earnings Retained. 'Big Five' car firms, 1947–56 176
Table 18. Funds Available, Internal and External (Long-term), 1947–56 ('Big Five' car firms) 177
Table 19. Net Assets, 1947–56 ('Big Five' car firms) 178

List of Charts, Figures and Tables

Table 20. Car Manufacturers—Sources and Uses of Funds, 1949–53 180

Appendix A—
Value of fixed assets per person employed and ratio of fixed assets to value added in motor and manufacturing industries (UK) .. 207
Ratio of total capital to output (1929 prices) in motor and manufacturing industries (USA) 208
Relation between numbers employed, capital and output in the motor industry (USA) 209

Appendix B—
Horse-power per 100 operatives in the UK and US motor industries 210
Number of vehicles produced per man per year in the UK and US motor industries 211

Appendix C—
Table 1. European car prices in various export markets, October 1956 216
Table 2. European cars—home market prices, October 1956 .. 218
Table 3. Estimated home market and landed prices of European cars, end 1956 219
Table 4. Estimated export prices as percentage of home market prices of European cars, end 1956 220
Table 5. European car prices in export markets, October 1956 222

Appendix D—
Table 1. UK Production of Motor Vehicles, 1913–57 223
Table 2. New Registrations of Motor Vehicles in the UK, 1927–57 224
Table 3. Vehicles in Use in the UK, 1913–57 225
Table 4. UK Exports of New Motor Vehicles, 1920–57 226
Table 5. Production of Cars—Chief Overseas Producers, 1929–57 227
Table 6. Production of Commercial Vehicles—Chief Overseas Producers, 1929–57 227
Table 7. Exports of New Cars and Car Chassis from UK and Chief Overseas Producing Countries, 1929–57 228
Table 8. Exports of New C.V.s and C.V. Chassis from UK and Chief Overseas Producing Countries, 1929–57 .. 228
Table 9. Profits of 'Big Six' Car Producers, 1929–57 229

R

INDEX

AC-Delco, Division of General Motors, Ltd., 30, 33, 129
Accessories, *see* Parts and Components
ACV Ltd., 24, 32, 152-5 *passim*, *see* AEC
Advertising, 34, 144-5, 193
AEC (ACV Ltd.), 24, 25, 61
Age of vehicles, 18, 18n, 39, 41, 55, 184
Aircraft Industry, 23, 152, 164, 207, 207n
Albion Motors Ltd. (Leyland Motors Ltd.), 24
Alford and Alder (Engineers) Ltd., 29
Allard Motor Co. Ltd., 23
Aluminium, 31, 53, 214
Alvis Ltd., 23, 155
American Motors Corporation, 83n
Andrews, P. W. S., *The Life of Lord Nuffield*, 102n, 109n, 110n, 162n, 230
Archdale, James, and Company Ltd., 59, 61
Armstrong Patents Company, Ltd., 30
Armstrong Siddeley cars (Hawker Siddeley Group Ltd.), 23
Assembly of vehicles, etc., 23, 54, 55, 55n, 63, 77-80, 83-4, 91, 92
Assembly plants, overseas, 54, 108, 183n, 193, 219, 219n
Aston Martin cars (David Brown Corporation Ltd.), 23
Austin Motor Company, Ltd., 22n, 100
   assets, 163, 178, 179n
   costs, 59, 91-2
   depreciation provisions, 162, 177
   dividends, 161-2, 176
   merger with Nuffield, 19, 170, 182
   models produced, 106, 107, 108, 109, 116, 120
   output, 12, 13, 15, 99, 183
   prices and price policy, 101, 104, 105, 112-17 *passim*, 120, 122, 137, 213n
   profits, 152-61 *passim*, 229
   recourse to capital market, 162-3, 176-7
   retained earnings, 161-3, 176-7
   return on capital, 160, 175
   share of market, 13, 15, 19, 20, 99, 107, 108, 117
   techniques of production used, 14, 58, 59, 60
Austin-Healey cars (British Motor Corporation Ltd.), 22n
Australia
   assembly plants, 54
   body-building plants, 55
   import restrictions, 18, 183
   preferential tariffs, 184
   prices of imported cars, 216, 217, 222
   vehicle production, 183, 183n
   vehicle taxation, 48
Autocar, The, 144n
Autolite Company, 84
Automation, 56-61, 78, 81 *et seq.*, 91-2
Automation and Technological Change, 78n, 81n, 83n
Automobile Engineer, 54n, 57n, 80n, 92n
Automobile Manufacturers' Association, *Automobile Facts and Figures*, 40n, 44n, 45n
Automotive Products Company, Ltd., 29-30
Avon India Rubber Company Ltd., 29
Axles, 29, 54, 79

Bain, Joe S., *Barriers to New Competition*, 98
Barna, T., *The replacement cost of fixed assets in British manufacturing industry in 1955*, 206, 207, 208
Batteries, *see* Electrical equipment
Battery Association, British Starter, 127, 129, 129n
Beans Industries Ltd. (Standard Motor Company, Ltd.), 29
Bentley cars (Rolls Royce Ltd.), 23, 140
Benz, Carl, 11
Bezier, P., *Automatic Transfer Machines*, 60n
'Big Five' car producers, 119, 188, 200, 202

Index

assets, 178 *et seq.*
car production, 22
commercial vehicle production, 24, 25, 147
costs, 62
depreciation provisions, 176 *et seq.*
dividends, 176 *et seq.*
foundry facilities, 29
methods of distribution, 34–7
models produced, 120–1
price of cars, 22
profits, 168–71, 229
recourse to capital market, 176 *et seq.*
retained earnings, 176 *et seq.*
return on capital, 174–6
share of market, 19, 22, 24, 32, 117, 120
suppliers of parts and components, 30
see British Motor Corporation, Ford, Rootes, Standard, Vauxhall, 'Big Six' car producers
'Big Six' car producers
assets, 163
depreciation provisions, 162
dividends, 161–3
models produced, 100 *et seq.*, 110–11
price of cars, 100 *et seq.*
profits, 153–9, 229
recourse to capital market, 162–3
retained earnings, 161–3
return on capital, 159–61
share of market, 107, 156
standardization, 135
see Austin, Ford, Morris, Rootes, Standard, Vauxhall, 'Big Five' car producers
Birfield Ltd., 30
Birmid Group, 29
Birmingham Aluminium Casting Company, Ltd., 29
Blanchard, Harold, 85n
BMC, *see British Motor Corporation Ltd.*
Bodies for vehicles, 29, 32, 34, 53
cost of, 19, 27, 28, 63, 64
manufacture and assembly of, 54, 79, 81 *et seq.*
suppliers of, 19, 28
mergers with vehicle manufacturers, 19, 118, 119, 131n, 204
variety of types, 110–11, 121
Borg and Beck Company, Ltd. (Automotive Products Ltd.), 30
Borg Warner Corporation, 33
Brakes, 27, 29, 31, 32, 63
Break-even point, 69 *et seq.*
Briggs Motor Bodies Ltd., 19, 28, 118, 133, 179, 230
Bristol Aeroplane Company, Ltd., 23
British Light Steel Pressings (Rootes Motors Ltd.), 28
British Motor Corporation Ltd., 84, 133, 202
assets, 178–9, 181
body manufacture, 19, 28
carburettor manufacture, 31n, 125
depreciation provisions, 177
dividends, 176
economies of scale, 192
expansion plans, 182
formation, 20, 200
mergers, 19
models produced, 120, 121, 140
output, 22, 25, 118, 175n, 182, 192
prices and price policy, 120, 140, 145
production overseas, 183, 184
profits, 143, 169–70, 229
recourse to capital market, 177
retained earnings, 176–7
return on capital, 174–5
share of market, 22, 25, 117
suppliers, 28, 30, 125
tractor manufacture, 26
turnover (sales), 170
see Austin, Morris
British Motor Syndicate, 11
British Motor Trade Association (BMTA), 147, 148, 149
Brown, Donaldson, *Pricing policy in relation to financial control*, 141n, 142
Brown, David, Corporation Ltd., 23, 26
Brunner, E., *The Life of Lord Nuffield*, 102n, 109n, 110n, 162n, 230
BSA (Birmingham Small Arms Company, Ltd.), 23
Burman and Sons Ltd., 30, 125

Cadillac cars (General Motors), 139, 140
Cam Gears Ltd., 30
Canada
 demand for vehicles, 38
 effect of hire purchase restrictions, 45
 motor industry
  effect of depression on, 14
  exports, 228
  output, 14, 16, 227
 vehicle taxation, 48
Capital employed
 effect of automation on, 59, 91
 future expansion in, 182
 return on, 142, 159–61, 174–6
 sources and uses of, 143, 161–3, 176–81
 value of, 163, 174, 174n, 175, 178–81, 206–9
 in producing parts and components, 12, 132
 in relation to labour employed, 206–9
 in relation to output, 206–9
 in relation to scale of production, 88, 90, 92, 123
Carburettors, 30, 31, 54, 125, 126
Cars
 materials in, 53
 number of parts in, 27n
 number of producers of, in UK, 13, 14, 21, 22
 output of, in UK, 12–17 *passim*, 22, 165, 182, 194, 223
 see Costs, Models produced, Price, Registrations, etc.
Cars, E., 57n, 58n
Castings, 27, 29, 30, 31, 53, 61, 77, 80, 90
Census of Distribution and Other Services, 1950, 35n
Census of Manufactures, 210n
Census of Production, 156, 158n, 166, 166n, 210n
Central Statistical Office, *National Income Statistics*, 47n
Champion Sparking Plug Company, Ltd., 30, 33, 129
Chassis, 54, 63, 78, 109, 110

Chevrolet cars (General Motors), 43, 79, 80, 110, 131, 139, 140, 213, 215
Chloride Batteries Ltd., 129
Chrysler Corporation, 77, 110, 192
Cincinatti Milling Machine Company, 92n
Citroen Ltd., 140, 141, 221
Clutch, 30, 63
Cohen, Ruth, *Effects of Mergers*, 19n
Commercial Vehicles
 heavy, 24, 25, 32, 35, 146–7, 165, 199
 light, 13, 24, 35, 146–7, 165
 costs of production of, 63, 67
 demand for, 47, 52, 185, 185n
 design of, 199
 exports of, 17, 182, 183, 184, 188, 226, 228
 government legislation concerning, 51–2
 output of, in UK, 12–17 *passim*, 24, 25, 164n, 165, 182, 194, 223
 producers
  number of, 15, 24, 202
  profits of, 151–5 *passim*, 162n, 164–5
  share of market by different producers, 13, 24–5
 suppliers of parts and components for, 31–2
 taxation of, 51, 51n
 see Distribution, Hire Purchase, etc.
Competition
 between vehicle manufacturers, 13, 19, 20, 32, 99–124, 135–47, 185, 195 *et seq.*
 foreign, 13, 186, 187
 oligopolistic, 72n, 124, 136
 long-period, 106, 115–16, 122
 short-period, 105, 115, 122
 in advertising, 144–5
 in dealer representation, 145–6
 in distribution of vehicles, 147–50, 195
 in export markets, 143–4, 184, 185, 186 *et seq.*
 in price, 15, 71 *et seq.*, 100 *et seq.*, 115 *et seq.*, 122–4, 136 *et seq.*, 141–3, 196
 in quality of models, 15, 106 *et seq.*, 118, 122 *et seq.*, 136 *et seq.*, 196–7, 199, 200

Index

in supply of parts and components, 27, 28, 125–35, 196
Components, *see* Parts and Components
Cook, P. Lesley, *Effects of Mergers*, 19n
Costs
  overhead (fixed), 26, 62 *et seq.*, 143n, 168, 172–4, 190, 191, 206n
  running, 46–9
  variable (direct), 62 *et seq.*, 74, 143n, 173–4
  changes in, 1930–37, 156–9
  changes in, 1947–56, 167–8, 170–1
  of assembly, 79, 80
  of changing models, 68, 68n, 79, 83, 120
  of labour, 59, 62 *et seq.*, 86, 88, 91, 92, 112, 168, 186, 212, 213
  of maintenance, 60, 91, 92
  of parts and components, 19, 26–32 *passim*, 62 *et. seq.*, 88–90, 96, 130, 208n
  of transport, 77, 80, 186, 203n, 218, 219, 220
  effect of automation on, 57, 59, 60, 91–2
  effect of changes in capacity working on, 63 *et seq.*, 66, 171–4, 191
  effect of changes in scale of production on, 74–98, 141–3, 159, 168, 190, 212
  in relation to prices in short-period 69 *et seq.*, 103, 105, 124
  in relation to size of car, 220n
  in British motor industry, 198, 199, 212–15, 221–2
  in French motor industry, 221–2
  in German motor industry, 201, 221–2
  in Italian motor industry, 221–2
  in US motor industry, 212–15
Covenant scheme, 148
Coventry, 11
Coventry Climax (Coventry Victor Motor Company, Ltd.), 23
Crank shaft, 53, 54
Creamer, David, *Capital and Output Trends in Manufacturing Industries, 1880–1948*, 207, 208, 209n

Crossley commercial vehicles (ACV Ltd.), 24
Cycles, 11, 23, 152, 164, 207
Cylinder
  block, 29, 53, 54, 59, 80, 81, 91
  head, 29, 54, 61

Dagenham, Essex, 14, 111, 118, 152, 155, 158, 161, 163
Daimler Company Ltd., 11, 23
Dartmouth Auto Castings Ltd., 29
Davis, J. D., 81
de Wolff, P., *Demand for Passenger Cars in the United States*, 38, 38n
Dealers, *see* Distribution of vehicles
Demand for vehicles, 14, 18, 38–52, 100, 122, 123, 184–5
Department of Scientific and Industrial Research, *Automation*, 60n
Depreciation provisions, 62 *et seq.*, 68, 153–4, 160, 161–3, 177 *et seq.*, 206, 207
Design of vehicles, 140–1, 187, 188, 195, 199, 200
Dies and tools, 82, 85, 86, 133, 153
Diesel engine, 15, 51, 61, 147, 171
Distribution of vehicles etc., 34–7, 127, 139, 145–50
  commercial vehicles, 35
  grades of dealer, 34
  manufacturers' agreements, 34, 36, 146
  number of dealers, etc., 35, 146, 147
  ownership links with manufacturers, 36
  competition in, 147–50, 195
  exclusive dealing in, 36–7
  manufacturers' policy regarding, 145–6, 193
  price maintenance, 34, 147–50, 195
  retail margins, 129, 147, 149, 193, 218
Dividends, 153–4, 161–2, 176 *et seq.*
Dunlop Rubber Company Ltd., 29, 32, 127
Dynamos, *see* Electrical equipment

Economic Journal, 159n, 160n

Economist, The, 13n, 15, 23n, 36n, 47n, 92, 93, 98, 110, 121n, 148n, 151, 152, 155, 163, 164, 165, 166, 168, 169, 185, 206n, 215, 222
Economist Intelligence Unit, *Britain and Europe*, 185n, 188n
'Economy' cars, 187, 187n, 200
Edison Swan, 129
Edwards, Corwin D., *Maintaining Competition*, 197n
Efficiency of motor industry, 187, 195, 197 *et seq.*
Elasticity of demand, 87
  income, 40, 41n
  price, 41, 70 *et seq.*, 141
Electrical equipment, 27, 28, 29, 31, 54, 63, 84, 129, 134
Employment, 11, 33, 34, 211
Engines for vehicles, 25, 27
  costs of production, 63
  effect of taxation on design, 49, 51
  'horse-power race,' 139, 215
  life, 85–6
  manufacture and assembly, 54, 79 *et seq.*
  suppliers, 23, 24, 26
  variety of types, 110–11, 121
Entry into motor industry, 135, 197
Europe
  Common Market, 188, 189
  Free Trade Area, 185n, 186, 187, 188–9, 201, 202, 203, 216
  motor industry, 78, 84
    car prices, 216–22
    exports to UK, 187
    integration, 33, 203
    models produced, 140–1
    output, 16, 17
    scale of, 187, 201
    supply of parts and components, 33, 132, 187
    use of diesel engines, 51
    vehicles in use, 48
  see France, Germany, etc.
Exports, 50, 112, 191, 193
  markets, 17, 18, 139
  methods of distribution, 35
  of UK motor industry, 11, 17, 18, 49, 50n, 111, 182–8 *passim*, 198–9, 226, 228
  of world motor industry, 17, 18, 184
  packaging methods, 54, 55
  prices, 143, 199, 216–22
  subsidies, 144, 221n

Farrell, M. J., *The Demand for Motor Cars in the United States*, 39n, 40, 43
Federal Trade Commission, *Report on the Motor Vehicle Industry*, 126n, 146
Ferguson tractors, 26, 126, 170
Fiat Ltd., 140, 141, 216–22 *passim*
Filters, oil, 30, 33
Firestone Tyre and Rubber Company Ltd., 29, 33
Fisher and Ludlow Ltd., 19, 28, 179
Fisher Body Division (General Motors), 79
Ford, Henry, 33, 78, 103, 136
Ford Motor Company Ltd. (UK), 20, 23, 81, 100, 119, 135, 196
  assets, 161, 163, 178 *et seq.*
  costs of production, 98, 111, 170–4
  depreciation provisions, 161–3, 177 *et seq.*
  dividends, 161–3, 176
  expansion plans, 182
  integration, 28, 29, 31
  location, 12, 14
  mergers, 19, 118, 133
  methods of production used, 59
  models produced, 12, 102n, 108, 109, 112, 116–18, 120, 121n, 140, 173n
  output, 12, 13, 15, 22, 25, 116, 118, 172–4, 175n
  ownership of share capital, 33
  policy of exclusive dealing, 36
  prices and price policy, 73–4, 101, 102–3, 104, 105, 112–18 *passim*, 120, 122, 137, 140, 172–4, 213, 214, 215, 216–22 *passim*
  profits, 73–4, 103, 142, 143, 152–61 *passim*, 169–74, 229
  recourse to capital market, 161–3, 177
  retained earnings, 161–3, 176–7
  return on capital, 160–1, 174–6

Index

share of market, 15, 22, 25, 102, 107, 117, 118, 182
tractor manufacture, 26, 118n
turnover (sales), 169–74, 175
Ford Motor Company (USA), 33, 43, 58, 60, 60n, 77, 78, 80, 81, 83, 84, 103, 108, 110, 111, 126, 136, 137, 192, 203, 213, 214, 215
Forgings, 27, 30, 31, 53, 84, 90
Foundries, 29, 31, 80, 83, 84, 90, 131
France
  motor industry, 58
  car prices, 216–22
  costs, 221–2
  exports, 183, 228
  models produced, 140–1
  output, 12, 14, 16, 17, 227
  supply of parts and components, 132
  taxation, 191, 218n, 221

Garage trade, *see Distribution of vehicles*
Gardner diesel engine, 24
Garringtons Ltd. (Guest, Keen and Nettlefolds Ltd.), 30
Gear box, 23, 54, 79
General Motors Corporation, 15, 30, 33, 77, 84, 108, 110, 131, 136, 139, 141, 142, 162, 176, 177, 183, 192, 193, 203
General Motors Corporation, *The Dynamics of Automobile Demand*, 38n, 40n, 42n, 45n, 70
Germany
Germany
  motor industry, 58
  car prices 216–22
  costs 221–2
  exports 17, 18, 183, 198, 228
  export subsidy, 144, 144n
  models produced, 140
  output, 14, 16, 17, 227
  productivity, 211
  supply of parts and components, 132
  vehicle taxation, 48, 192
Girling Ltd. (Joseph Lucas Ltd.), 30
Goodyear Tyre and Rubber Company Ltd., 29, 33

Goods vehicles, *see Commercial vehicles*
Griffith, F., *Why Austin developed Unit Construction Transfer Machines*, 59n, 91n
Guest, Keen and Nettlefolds Ltd., 29, 30

Hancock, E. W., 27n
Hardy Spicer Ltd. (Birfield Industries), 30
Hawker Siddeley Group Ltd., 23
Hillman cars (Rootes Motors Ltd.), 22n, 100, 101, 104, 106, 108, 109, 112, 114, 115, 117, 120, 121
Hire purchase
  effect on vehicle sales, 44–5, 190, 191
  number of agreements, 44
  restrictions on, UK, 19, 44n, 45, 185
Hoffman, Paul, 71, 83, 137, 187n
Holden car (General Motors), 183, 183n
Hope, Ronald, *Profits in British Industry from 1924 to 1935*, 151n, 155n, 161n
Hudson Motor Co., 83n
Humber Ltd. (Rootes Motors Ltd.), 11, 22n, 120
  assets, 163
  depreciation provisions, 162
  dividends, 161–2
  profits, 152–61 *passim*, 230
  recourse to capital market, 161–3
  retained earnings, 161–3
  return on capital, 159–61, 175
  see Rootes Motors Ltd.

Imperial preference, 111, 184, 186, 216
Imports
  duties on, 13, 50, 54, 111
  into UK, 13, 187, 189
  restrictions on, 17, 18, 183, 198
  see Exports
Inland Revenue, Commissioners of, 167n
Innovation, 23, 97, 100, 122, 198, 201
Institution of Production Engineers, *The Automatic Factory. What does it mean?* 60n
Instruments, vehicle, 30, 31, 33
Insurance of vehicles, 48, 49

240   *The Motor Industry*

Integration
  effect on cost structure, 31
  horizontal, 19, 32, 202, *see Mergers*
  vertical, 19, 28–32 *passim*, 36, 84, 93n, 95, 131, 133–4, 193, 203–5
International Harvester Ltd., 26
Italy
  motor industry
    car prices, 216–22
    costs, 221–2
    exports, 183, 228
    models produced, 140–1
    output, 16, 17, 227
    motoring taxation, 48, 191, 192, 218n, 221

Jaguar Cars Ltd., 22, 23, 37, 197, 202
Jowett Cars Ltd., 19, 106, 119

Kaldor, N., *An Expenditure Tax*, 161
Kelsey-Hayes Wheel Company, 29
KLG sparking plugs (S. Smith and Company), 129

Labour, 112, 133, 193, *see Costs*
Lagonda cars (David Brown Corporation Ltd.), 23
Lanchester, F. W., 11
Lea-Francis Cars Ltd., 119
Lenoir, Etienne, 11
Leyland Motors Ltd., 24, 25, 32, 147, 152–3 *passim*, 202
Liesner, H. H., 188
Lloyds Bank Review, 98
Location of UK motor industry, 33
Locomotive on Highways Act, 11
Lodge Plugs Ltd., 129
Lord, Sir Leonard, 110
Lotus cars, 23
Lucas, Joseph, Ltd., 14, 28, 30, 32, 84, 129, 134–5

Machine-tools, 15, 23, 53, 56 *et seq.*, 62, 112, 121
Machining of vehicle parts, 27, 53, 55, 55n, 56 *et seq.*, 77, 79, 80 *et seq.*, 92
Machinist, The, 27n, 59n, 81n, 91n
Management, 109–10, 192–3, 212
Market for vehicles in UK, 14, 17, 18, 24, 138, 139, 184–5, 190, 191, 194

Market shares, *see Share of Market*
Mass-production, 14, 22, 24, 27, 32, 67, 68, 69, 75 *et seq.*, 90, 103, 137 *see Automation, Production (flow)*
Materials, *see Parts and Components*
Maudslay Motor Company Ltd. (ACV Ltd.), 24
Maxcy, George, 19n
Meadows, Henry, Ltd., 24
Mechanization, 55 *et seq.*, 78 *et seq.*, 91, 210–11
Mergers, 19, 20, 28, 33, 83, 118, 119, 131n, 133, 170, 182, 188, 200, 202, 205
Metalworking Production, 57n, 58n, 60n, 61n
MG cars (British Motor Corporation), 22n
Michelin Tyre Company Ltd., 29
Midland Motor Cylinder Company Ltd., 29
Models produced, 112
  agreements on, 124, 196
  annual output, 75 *et seq.*, 110, 123, 187
  changes in, 85–6, 102 *et seq.*, 115 *et seq.*, 119 *et seq.*, 123, 138
  cost of changing, 68, 79
  design of, 140–1, 187, 188, 195, 199, 200
  effect of new models on demand, 42, 43
  variety of, 15, 20, 21, 25, 49, 50, 100, 109–11, 119–21, 123, 138–40, 188, 194–5, 200 *et seq.*
Monopolies and Restrictive Practices Commission, *Report on the Supply and Export of Pneumatic Tyres*, 29, 127, 128, 130, 149
Monopoly, 28, 89, 90, 125, 134, 196, 204n
Moody's Services Ltd., 160n, 163, 178, 230
Morgan Motor Company Ltd., 23
Morris Motors Ltd., 22n, 100, 103, 183
  assets, 163, 178, 179n
  Austin merger, 19
  depreciation provisions, 162, 177
  dividends, 161–2, 176
  integration, 19

Index

management difficulties, 109–10
models produced, 102, 106–10 *passim*, 115, 118, 120
output, 12, 13, 99
prices and price policy, 101, 104, 105, 112, 113, 114, 116, 120, 213n, 216–22 *passim*
profits, 103, 152–61 *passim*, 229
recourse to capital market, 161–3, 177
retained earnings, 161–3, 176–7
return on capital, 159–61, 175
share capital, 162
share of market, 13, 99, 107, 108
suppliers of parts and components, 13
techniques of production used, 14, 58, 59, 102
Morris, William (Viscount Nuffield), 13, 109
Motor Business, 184n, 185n
Motor Critic, 85n
Motor Industry Research Association, 135
Motor Show, 21, 42, 105, 115, 135
Motor, The, 86n, 101, 104, 113, 114
Mulliners Ltd. (Standard Motor Company Ltd.), 28

Nash-Kelvinator Corporation, 83n
National Advisory Council for the Motor Manufacturing Industry, 135
 Report on Proceedings, 50n, 68, 68n, 75, 87n, 92, 96, 110
National Institute of Economic and Social Research, 164, 165, 165n, 166n, 179
National Used Car Price Book, 147
Nationalization, 52, 200
Netherlands, 216–22 *passim*
New Zealand, 183
Nuffield Organization, 15, 20, 107, 117, 117n, 170, 182
 see Morris Motors Ltd.
Nuffield, Viscount (William Morris), 13, 109

Office of Business Economics (US Department of Commerce), 40, 41

Oil, 35, 36n, 51, 207
Oldham and Sons Ltd., 129
Oligopoly, 72n, 124, 129, 136, 140
Opel cars (General Motors), 216–22 *passim*
Optimum output, 75–86, 192–5, 200, 201, 202, 203
 see Production, economies of large-scale
Organization for European Economic Co-operation (OEEC)
 Situation in the Automobile Industry in Member Countries in 1950, 144n
 Some Aspects of the Motor Vehicle Industry in the USA, 77n, 81, 82, 97n, 131n, 132n
Original equipment market, 28, 29, 33, 127–9
Otto, Dr A. N., 11
Oxford Economic Papers, 150n

Packard Motor Corporation, 83n
Parts and Components
 assets employed in manufacture of, 207n
 competition in supply of, 125–35
 cost of bought-out parts, 27, 28, 30, 31, 62 *et seq.*, 78, 96
 distribution, 35
 economies of scale in manufacture, 84, 88–90, 95–6, 132
 manufacture and assembly, 12, 34, 84
 patents, 126
 price agreements, 127, 129
 prices, 128, 134
 production by vehicle manufacturers, 125, 130 *et seq.*, 157, 171, 171n, 203–4
 profits of manufacturers, 128, 130, 134
 standardization, 20, 26, 187, 194, 204–5
 suppliers, 12, 13, 14, 27, 28, 30, 31, 33
  relations with vehicle manufacturers, 90, 130 *et seq.*
 technical progress in manufacture, 97, 132
 trade associations, 127–9

242   The Motor Industry

Patents, 11, 126–7, 132
PEP (Political and Economic Planning), Motor Vehicles, 25n, 26, 42n, 49n, 53n, 111, 134n, 144n
Perkins, F. Ltd., 24
Petrol, 19, 35, 36n, 39, 49, 49n, 50, 51, 191
Peugeot Ltd., 140, 216–22 passim
Picard, M., 98
Platt, Maurice, 86n
Plymouth cars (Chrysler Corporation), 43, 110
Pressed Steel Company Ltd., 19, 28, 32
Pressings for vehicles, 32, 54, 55, 55n, 77, 79, 81 et seq., 92
Prest, A. R., 159n
Price, 159n
   of new cars in UK, 14, 18, 22, 23, 24, 100 et seq., 112 et seq., 137, 185, 213–5, 216–22
   of second-hand cars in UK, 18
   of commercial vehicles, 25
   of all new vehicles in UK, 156, 157, 166, 168
   of parts and components, 128, 134
   of raw materials, 186
   wholesale, 18, 166, 168, 218–21 passim
   in export markets, 143, 187, 199, 216–22
   effect of changes in variable costs on, 74, 115, 123, 142
   method of formation, 142–3
   relationship to costs of production, 64, 69 et seq., 142–3, 172–4
   agreements, 105, 115, 124, 129, 196
   competition, 15, 100 et seq., 115 et seq., 122–4, 136 et seq., 141–3, 196
   cutting, 69 et seq., 124, 129
   discrimination, 143, 217, 220
   leadership, 105, 106, 115–17, 123–4
   maintenance, 34, 147–50, 195
   stability, 105, 122–4, 136–7
   in relation to horse-power, 214–15
   in relation to weight, 213–15, 216–17
   see Elasticity of Demand
Production
   annual, 75 et seq., 93, 123, 187, 192
   batch, 25, 56, 60, 61, 77, 78, 92

flow, 14, 25, 27, 56 et seq., 64, 77 et seq., 92, 132, 208
economies of large-scale, 33, 55 et seq., 74, 75–98, 100, 110, 123, 132, 134, 190, 191–5, 202, 212
expansion of, 182, 191
index of, 156, 164n, 166
in relation to profits, 156–9, 165–71
capacity, 15, 65n, 112, 168, 182, 185, 186
length of run, 86, 121
methods, 25, 26, 32, 53–61, 76 et seq., 90, 91
see Mass Production
Production Engineering Research Association, 60
Productivity
   of machines, 92, 209
   of labour, 209, 211–12
Profits, 197
   industrial, 151–2, 164
   overseas, 184
   retained, 161–3, 176–9
   in distribution of vehicles, 147, 193
   in export markets, 143
   of car producers, 151–9, 163–74, 229
   of commercial vehicle producers, 26, 152–5 passim, 164–5
   of motor, cycle and aircraft companies, 151–2, 164
   of parts and components manufacturers, 128–30, 134, 165, 204
   in relation to capital employed, 159–61, 174–6
   in relation to costs and prices, 69 et seq., 142–3, 171–4
   in relation to vehicle output, 156–9, 165–71, 191
   in relation to the value of vehicle sales, 156–9, 165–71
Pumps, fuel, 30, 31, 33
Purchase Tax, 18, 48, 49, 119, 190, 191, 192, 194, 218, 219

Racing cars, 22, 23
Railway rates, 52
Registrations, new
   cars, 17, 18, 19, 47, 50, 102, 159, 224
   commercial vehicles, 17, 18, 19, 47, 224

Renault Ltd., 59, 60, 91, 92, 98, 140, 141, 187, 216–22 *passim*
Research, 97, 108, 132
Restrictive Trade Practices Act, 1956, 148, 195
Retail motor trade
see Distribution of vehicles
Reuther, Walter, 83
Riley cars (British Motor Corporation), 22n, 155
Road and Rail Traffic Acts, 51
Rolls-Royce Ltd., 23, 24, 140
Roos, C. F., *Factors governing changes in domestic automobile demand*, 38n, 40, 41, 41n, 42
Rootes Motors, Ltd., 27n, 86n, 100, 152n
  assets, 178 *et seq.*
  body manufacture, 28
  depreciation provisions, 177 *et seq.*
  dividends, 176
  integration with retail trade, 36
  mergers, 119
  models produced, 108, 109, 120, 139
  output, 15, 22, 25, 176n
  prices and price policy, 114, 120, 213n
  profits, 143, 170, 229
  recourse to capital market, 176 *et seq.*
  retained earnings, 176–7
  return on capital, 174–6
  share of market, 15, 22, 25, 107, 117
  techniques of production used, 58
  see Hillman, Humber
Rostas, L.
  Comparative Productivity in British and American Industry, 210, 211, 212n
  Industrial Production, Productivity and Distribution in Britain, Germany and the United States, 211n
Rover Company Ltd., 11, 12, 22, 23, 24, 25, 37, 106, 155
Rowe, D. A., *The Market Demand for Durable Goods*, 39n
Rubery Owen and Company Ltd., 29

Sankey, Joseph, and Sons Ltd. (Guest, Keen and Nettlefolds Ltd.), 29

Sara, E. T., *Free Trade in Steel?*, 186n
Scale of production, *see* Production
Scoville, J. W.
  Behaviour of the Automobile Industry in Depression, 41
  Reasons for the fluctuations in automobile production, 39n, 46n
Scrapping of vehicles, 40, 41
Seasonal demand for vehicles, 42–3
Second-hand cars
  competition with new cars, 137
  demand for, 39, 40, 40n
  hire-purchase sales, 44–5
  part-exchange allowances, 40, 147, 149
  prices, 18, 40
Selden patent, 126
Share of market
  cars, 13, 15, 19, 20, 22, 99, 102, 107 *et seq.*, 110–11, 117 *et seq.*, 140, 182, 185
  commercial vehicles, 13, 15, 24, 25
  exports, 17, 18
  tractors, 26
Shift working, 80
Shock absorbers, 29, 30, 89
Silberston, A., 160n
Simca Ltd., 140
Simms, F. R., 11
Singer Motors Ltd., 12, 13, 19, 99, 106, 119, 120, 121
Smith, Sir Rowland, 81
Smith, S. and Sons Ltd., 30
Society of Motor Manufacturers and Traders (SMMT), 27, 127, 135
  Motor Industry of Great Britain, 14n, 48, 50n, 156, 228n
Solex Ltd., 30, 126
Solomons, D., 160n
South Africa, 48, 54
Spare parts, 34, 55, 69, 157, 171, 171n, 172
Sparking plugs, 30, 31, 33, 128, 129
Specialist car producers, 25, 32, 99, 106, 119, 120, 202
  methods of distribution, 35, 37
  output, 22–3
  prices, 140
  profits, 155, 155n
  share of market, 22, 24

suppliers, 118, 119
Speed limit, 52
Sports cars, 22, 23
Standard Motor Company Ltd., 100
    assets, 163, 178 *et seq.*
    body supplies, 28
    depreciation provisions, 162, 177
    dividends, 161, 176
    mergers, 28n, 29
    models produced, 106, 108, 109, 116, 120, 174n
    output, 15, 22, 24, 175n
    prices and price policy, 101, 104, 105, 112, 113, 114, 116, 120, 215
    profits, 143, 152–9 *passim*, 169–70, 229
    recourse to capital market, 162–3, 177
    retained earnings, 161–3, 176–7
    return on capital, 159–61, 174–6
    share of market, 15, 22, 107, 108, 117
    techniques of production used, 58
    tractor manufacture, 26, 170
    turnover (sales), 170, 170n
Standardization
    effect on methods of production, 56
    of engines, 84
    of machine-tools, 58
    of parts and components, 12, 13, 20, 84, 89, 132, 134, 194, 204, 205
    of vehicles, 15, 20, 24, 85, 96, 109, 110–11, 120–2, 135, 146, 194–5
Starter motors, *see Electrical equipment*
Steel, 11, 16, 19, 31, 53, 54, 89, 90, 95, 100, 112, 186n
Steering gears, 30, 31, 63, 125
Sterling Metals Ltd., 29
Stocks
    in process, 56, 61
    of parts, 133, 145, 146
    of vehicles, 34, 35, 41, 47
    value of, 179, 180, 181
Stone, Richard, *The Market Demand for Durable Goods*, 39n
Structure of motor industry, 13, 21–37, 99, 195–6, 200
Studebaker Corporation, 71, 83, 83n, 137

SU Carburettor Company Ltd. (British Motor Corporation), 30, 31n, 125
Sub-contracting, 12, 13, 132–3
Subsidy schemes, 12, 144, 144n
Sunbeam cars (Rootes), 22n
Suspension for vehicles, 27, 29, 31, 63
Swift cars, 106
Switzerland, 215, 216–22 *passim*
Szeliski, Victor von, *Factors governing changes in domestic automobile demand*, 38n, 40, 41, 41n, 42

Tariffs, 13, 111, 184, 186, 189, 218, 219
Taxation, 46, 47, 48–51, 96, 152–5 *passim*, 180, 185, 187, 192, 218n, 221, *see Purchase Tax*
Technique of production, *see Production, methods*
Temporary National Economic Committee (TNEC), 72n, 83, 83n, 90n, 106n, 137
Thornycroft (John I.) and Company Ltd., 12
Tractors, 15, 16, 23, 26, 31, 32, 51, 164n, 166, 223
Trade cycle
    effect on motor industry, 13, 14, 39, 151–5 *passim*
    relationship to price policy, 71, 72
Transmission, vehicle, 33, 63, 215
Triplex Safety Glass Company Ltd., 125
Triumph cars (Standard Motors Ltd.), 22n, 23, 106, 112n, 174n
Trucks, *see Commercial vehicles*
Turnover (sales), 69, 156–9, 166–74 *passim*
Tyre Manufacturers' Conference, 127
Tyres, 27, 28–9, 31, 32, 33, 62, 63, 89, 127–8, 129, 130, 149, 195

United States
    demand for vehicles, 38–43 *passim*
    imports of cars, 18, 184
    instalment sales, 44, 45
    market for vehicles, 33, 136, 138
    motor industry, 90, 97
        capital/output ratio, 208–9
        competition in, 136–7, 144, 215
        costs, 70, 92, 212–15

exports, 17, 111, 198, 228
foundries, 80
frequency of model changes, 43
 85–6, 122, 123
integration, 32, 33, 203
labour costs, 210, 212, 213
managerial efficiency, 212
mechanization, 210–11
methods of production, 54, 58, 61,
 78, 80 *et seq.*
output, 12, 14, 15, 16, 38, 99, 227
overseas subsidiaries, 33, 108
patents, 126
prices, 213–15
productivity, 209, 211–12
relations of manufacturers and
 distributors, 34n, 146
supply of parts and components,
 11, 132, 203
type of vehicles produced, 198,
 212n, 215
use of diesel engines, 51
variety of models produced, 15,
 110, 111, 139, 140
running costs of cars, 46n
vehicle taxation, 48, 192, 213n
vehicles in use, 47–8
Used cars, *see Second-hand cars*

Vance, H. S., 106n
Vanderblue, Homer B., 141n
Variety of models produced, *see Models produced*
Vauxhall Motors Ltd., 20, 86n, 100
 assets, 160, 163, 175, 178–9, 181
 body manufacture, 28
 costs of production, 170–1, 220n
 depreciation provisions, 160, 162–3, 177

dividends, 161, 176–7
expansion plans, 177, 182
lack of foundry, 29, 80
methods of production used, 58, 59
models produced, 108, 108n, 109,
 117, 120, 121n, 139, 159
output. 15, 22, 25, 169, 175n, 182
ownership, 14, 33, 196
prices and price policy, 101, 104, 108,
 112, 113, 114, 117
profits, 143, 152–9 *passim*, 169–71,
 229
recourse to capital market, 161–3,
 176–9
retained earnings, 161–3, 176–7
return on capital, 159–61, 174–6
share of market, 15, 22, 25, 107, 117,
 182
suppliers, 30
turnover (sales), 169–71, 175
Vehicles in use, 18, 18n, 39, 47–8, 225
Volkswagenwerk G.m.b.H., 140, 187,
 192, 199, 201, 216–22 *passim*

Wage-rates and earnings, 168, 186, 213
Wansbrough, G., *Automobiles: The
 Mass Market*, 98
War, effect on motor industry, 13, 15
Wheels, 27, 28, 29, 31, 63
Wico-Pacy Sales Corporation Ltd., 129
Wolseley Motors Ltd., 12, 22n
Woollard, F. G.
 Machines in the Service of Men, 60n
 *Principles of Mass and Flow Pro-
 duction*, 56n

Zenith Carburettor Company, Ltd.,
 30, 125, 126

GEORGE ALLEN & UNWIN LTD
London: 40 Museum Street, W.C.1

Auckland: 24 Wyndham Street
Bombay: 15 Graham Road, Ballard Estate, Bombay 1
Calcutta: 17 Chittaranjan Avenue, Calcutta 13
Cape Town: 109 Long Street
Karachi: Metherson's Estate, Wood Street, Karachi 2
New Delhi: 13–14 Ajmeri Gate Extension, New Delhi 1
São Paulo: Avenida 9 de Julho 1138–Ap. 51
Singapore, South East Asia and Far East: 36c Princep Street
Sydney, N.S.W.: Bradbury House, 55 York Street
Toronto: 91 Wellington Street West

EFFECTS OF MERGERS
P. LESLEY COOK AND RUTH COHEN

The concentration of industry has been viewed with suspicion particularly where that concentration has been brought about by means of mergers. This book examines the history of six industries with a view to showing the effects of mergers. To do this it is necessary to try to find the differences between what actually happened after the mergers and what might have happened in their absence. The conclusions must depend upon predictions or even guesses about alternative patterns of development and much of the book is devoted to the study and weighting of the major influences at work in the different industries covered—cement, calico printing, soap, flat glass, motor cars and brewing.

The study deals both with the long term and short term effects of changes in the structure of industry; judgment as to whether or not any particular merger is in the public interest is difficult but it is this question which should be tackled. In many cases a verdict of not proven must be accepted but these studies suggest that mergers are not very often against the public interest.

The form of the analysis of mergers can readily be adapted to the study of other structural changes, and this book will be read by those studying the development of industries and those interested in various forms of organisation such as monopoly, price leadership and price agreement.

Cambridge Studies in Industry. *Demy 8vo. 42s. net*

COMMON SENSE ABOUT THE COMMON MARKET
E. STRAUSS

The Common Market between France, Western Germany, Italy and the 'Benelux' countries is not merely a reshuffle of tariff rates and trade agreements but a political milestone in post-war history. Its effects will be felt throughout the world, and not least in Britain and the Commonwealth.

This book surveys the pre-history of the Common Market from the German Zollverein to the abortive customs union with Austria in 1931, and traces its roots amongst the tangled post-war politics of occupied Germany, the Ruhr Authority and the Coal and Steel Pool.

Finally, the author deals with the challenge of the new developments to Great Britain. He rejects the original conception of an industrial free trade area as unrealistic and calls for a broad extension of mutual preferences as a possible remedy for the potential dangers of the Common Market.

'Intelligent, stimulating, but perverse.' *Financial Times.*

Demy 8vo. 15s. net

AMERICAN INVESTMENT IN BRITISH MANUFACTURING INDUSTRY
JOHN H. DUNNING

Investment by United States' business interests in British manufacturing industry now exceeds $1,200 million and is increasing at the rate of 10 per cent per annum. At present, more than 300 branch subsidiaries of American corporations and jointly financed Anglo-American concerns give employment to close on 350,000 people and produce a wide range of consumer and capital goods. In 1956, the gross sales turnover of such firms was over £850 million, and their export contribution accounted for one-tenth of all British manufacturing exports. Each year, the parent companies of these concerns spend more on research and development than the whole of British industry (on private account) combined.

These are just a few of the findings of a three-year research project conducted by the author into the nature, extent and economic significance of US direct participation in British industry. They are here presented without bias and their implications for the British economy carefully examined.

Demy 8vo. About 35s. net

PRODUCTIVITY AND ECONOMIC INCENTIVES
J. P. DAVIDSON, P. SARGENT FLORENCE, BARBARA GRAY AND NORMAN ROSS

This book gives the results of 'fieldwork' investigations in factories, laundries and Co-operative shops, conducted by members of the Faculty of Commerce and Social Science at the University of Birmingham. By means of statistics of output before and after a change in methods of wage-payment and of interviews with the individual workers actually concerned, it was found that the productivity of labour, so important to the national economy, can be very greatly increased, together with an increase in earnings, without workers complaining of undue strain. The conditions are given in detail under which the increase in productivity was obtained, varying from 7 per cent to over 200 per cent and resulting in lowered cost of production. These conditions include the procedures, found so necessary, for obtaining the workers' consent. P. Sargent Florence, now Emeritus Professor, supplies an introductory chapter reviewing to date productivity studies, in many of which he has, since 1913, participated, and also discusses the extension of piece-rates to jobs where hitherto they have not been applied.

Demy 8vo. About 35s. net

GEORGE ALLEN & UNWIN LTD